Modern Protestant Theology

Modern Protestant Theology

Introducing the Classics

Wesley Vander Lugt

t&t clark
NEW YORK • LONDON • OXFORD • NEW DELHI • SYDNEY

T&T CLARK
Bloomsbury Publishing Plc, 50 Bedford Square, London, WC1B 3DP, UK
Bloomsbury Publishing Inc, 1359 Broadway, New York, NY 10018, USA
Bloomsbury Publishing Ireland, 29 Earlsfort Terrace, Dublin 2, D02 AY28, Ireland

BLOOMSBURY, T&T CLARK and the T&T Clark logo are trademarks of Bloomsbury Publishing Plc

First published in Great Britain 2026

Cover design: Elena Durey
Cover image © Henry B/Unsplash

A catalogue record for this book is available from the British Library.

A catalog record for this book is available from the Library of Congress.

ISBN: HB: 978-0-5677-1801-3
PB: 978-0-5677-1800-6
ePDF: 978-0-5677-1803-7
eBook: 978-0-5677-1802-0

Typeset by Deanta Publishing Services, Chennai, India
Printed and bound in Great Britain

For product safety related questions contact productsafety@bloomsbury.com.

To find out more about our authors and books visit www.bloomsbury.com and sign up for our newsletters.

To my students at Gordon-Conwell Theological Seminary
who are all theologians seeking to know God and make God known

Contents

Foreword

Kelly M. Kapic

Many in recent history, including me, have assembled volumes seeking to introduce students to theology from the last two centuries.[1] These large, technical books are usually arranged either historically or thematically: each serves its purpose and can be genuinely helpful. Both types, however, tend to be highly demanding and too often overwhelm readers new to the field with a labyrinth of nuanced ideas, endless names, historical contingencies, and philosophical presuppositions. While I still believe such volumes are valuable, they are rarely accessible to undergraduate students or other nonspecialists just beginning to explore the topic.

Thankfully, Wesley Vander Lugt's approach is inviting and genuinely accessible, offering a fresh overview of the period based on a sampling of an author and their key work. Consequently, readers are introduced to a variety of thinkers, such as Friedrich Schleiermacher, Charles Hodge, James Cone, Sallie McFague, and Kwame Bediako. Each figure is helpfully introduced by a detailed treatment of a representative classic that they wrote. This allows students to follow how arguments unfold within a work and learn the emphases and concerns that shape a particular classic. Readers walk away from Vander Lugt's book conversant with a sampling of fifteen key texts from the past 200 years, and with that knowledge, they are equipped to engage the larger theological conversation of this period and to approach current debates with a greater sense of the unfolding dialogue.[2]

1 For example, Rachel Muers and Ashley Cocksworth with David Ford, *Ford's The Modern Theologians: An Introduction to Christian Theology since 1918*, 4th ed. (London: Wiley-Blackwell, 2024); John E. Wilson, *Introduction to Modern Theology: Trajectories in the German Tradition* (Louisville: Westminster John Knox Press, 2007); Kelly M. Kapic and Bruce L. McCormack, eds., *Mapping Modern Theology: A Thematic and Historical Introduction* (Grand Rapids: Baker Academic, 2012).

2 Twelve of Vander Lugt's chapters were originally found in a much larger volume organized along these lines, only that book covers twenty centuries, not just two. See Kelly M. Kapic and Hans Madueme, eds., *Reading Christian Theology in the Protestant Tradition* (London: Bloomsbury T&T Clark, 2018), with the relevant Vander Lugt material on pp. 625–772.

For a reader new to this field, a brief bit of historical background can serve you well, so what follows is a sketch that may prove useful in preparing you for the journey you are about to take. During the nineteenth and twentieth centuries, early modern tendencies that developed in the seventeenth and eighteenth centuries were affirmed by some but passionately questioned by others. Many remained confident in the role of reason in their quest to affirm a respectable religion, while others (e.g., Romanticists) began to argue that following the Enlightenment path of rationalism led not to the Divine but instead to a dehumanized religion. While early modernity assumed that the "universal" and "rational" were proper goals, presupposing an underlying uniform reality, new doubts about the possibility of such goals emerged by the end of the twentieth century: Scholars grew convinced that concepts like "nature" and "objectivity" were far more culturally and experientially shaped than had been earlier imagined. And given this volume's focus on Protestant theology, how did these Christian thinkers fit into this discussion?

The Enlightenment habit of questioning authority and tradition led many nineteenth-century biblical scholars to investigate the biblical texts as scientifically as possible, as if putting together an ancient puzzle (e.g., JEDP theory). They were looking for evolutionary patterns in the ancient faith(s) of Judaism and Christianity, often focusing on the developments and differences that arose (e.g., history of religions school). During this period, scholars and even church leaders grew more comfortable with apparent tensions and assumed inconsistencies within those texts. These sacred writings increasingly were treated as either merely interesting on a historical level or possibly of abiding ethical value, but assuming that they contained *revelation* from the Divine became a ditch too vast for many to jump across. How could knowledge of the transcendent be discovered within the realm of history? Maybe what Christianity taught us was more about ourselves than God?

Some thinkers reacted against rationalism and its cold objectivity by investigating the function of the individual believer's subjectivity. This turn toward the subjective both grew out of rationalism and eventually exposed the Enlightenment's reliance upon the supposed neutrality of reason. Friedrich Schleiermacher, for example, addressed some of his work to the "cultured despisers of religion," encouraging them to see that God was discovered in that feeling (*Gefühl*) of absolute dependence, which was one's consciousness of the divine. While Schleiermacher could speak of God in a way that other Romantics of the period resonated with, his critics asked if he was losing Christianity in the process. *The Christian Faith* was an attempt to answer questions like this. Even with this, however, we must ask whether—to paraphrase Barth's later and memorable critique—his attempts to speak about God were no more than speaking in a loud voice about humans. Or did Schleiermacher see something more profound, creatively articulating the Christian faith in a way that moved beyond the ancient grammar of Nicaea and Chalcedon, but that still pointed to the same divine reality?

Hegel joked (unfairly!) that if Schleiermacher's religious ideal of absolute dependence was correct, then a dog was the most faithful example to follow. By way of contrast, Hegel spoke with massive, even cosmic, confidence, believing that God's revelation is found in history, process, and development. By observing the dynamics of historical processes, we will discover not merely historical events but nothing less than the Divine disclosing itself through events happening in a pattern of thesis, antithesis, and synthesis. But again we must ask, amid this stunning creativity and genius: was the uniqueness of Jesus at risk of being lost?

Other theologians tried to remain tied to the orthodoxy of previous centuries while playing by as many Enlightenment rules as possible. They believed in miracles, and they affirmed the incarnation and resurrection, but they organized and communicated their theology in a very "scientific" manner. Such orthodox approaches to theology are worth recognizing, because in telling the story of modern theology there is a tendency to highlight only what is new or different, rather than what affirms inherited and confessional traditions. But for Protestant theology in the nineteenth and twentieth centuries, it would be an incomplete story if we only observed those who called into question the Orthodox theology they received. For example, at Princeton Seminary, Charles Hodge used his powerful intellect to defend what he saw as historical orthodox Protestant Christianity. In this work, he was not simply repeating the past but trying to sing this inherited theology to a slightly modernist tune. His conservative *Systematic Theology* made intentional links between the past and the currents of his own day.

Danish philosopher Søren Kierkegaard, in his context, worried that the Christianity of the nineteenth century was no longer true Christianity. While there was much religion around him, he did not hear the living, demanding, personal God of Abraham, Isaac, and Jesus proclaimed by the institutional churches of Denmark. In response, he called for people to recognize the paradox of Christ and the demands of God's call, to take a leap of faith by submitting to a crucified Messiah. While not hugely influential in his day, Kierkegaard would become a major voice in the twentieth century, influencing many theologians, and even non-Christian existentialists, in the early part of the twentieth century.

Familiar with the realities of poverty, depression, and disenfranchisement, Walter Rauschenbusch also pushed hard against the status quo and Christian complacency. He wanted his Christian audience to rediscover that Jesus was a King who brought restoration by healing the sick and feeding the hungry. Here was a political Savior who was certainly occupied with earthy practical concerns rather than abstract academic debates. His church, therefore, best exhibits faithfulness not by doctrinal precision but by going to the margins, demonstrating concern for the needy and seeking to meet the social crises of the day.

Swiss theologian Karl Barth began his career having been soaked in the dominant theological Liberalism passed down from the Ritschlian school. The Great War, however, revealed the dependence of this liberalism on the failed cultures of Europe—especially as he saw his respected German theological professors supporting the German war effort. Preaching through Romans, he rediscovered the demands of the God of the apostles and prophets, who was not distant, who was not bourgeois, but a present and confrontational God, breaking in and making demands, the very demands that God himself, and he alone through his Son, could fulfill. Moving from *destruction*—showing the weaknesses of Liberal theology—to *construction*—positing a theology for the church—was not an easy venture. Nevertheless, Barth attempted to rediscover and represent orthodoxy to his age.

Paul Tillich, a German theologian who taught for many years in the United States, went the opposite direction of Barth, doing everything he could to contextualize Christianity to the modern world. The goal was not to affirm ancient beliefs and practices, but to take the abiding truths behind Christianity and make sense of them for his own twentieth-century readers. Faith was not about affirming the eternal Son of God who became fully human, bringing redemption through his historic death and bodily resurrection; instead, the faith of Christianity meant having the courage to discover real existence: God is called the "ground of being" in Tillich's attempt to make his Protestant faith relevant to mid-twentieth-century listeners.

The optimism and ethics of the nineteenth century quickly receded after the two World Wars. As the power of Modernity began to fade—or, as others convincingly argue, as Modernity fully blossomed—confidence in objective reason and universal norms became increasingly suspect. Was this "Post"-Modernity? When examined closely, too many "norms" turned out not to express underlying universal truths but to be expressions of power and manipulation; furthermore, the face giving voice to those "truths" was almost always a white, educated male.

A new appreciation for the global nature of the Christian faith and the diversity of believers began to find voice in various new leaders. For example, James Cone did not simply raise consciousness about hidden "white" presuppositions, but he also argued for the value of "black" perspectives on this ancient faith. In England, playwright and novelist Dorothy Sayers wrote popular theological essays in a culture dominated by male voices, and her creative, interdisciplinary approach made theological wisdom available to those without formal theological training, while also being praised by theologians and clergy. Argentinian theologian José Míguez Bonino worried that observing the status quo meant that the church had too often sided with those in power rather than with the poor and oppressed, and he wondered if the gospel were lost in the process: *Doing Theology in a Revolutionary Situation* called for fresh thinking and action that had too often been neglected. Japanese author Kosuke Koyama highlighted the place of humility by seeking to focus on the local rather than the universal, learning more from people on the ground than from university theology professors. Similarly, Ghanaian theologian Kwame Bediako focused on contextual theology in a postcolonial world, arguing for a continuity between primal African religions and the revelation of God in Christ. Both Koyama and Bediako were passionate about doing theology in ways uniquely adapted and relevant to their non-Western contexts. In the American context, Sallie McFague asked uncomfortable questions about inherited Christian conceptions of God, taking seriously what had been missed as a result of the silencing of women through the ages, which dovetails with how we treat the earth. These concerns were not merely about how one lives but also about who one imagines God to be and how people might relate to that God and the rest of creation. And finally, Delores Williams takes up the plight of Black women and the "challenges of womanist God-talk" in her groundbreaking book *Sisters in the Wilderness*. Williams shows how social location and gender identity influence how one reads the text, and how biblical stories, particularly a story like Hagar's, provide an enduring resource for liberation and endurance.

George Lindbeck represents a mediating postliberal approach, offering a cultural-linguistic model of theology. He begins by incorporating the insights of those who emphasized embodied Christian communities as legitimately providing and shaping beliefs. Next, he recognizes that these were not merely tribal imaginations but practices shaped around the narrative of the biblical texts. Thus, even amid differences through the ages and cultures, one could enter into this living faith that rightly centers on Jesus the Christ with his continuing authority found in the community shaped by this distinctive narrative.

Modern Protestant theology is no uniform movement, but rather a vibrant, ever-changing phenomenon. Tracing its roots back to the ancient church and then in reaction to certain perceived abuses from the late medieval period, this expression of the Christian faith has now developed its own tradition(s). While Presbyterians, Pentecostals, Lutherans, Methodists, and more are all considered "Protestant," each expression of faith has developed its own instincts and practices, and normally even within these traditions there is wide latitude between those who claim the label (e.g., among Baptists). Some Protestants advocate that the way forward is by looking back to the wisdom of the early church. Others argue that survival of this faith comes only by taking more seriously the pressures and apparent insights of the twenty-first century and beyond. While one group pushes for renewed commitment to sacred texts, others demand greater appreciation of the reality that biblical texts are not ahistorical nor are their contemporary readers: Greater attention is needed not merely to the ancient context but also to our own. And so, the conversation continues. And you are invited to join the conversation.

Acknowledgments

My first expression of gratitude extends to Kelly Kapic, who initially invited me to write twelve of these essays as one of five parts in *Reading Christian Theology in the Protestant Tradition*.[1] He took a risk on a young theologian just finishing a PhD and guided me through that process with acute intelligence and pervasive kindness. Writing those original essays was a significant stage in my own theological development, and as other theological writers can attest, I'm grateful for the opportunity to research, write, pray, and revise my way toward greater theological understanding and wisdom. I'm also thankful for keen editorial comments from Mel Webb and Hans Madueme, who helped guide that project to completion, as well as research assistance from Jimmy Myers.

Anna Turton at T&T Clark graciously considered my proposal to take those original twelve essays, add three more, and publish a stand-alone volume on modern Protestant theology. I appreciate her patience and persistence as I considered which additions were most fitting—Sayers, Bediako, and Williams making the final cut—and labored to make the deadline amid many other responsibilities. I'm grateful for her leadership, the editorial assistance of Jack Curtin, and the whole team at T&T Clark. In writing the essay on *Sisters in the Wilderness* by Delores Williams, I received generative feedback and encouragement from Dianne M. Stewart at Emory University, who was Williams's student and has written arguably the best and most accurate introduction to her work as a contribution to the *T&T Clark Handbook of Modern Theology*.[2]

Teaching theology at Gordon-Conwell Theological Seminary is a deeply rewarding experience, and I'm grateful for students who embrace with vigor and curiosity the challenge of reading Søren Kierkegaard, Karl Barth, Kosuke Koyama, and other theologians featured in this volume. My students from the Majority World, particularly the cohorts of Ghanaian students, have and continue to stretch me to consider the biblical, historical, and contextual dimensions of theology and make me increasingly passionate to introduce them and others to Majority World theologians like Kwame Bediako. This volume is dedicated to these students, who are passionate about knowing

[1] Kelly M. Kapic and Hans Madueme, eds., *Reading Christian Theology in the Protestant Tradition* (London: Bloomsbury T&T Clark, 2018).

[2] Dianne M. Stewart, "Delores Williams," in *T&T Clark Handbook of Modern Theology*, eds. Philip G. Ziegler and R. David Nelson (London: Bloomsbury T&T Clark, 2025).

God and making God known and who inspire my own journey as a pastor-theologian.

Finally, I want to thank my small and faithful circle of friends and family who graciously ask questions about my teaching and writing life and then listen patiently as I try to explain projects like this without using too much theological lingo, which I inevitably do. My attempt to write about these fifteen classics of modern Protestant theology in an accessible way was tested and strengthened by these conversations with friends and family. I hope these essays inspire similar conversations in other contexts, whether around a table, on a walk, or by a fire. We are all theologians after all, and the conversation is never over.

Introduction

Locating Modern Theology

What is modern theology? Theologians and historians have offered various and complex definitions, but the simplest way of answering that question is to identify modern theology as any way of thinking and writing about God that engages with the Christian tradition as well as the dynamics of modernity—the philosophical, scientific, and cultural shifts spanning from the late eighteenth century to the present. David Ford, in his seminal introduction to modern theology, explains that some forms of theology ignore the challenges of modernity while others give a mere passing glance at the Christian tradition, neither of which are properly *modern* and *theological*.[1] Similarly, Rachel Muers and Ashley Cocksworth, who edited and expanded the latest edition of Ford's original work, locate modern theology as attempts to grapple with features of modernity such as the prominence of the human subject, multiple ways of knowing, and the contextual, hermeneutical, and public dimensions of the theological task.[2] Roger Olson takes a similar approach, defining modern theology simply as "thinking about God in the context of modernity."[3]

However accurate this description may be, it is also difficult to conceive of any theologian who can escape or ignore the context of modernity, especially in our globalized world, so it may be helpful to add one more identifying mark. Bruce McCormack, in his introduction to a thematic and doctrinal introduction to modern theology edited with Kelly Kapic, explains how most modern theologians bring the Christian tradition into dialogue with

1 David F. Ford, ed., *The Modern Theologians: An Introduction to Christian Theology in the Twentieth Century*, 2 vols., 1st ed. (Oxford: Basil Blackwell, 1989), 2. David Ford draws on Hans Frei's theological typology, arguing that types one and five in Frei's typology are either too modern or too theological, while types two, three, and four (which Frei identifies with David Tracy, Friedrich Schleiermacher, and Karl Barth respectively) are proper and distinct ways of doing modern theology. Hans Frei, *Types of Christian Theology*, eds. George Hunsinger and William C. Placher (New Haven: Yale University Press, 1992).

2 Rachel Muers and Ahsley Cocksworth, eds., *Ford's The Modern Theologians: An Introduction to Christian Theology since 1918*, 4th ed. (Oxford: Wiley-Blackwell, 2024), 2–3.

3 Roger E. Olson, *The Journey of Modern Theology: From Reconstruction to Deconstruction* (Downers Grove: IVP Academic, 2013), 18.

the dynamics of modernity by utilizing "a heuristic and critical principle" as a form of mediation.[4] For example, in seeking to alleviate conflict between modern science and the Christian faith, Friedrich Schleiermacher utilized "the feeling of absolute dependence" as a norm for reinterpreting Christian doctrine and practice. McCormack points out that even a theologian like Karl Barth, who opposed any natural correlation between theology and modern culture, still utilized a heuristic and critical principle in his theological project, namely, his concept of revelation. Similarly, the works of theology explored in this volume may be identified as *modern* theology to the extent that they utilized a critical, organizing principle for their work such as biblical data (Charles Hodge), Blackness (James Cone), ultimate concern (Tillich), or survival and quality of life (Delores Williams). These theologians all wrestled with the conditions of modernity in different ways, some oriented more to the canon of Scripture and theological tradition and others oriented more toward the context and realities of race, class, politics, and gender. But they all were "thinking about God in the context of modernity" and doing so by drawing on heuristic principles.

Telling the Story of Modern Theology

Modern theology, which spans the last 250 years, is a sprawling phenomenon and easily overwhelming to curious learners, theology students, and those tasked with teaching on the topic. There are many laudable introductions to modern theology, but given the enormous task of summarizing such a large and burgeoning movement, these introductions are inherently selective and utilize various organizational schemas.

One approach is to introduce leading theologians, like Hugh Ross Mackintosh's *Types of Modern Theology* (1937), Karl Barth's *Protestant Theology in the Nineteenth Century* (1947), William Fletcher's *The Moderns: Molders of Contemporary Theology* (1962), and *Theologians of Our Time* (1964), which was one of the first volumes to incorporate Catholic theologians into the story of modern theology.[5] Perhaps the most widely read introduction of this kind, which also organizes theologians geographically and according to theological

4 Bruce L. McCormack, "Introduction: On 'Modernity' as a Theological Concept," in Kelly M. Kapic and Bruce L. McCormack, *Mapping Modern Theology: A Thematic and Historical Introduction* (Grand Rapids: Baker Academic, 2012), 7.

5 H. R. Mackintosh, *Types of Modern Theology; Schleiermacher to Barth* (London: Nisbet and Co., distributed by Scribner, 1937); Karl Barth, *Protestant Theology in the Nineteenth Century: Its Background and History*, trans. Brian Cozens and John Bowden, rev. ed. (Grand Rapids: Eerdmans, 2002); William C. Fletcher, *The Moderns: Molders*

traditions, is the aforementioned volume by David Ford, *The Modern Theologians* (1989), now in its fourth and greatly expanded edition.[6] This volume does not trace the roots of modern theology in the late eighteenth and nineteenth centuries as many of the others do, but the newest edition in particular shows the expansive, diverse, interdisciplinary, and global nature of modern theology. The most comprehensive coverage of key modern theologians to date, however, is the *T&T Clark Handbook of Modern Theology*, which also includes a robust unit on key themes in modern theology.[7]

Another approach is to trace the historical development of modern theology. Some volumes that take this approach focus on certain geographical areas, such as John E. Wilson's *Introduction to Modern Theology: Trajectories in the German Tradition* (2007); others focus on the Western context as a whole, such as Claude Welch's *Protestant Thought in the Nineteenth Century* (1972), *Modern Christian Thought* by James Livingston and Francis Schüssler Fiorenza (2006), and Roger Olson's *The Journey of Modern Theology* (2013), while others expand the scope into global contexts, such as Hans Schwarz's *Theology in a Global Context: The Last Two Hundred Years* (2005).[8]

A third approach to introducing modern theology is to organize the material thematically while integrating a historical perspective. One popular example is *20th-Century Theology* (1992) by Stanley Grenz and Roger Olson, which tells the story of modern theology through the interplay of divine transcendence and immanence.[9] *The Blackwell Companion to Modern Theology* (2007) covers

of Contemporary Theology (Grand Rapids: Zondervan, 1962); Leonhard Reinisch, ed., *Theologians of Our Time* (Notre Dame: University of Notre Dame Press, 1964).

6 See references in the first two footnotes. An accompanying volume is *The Modern Theologians Reader*, which provides selections from a vast array of theologians from Karl Barth onward. David F. Ford, Mike Higton, and Simeon Zahl, eds., *The Modern Theologians Reader* (Oxford: Wiley-Blackwell, 2012).

7 Philip G. Ziegler and R. David Nelson, eds., *T&T Clark Handbook of Modern Theology* (London: Bloomsbury T&T Clark, 2025).

8 John E. Wilson, *Introduction to Modern Theology: Trajectories in the German Tradition*, 1st ed. (Louisville: Westminster John Knox Press, 2007); Claude Welch, *Protestant Thought in the Nineteenth Century*, 2 vols. (repr; New Haven: Yale University Press, 1985); James C. Livingston and Francis Schüssler Fiorenza, *Modern Christian Thought*, 2 vols., 2nd ed. (Minneapolis: Fortress Press, 2006); Olson, *The Journey of Modern Theology*; Hans Schwarz, *Theology in a Global Context: The Last Two Hundred Years* (Grand Rapids: Eerdmans, 2005). Both Livingston/Fiorenza and Roger Olson engage with Latin American liberation theology but otherwise do not address the development of modern theology in the Majority World. Roger Olson acknowledges this but explains the gap in part because in his estimation, many Majority World theologians are often not wrestling with modernity. Olson, *The Journey of Modern Theology*, 13.

9 Stanley J. Grenz and Roger E. Olson, *20th-Century Theology: God & the World in a Transitional Age* (Downers Grove: InterVarsity Press, 1992). Roger Olson's book *The Journey of Modern Theology* is an updated version of this book that leaves behind the thematic schema of divine transcendence and immanence.

themes and issues but is sometimes curiously selective, especially when compared to the extensive coverage in the new *T&T Clark Handbook of Modern Theology*.[10] Other helpful volumes with a thematic schema include *Modern Theology* (2012) by Rachel Muers and Mike Higton, which also includes a section on key figures, and *Mapping Modern Theology* (2012) edited by Kelly Kapic and Bruce McCormack, which shows the development of modern theology in relation to doctrinal topics such as soteriology and eschatology.[11]

My approach in this volume is to tell the story of modern theology in its Protestant form through the lens of fifteen classics, a "great books" approach if you will, and to include a wide range of contributions from a variety of contexts. This kind of introduction has its own challenges in terms of selectivity, but I think it has value for several reasons. First, as a teacher, scholar, and reader, I am passionate about engaging with primary sources but find that many are tempted to skip over the primary sources of modern theology, especially the more difficult and voluminous works. By introducing readers to these fifteen classics, my goal is to drive more engagement with and enjoyment of the primary sources and to encourage readers to peruse additional works by their favorite authors. Second, by calling these fifteen works "classics," I am both affirming and challenging the canon of modern theology, including some books and theologians ubiquitous in the surveys (e.g., Schleiermacher, Barth, Tillich) while including others—like Dorothy L. Sayers's *The Mind of the Maker*, Kwame Bediako's *Theology and Identity*, and José Míguez Bonino's *Doing Theology in a Revolutionary Situation*—which are rarely if ever engaged at this level. In doing so, I am recognizing the contributions of lay theologians like Sayers as well as Majority World theologians like Bediako and Bonino who often get eclipsed by other theologians (e.g., John Mbiti and Gustavo Gutiérrez) whose writing engages with a wider range of theological topics. Third, as the title clearly indicates, this volume focuses on *Protestant* classics in modern theology, partly to give room for contributions like the ones above but also because there is value in tracing the trajectories and developments within this singular theological tradition stemming from the Protestant Reformation, as diverse as that tradition may be. Additional volumes introducing classics in modern Catholic theology and modern Orthodox theology would be equally important and instructive, but those are not the traditions I know best.

In writing on these classics of modern Protestant theology, my aim was to be descriptive rather than prescriptive, presenting as accurately as possible

[10] Gareth Jones, ed., *The Blackwell Companion to Modern Theology* (Oxford: Blackwell Publishing, 2007).

[11] Rachel Muers and Mike Higton, *Modern Theology: A Critical Introduction* (London: Routledge, 2012); Kelly M. Kapic and Bruce L. McCordmack, *Mapping Modern Theology: A Thematic and Historical Introduction* (Grand Rapids: Baker Academic, 2012).

what these theologians communicated, not whether I think their theological proposals are right or wrong. While to a certain extent it is inevitable for one's own principles and perspectives to impact the interpretive process, my task was to present the arguments and themes of each work without evaluation or judgment, leaving that next step to readers and their own interpretive frameworks. At times I have highlighted common critiques levied by other theologians or sub-traditions within Protestant theology, but only to the extent that it aids further understanding of the work itself and its impact on modern Protestant theology. In doing so, I am seeking to model a hospitable method of literary and theological engagement that involves careful attentiveness, listening, and understanding someone on their own terms.

Each chapter begins with a brief sketch of the theologian's life and development, situating the chosen "classic" in biographical, historical, geographical, and cultural context. In some cases, the classic is a theologian's first monograph (e.g., Cone, Bediako, and Williams); for others, the classic represents the culmination of their life's work (e.g., Schleiermacher, Barth, and Hodge); still, for others, the classic is a significant mid-career contribution (e.g., Kierkegaard, Tillich, and McFague). Whatever the case, each work in some way shows a heuristic principle at play that distinguishes it as a work of modern theology and wields influence on the development of modern Protestant theology. After the biographical introduction, each chapter proceeds to summarize the work, progressing more or less sequentially through the volume to give a sense of the development of theological ideas, providing parenthetical page references to the primary source for easy reference. Finally, each chapter concludes by indicating the impact of the theologian and their approach on other theologians and on modern Protestant theology as a whole, providing suggestions for avenues to explore and a select bibliography for further reading.[12]

Hopes and Encouragements

As already indicated, one hope I have is that this introduction to classics of modern Protestant theology will spur readers to take up and read the primary sources. A common pitfall is to either affirm or critique a work and

[12] Of course, not nearly all the classics of modern Protestant theology could be covered in this volume, but the concluding sections of each chapter attempt to recognize and place the contributions of others such as Abraham Kuyper, Rudolf Bultmann, Reinhold Niebuhr, Dietrich Bonhoeffer, Thomas F. Torrance, Wolfhart Pannenberg, Jürgen Moltmann, Kwok Pui-lan, Desmond Tutu, and many other theologians who have shaped the trajectory of modern Protestant theology.

its author without reading it, touting opinions acquired from theological institutions, church traditions, or authority figures. Even if these affirmations and critiques are legitimate, there are always insights to glean and ways to grow and be challenged when reading primary sources.

When you do so, my encouragement is to try as much as possible to recognize biases, assumptions, and your own contextual frameworks and critical principles that influence how you read and understand. Some assumptions and principles are fundamentally healthy, such as the commitment to believe in order to understand (following Anselm's famous dictum: *fides quaerens intellectum* or *faith seeking understanding*) and to recognize how all theological reflection is embedded within the journey of trusting and wrestling with God. Other assumptions and principles, however, can be fundamentally unhealthy, like whiteness seeking confirmation, biblicism seeking proof, or humanism seeking respectability. The goal is to distinguish between healthy and unhealthy assumptions and how they impact the hermeneutical and theological process.

Ultimately, as you take up this book, I hope that you will recognize that whatever your life situation and vocation, you are a theologian who is invited to answer Jesus's question: "Who do you say that I am?"[13] Theology is not just reserved for professional theologians, but for anyone who encounters and thinks about God. As Kelly Kapic writes, theology is "an aspect of thought and conversation for all who live and breathe, who wrestle and fear, who hope and pray."[14] The fifteen classics in this book all seek to make sense of Jesus, the revelation of God, and human experience in the modern world, which is the responsibility of every individual and community in every context. While there are compelling responses to Jesus's question that continue to resonate across various times and places, these responses are neither definitive nor complete. The work of theology continues as the modern world continues to unfold and present new challenges and as God continues to encounter us along the way.

[13] Mt. 16:15; Mk 8:29; Lk. 9:20.

[14] Kelly M. Kapic, *A Little Book for New Theologians: Why and How to Study Theology* (Downers Grove: InterVarsity Press, 2012), 15–16.

1

Friedrich Daniel Ernst Schleiermacher, *The Christian Faith*[1] (1821)

Schleiermacher: The Father of Modern Theology?

In the preface to the second edition of *The Christian Faith*, Friedrich Schleiermacher (1768–1834) protested those who described him as the founder of a new theological school of thought. Nevertheless, to this day he is widely referred to as "the father of modern theology," due in large part to his monumental reshaping of theological method and Protestant theology in *The Christian Faith*. Does Schleiermacher deserve this title, and if so, how does *The Christian Faith* lay a foundation for modern Protestant theology? To address these questions, we must begin with understanding Schleiermacher in his context.

Friedrich Schleiermacher was born in 1768 in Breslau, Prussia (present-day Wroclaw, Poland) to parents firmly situated within the Reformed tradition. His father, Gottleib Schleiermacher, was a Reformed pastor, a chaplain in the Prussian army, and himself the son of a Reformed pastor. Having experienced religious renewal through contact with the Moravian Brethren, Friedrich's parents decided to send him to the Moravian boarding school in Niesky in 1783. During these and subsequent years at the Moravian Seminary in Barby, Schleiermacher imbibed a deep piety that would influence the rest of his life, although he would eventually classify himself as a "Moravian of a higher order." During his stint at Barby, this budding Pietist was plagued with doubts about traditional methods and forms of expressing the Christian faith. These doubts motivated him to transfer to the University of Halle in 1787, where he immersed himself in the works of leading thinkers of his day, most notably the philosopher Immanuel Kant. After finishing his studies at Halle, Schleiermacher began the process of becoming a minister

[1] Translated from *Der christliche Glaube nach den Grudsätzen der evangelischen Kirche im Zusammenhange dargestellt*; hereafter, all references to Friedrich Schleiermacher, *The Christian Faith*, eds. H. R. MacKintosh and J. S. Stewart (London: T&T Clark, 1999) shall be noted by employing in-text parenthetical citations of sections sometimes followed by particular page numbers (e.g., §62, 261).

of the Reformed Church and worked as a tutor for the aristocratic Dohnas family (1790–4). Once he completed the ordination process, Schleiermacher served as an assistant pastor of a Reformed Church in Landsberg (1794–6) and then as chaplain to Charité Hospital in Berlin (1796–1802).

Moving to Berlin was a significant event in Schleiermacher's life, as it placed him in contact with the leading intellectuals of his day, including defenders of rationalism and romanticism. Exacerbated by these intellectuals' dismissal of religion, Schleiermacher wrote *On Religion: Speeches to Its Cultured Despisers* (1799) in hopes of confronting their "enlightened" slumber. This work wielded an enormous impact, leading eventually to Schleiermacher's appointment as a professor and university preacher at the University of Halle in 1804. Napoleon's invasion of Halle in 1806 and its detachment from Prussia, however, motivated Schleiermacher to move to Berlin. There he married Henriette von Willich (1809), served as a minister of Trinity Church (1809 until his death), and became involved in the formation of the University of Berlin, which opened in 1810 with Schleiermacher as a professor and dean of the theological faculty.

During his 24 years as a professor at the University of Berlin, Schleiermacher lectured on an array of topics, including hermeneutics, psychology, pedagogy, aesthetics, ethics, dialectics, and politics. He approached his lectures on theology with the same rigor devoted to these other topics and with an overarching concern for knowledge advancement and practical instruction. His *Brief Outline on the Study of Theology* (1811) divides theology into three categories—philosophical, historical, and practical—with historical theology including exegetical theology, church history, and dogmatic theology. Dogmatic theology is further subdivided into Christian doctrine (the science of faith, or *Glaubenslehre*) and Christian ethics (the science of morality, or *Sittlichkeit*). This explains why in *The Christian Faith*, which Schleiermacher referred to as his *Glaubenslehre* (or Doctrine of Faith), he defines dogmatic theology as "the science which systematizes the doctrine prevalent in a Christian Church at a given time" (§19). In short, this is theology done within a socio-historical framework rather than deduced from philosophical principles.

The purpose of *The Christian Faith*, therefore, is to present a system of doctrine that arises out of the particular faith experience of the church Schleiermacher called home most of his adult life and where he preached, namely, Trinity Church (*Dreifaltigheitskirche*) in Berlin. Originally a Reformed Church, Schleiermacher urged the congregation to join the Evangelical Church of the Old Prussian Union in 1817 (*Evangelische Kirche der altpreußischen Union*), a union of the Lutheran and Reformed traditions. *The Christian Faith* shares this unifying objective, while at the same time presenting a way forward for Protestant theology in the wake of rationalism and skepticism. The first German edition appeared in 1821–2 entitled *Der christliche Glaube nach den Grudsätzen der evangelischen Kirche im Zusammenhange dargestellt* (*The Christian Faith Presented as a Coherent Whole According to the Fundamental Principles of the Evangelical Church*) but was significantly revised in 1830–1 to reflect Schleiermacher's ongoing struggle and desire to match doctrinal expression with his experience of faith. Despite its widespread impact, *The Christian Faith* was not translated into English until 1928, but it had already influenced a whole new generation of theologians seeking to articulate Christian belief in the shadow of the Enlightenment.

Religion Within the Limits of Feeling

In the Introduction to *The Christian Faith*, Schleiermacher explains that, at its core, religion is a matter of feeling. This perspective was particularly at odds with the rationalists in nineteenth-century Europe who, following Kant, believed that religion was primarily a product of reason. In referring to "feeling," Schleiermacher does not merely mean emotions but a more basic level of feeling he calls "immediate self-consciousness" (§3). Having self-consciousness entails being aware of the capacity to act but also the reality of being acted upon. In other words, self-consciousness involves the feeling of freedom and the feeling of dependence on everything outside the self. It is a sense of active spontaneity and passive receptivity. Since it is impossible to be absolutely spontaneous and absolutely receptive at the same time, receptivity or dependence is ultimately determinative. For Schleiermacher, this "feeling of absolute dependence" is the same as being conscious of God. In fact, "God" is the term he uses to describe the feeling of absolute dependence, which is the core of all religions.

Just as Schleiermacher views "God" as a description of the feeling of absolute dependence, he similarly explains all doctrines as religious feelings expressed in language (§15). For example, the doctrines of divine attributes—God's eternity, omnipresence, and so on—do not represent something special in God but are simply different ways of describing the feeling of absolute dependence (§50). In addition, to say that God is Creator or Sustainer of the universe is not to articulate the truth of God's historical action in the world, but rather it is an appropriate way of expressing the entire world's dependence on God (§36).

If doctrines are ways of describing the feeling of absolute dependence, then some doctrines may be particularly useful while others may be considered superfluous. As Schleiermacher progresses through the traditional topics of

Christian theology, he devotes attention to delineating doctrines related to the feeling of absolute dependence—such as absolute divine causality (§51)—but hurries quickly over other doctrines he deems irrelevant. For instance, since the existence of angels has no impact on or relevance to religious experience, they have no dogmatic importance (§43). Similarly, a historical account of creation is not necessary because it would not clarify the feeling of absolute dependence (§40.2). Furthermore, a doctrine such as the virgin birth of Jesus is superfluous because all that is really necessary is the divine power to enable a supernatural conception ensuring the perfection of a Redeemer (§97.2). One final example is the doctrine of last things or eschatology to which Schleiermacher assigns lesser value because these doctrines do not arise from the inner life; rather, they are the "efforts of an insufficiently equipped faculty of premonition" (§159.2, 706).

By grounding doctrine in feeling, Schleiermacher not only gives rationale for dividing useful from superfluous doctrine, but he also provides a defense of doctrinal change and adaptation. Perhaps the most well-known example in *The Christian Faith* in this regard is Schleiermacher's resistance to two-nature formulations of Christology and his alternative proposal. In his opinion, the language of Christ having a divine nature and human nature, indivisibly yet distinctly united in one person, is unnecessarily confusing and only leads to inevitable errors. If the confluence of divinity and humanity in the person of Christ is understood in terms of Christ's perfect God-consciousness, argues Schleiermacher, not only does this make more sense, but it also directly relates to our feeling of fellowship with God (§96). Schleiermacher's Christology will be explored further below, but at this point, it is instructive to observe how constructing doctrine from the foundation of feeling influences his perspective at every juncture.

It might be tempting to assume that if religion and doctrine function within the limits of feeling, Schleiermacher has little concern for Scripture. The opposite is the case, and he boldly confesses the sufficiency of the Holy Spirit working through Scripture. In typical Reformed fashion, he affirms the efficacy of the Scriptures: "So that if one day there should exist in the Church a complete reflection of Christ's living knowledge of God, we may with perfect justice regard this as the fruit of Scripture, without any addition of foreign elements having had to come in" (§131.2, 606). Schleiermacher's reasons for affirming the authority of Scripture, however, differ from the defense of *sola scriptura* during the Protestant Reformation. Essentially, he affirms the normativity of Scripture because it is the expression of original Christian consciousness into language. Because this Christian consciousness only arose after Jesus, it is possible to see why, although Schleiermacher views Scripture as a norm, the Old Testament is not nearly as relevant or normative as the New Testament. Earlier in *The Christian Faith*, he all but dismisses the Old Testament as completely superfluous (§27.3). In a later section, however, Schleiermacher clarifies that the Old Testament is useful to the extent that it illuminates the New (§132). Overall, it is faith in Christ, as present among the early church, which grounds the authority of Scripture, not Scripture which grounds faith in Christ.

Just as Schleiermacher both affirms and revises the doctrine of Scripture within the limits of feeling or consciousness, the same is true with his understanding of faith itself. It is significant to note that the title page of the German original contains two quotes from Anselm: "Nor do I seek to understand in order that I may believe, but I have faith in order that I may understand," and "For he who does not believe does not experience, and he who does not experience, does not understand." By placing these two quotes together, Schleiermacher is making two important points. First, faith is primarily about experience, or more specifically, it is an inward "certainty concerning the feeling of absolute dependence" (§14.1, 68). Second, faith is the ground of knowledge and understanding, which brings us back to the centrality of feeling in Schleiermacher's entire project. Feeling is the foundation on which everything rests, and it leads him to a unique explanation of Christianity as a religion of redemption.

Christianity as a Religion of Redemption

Christianity is unique among religions, according to Schleiermacher, because it relates everything to the redemption accomplished by Jesus of Nazareth (§11). Before discussing the place of Jesus and Christology in *The Christian Faith*, however, it is helpful to grasp how Schleiermacher articulates the need for and nature of redemption. He begins by showing how the feeling of absolute dependence always includes both a feeling of turning away from God and a feeling of drawing near to God (§62, 261). This feeling of alienation from God is the essence of sin, stemming from our own lack of God-consciousness. The feeling of fellowship with God is something that comes from God himself, and this is what Schleiermacher calls grace (§63). The second part of *The Christian Faith*, which is by far the largest part, is structured by exploring this antithesis of sin and grace, which are present at every moment of the Christian life.

Schleiermacher insists that any feeling of fellowship is a Redeemer-communicated grace (§91), whereas any feeling of alienation, any feeling not oriented toward consciousness of God, is a self-originating sin (§66). Much of what Schleiermacher says about sin matches traditional Reformed and

Lutheran perspectives, such as the existence of original sin, the inevitability of actual sin, and the hopelessness of achieving redemption apart from the gracious work of the Redeemer. The biggest difference is that he takes this traditional presentation and translates it as lack of God-consciousness. Thus, original sin is the lack of God-consciousness that exists in every individual and makes apparent the universal need for redemption (§70–1). Similarly, actual sin is every human person's active suppression of or lack of desire for a perfect God-consciousness, flowing from our natural incapacity for fellowship with God. While traditional perspectives link original sin with Adam and Eve's first sin, Schleiermacher identifies original sin as an inherent incapacity for good, which, along with the inherent capacity for God-consciousness, constitutes universal human nature (§72). Consequently, there is no imputation of the first parents' sin to the rest of humanity, which would make sin—and, by implication, the work of redemption—something external rather than an internal reality (§72.4, 300–1).

As such, Schleiermacher views redemption as an inward process of being drawn toward greater consciousness of God. More precisely, it is the process of being drawn into the power of the Redeemer's own perfect consciousness of God that we could never achieve with our own power. Only through receptivity to the Redeemer can humans experience living fellowship with God. In this way, fellowship with God is the same as fellowship with the Redeemer. Schleiermacher repeatedly emphasizes that this redemption never occurs in isolation but always involves being assumed into reconciled fellowship with others who are experiencing the Redeemer's blessings (§101). As a result, Schleiermacher's view of redemption is inherently relational, and at the hub of all these relationships is the Redeemer himself. This leads us to consider at greater length the significance of Jesus and the extent to which *The Christian Faith* can be considered a Christ-centered work of theology.

The Uniqueness of Christ the Redeemer

One of Schleiermacher's most influential students, David Friedrich Strauss (1808–74), once commented that *The Christian Faith* has a single dogma: the person of Christ.[2] This can already be seen by the fact that Schleiermacher believed that every element of Christianity is related to the Redeemer's person and work. What makes the Redeemer unique, and the crux of Schleiermacher's

[2] David Friedrich Strauss, *The Christ of Faith and the Jesus of History: A Critique of Schleiermacher's Life of Jesus*, trans. Leander E. Keck (Philadelphia: Fortress Press, 1977), 4.

Christology, is "the constant potency of His God-consciousness, which was a veritable existence of God in Him" (§94). In other words, Christ is unique and can be distinguished as the Redeemer because he perfectly experienced the feeling of dependence on and fellowship with God, so much so that this is how we should understand Christ's divinity.

Schleiermacher is uncomfortable with the traditional language of Christ having two natures—divine and human—in one person. He thinks this language is misplaced because it confuses and distracts us from what really makes Christ unique, namely, "the innermost fundamental power within Him, from which every activity proceeds and which holds every element together" (§96.3, 397). Therefore, he deems it legitimate to speak of Christ as "the Word become flesh" or "the image of the invisible God" because Christ's constantly perfect God-consciousness is the very meaning of God becoming incarnate.

The power of God in Christ—Christ's perfect feeling of fellowship with God—is what makes redemption possible for the rest of humanity. In articulating the details of how Christ assumes people into his perfect fellowship with God, Schleiermacher critiques the Protestant notion of vicarious satisfaction, preferring to speak of Christ as a "satisfying representative" (§104.4, 461). Christ does not make satisfaction for our lack of God-consciousness to the extent that we no longer have any responsibility to pursue fellowship with God. Rather, Christ represents "the perfecting of human nature" (§104.4, 461) and by his free surrender to death frees people from their inability—with its accompanying guilt—to eradicate the feeling of alienation.

The Redeemer assumes believers into his perfect fellowship with God through an ongoing and comprehensive process, but Schleiermacher does pinpoint some particular moments. He recognizes a turning point—regeneration—at which the Redeemer's God-consciousness begins to influence others, although this turning point cannot be isolated from the overall process of experiencing the blessedness of the Redeemer (§106.1, 476–7). Likewise, Schleiermacher explains conversion as the moment when a passive consciousness is transformed into an active consciousness. Attempting to identify the precise time and place of conversion, however, is an "arbitrary and presumptuous restriction of divine grace," since the activation of God-consciousness can take many different forms (§108.3, 487). Justification is interdependent with conversion as God's act of changing our relation to him, but embedded within this relational reorientation is the ongoing influence of Christ's power on our consciousness (§109.3, 502–3). Justification and sanctification are therefore part of the same process of growing in Christlike fellowship with God, although sanctification stresses the progressive nature of this growth (§110).

It is important to stress that Schleiermacher views all these elements and moments of redemption as happening not just within individuals but within the common life of believers. All those who are experiencing the process of sanctification have a mutual influence on one another, so much so that Schleiermacher identifies the mutuality that develops among the fellowship of believers as the communication of the Holy Spirit (§121). In other words, the Holy Spirit is none other than the common Spirit present among those who experience living fellowship with the Redeemer (§123–4). By describing the Spirit in this way, Schleiermacher places pneumatology in a symbiotic relationship with ecclesiology, which naturally raises the question: what implication does this have for Schleiermacher's understanding of the Trinity?

Schleiermacher places his short discussion of the Trinity at the very end of *The Christian Faith*, primarily because it does not express anything immediately arising from the feeling of absolute dependence. Instead, it is a doctrine that culminates from the articulation of other doctrines, such as Christology and ecclesiology (§170). The Trinity is not a foundational doctrine on which all other doctrines rest, but the "coping-stone" or capstone of Christian doctrine (§170.1, 739). Many theologians have critiqued Schleiermacher for relegating a full discussion of the Trinity to a short conclusion in a massive work of dogmatic theology, but Schleiermacher did not make this decision because he thought this doctrine to be unimportant. On the contrary, take away the Trinity as three equal Persons in one divine essence, he claims, and "everything most important in Christianity would be changed" (§171.1, 742–3). Schleiermacher was hoping for a transformation of trinitarian theology, and subsequent theologians have taken up his challenge, both those who share his fundamental principles and those who categorically disagree, such as Karl Barth.

Mention of Karl Barth brings us back to Schleiermacher's Christology, for despite the vast differences between these two seminal theologians, both have been described as placing Christ at the center of their theological projects. An important difference, however, is that Schleiermacher does not begin with Christ; as we have seen, his starting point is the feeling of absolute dependence and the consciousness of a Creator God. Accordingly, Christ is the measure of true humanity, the one who possesses perfect God-consciousness and through whom all humanity can experience a new life of receptivity to God. As such, Richard Niebuhr identified Schleiermacher's theology as "Christo-morphic" rather than Christo-centric, since his system does not resemble "the artificial simplicity of a circle."[3] Therefore, whereas it

3 Richard R. Niebuhr, *Schleiermacher on Christ and Religion* (London: SCM Press, 1964), 212.

might not be accurate to agree with Strauss that Christology is the one single dogma of *The Christian Faith*, it is possible to conclude that the overarching purpose of this work is to present the possibility and indeed the necessity of living fellowship with Christ the Redeemer.

Protestant Theology After Schleiermacher

Whether or not Schleiermacher intended to found a new theological movement, *The Christian Faith* charted a new way of doing theology in the modern world. Rather than reacting with skepticism to the limits of human knowledge, Schleiermacher showed how it is possible to ground theology in religious experience and to connect doctrine intrinsically to the life of faith. He inspired the main proponents of what would eventually be considered liberal Protestant theology in Germany and beyond, as represented by Albrecht Ritschl (1822–89) and later Rudolf Bultmann (1884–1976) and Paul Tillich (1886–1965). But even more than that, he influenced new trends in the social sciences and arts more broadly, as evident in the work of Wilhelm Dilthey (1833–1911).

The fact that even some of Schleiermacher's strongest critics in the twentieth century—such as Karl Barth (1886–1968) and Emil Brunner (1889–1966)—were committed to understanding and lecturing on *The Christian Faith* shows its enduring significance. Despite his radical opposition to Schleiermacher's methodology, Barth confessed the genius of Schleiermacher: "All the so-to-speak official impulses and movements of the centuries since the Reformation find a center of unity in him: orthodoxy, pietism, the Enlightenment."[4] Indeed, *The Christian Faith* shows how Pietism could survive in the shadow of the Enlightenment, although the extent to which Schleiermacher preserved orthodoxy has been an ongoing debate between his ardent appreciators and disgruntled detractors.

What is not subject to debate, however, is the fact that *The Christian Faith* arose out of and fed back into the life of the church. From the beginning to the end of his career, Schleiermacher was committed to the local church, dedicated to ecumenical efforts in uniting Lutheran and Reformed traditions, and devoted to preaching in a way that connected with the affections and intellects of his congregations. In his *Brief Outline on the Study of Theology*, he posited that someone who combined religious and scientific

[4] Karl Barth, *The Theology of Schleiermacher: Lectures at Göttingen, Winter Semester of 1923–24*, ed. Dietrich Ritschl and trans. Geoffrey W. Bromiley (Grand Rapids: Eerdmans, 1982), xv.

sensibilities and who was capable of serving both theoretical and practical purposes deserves the title "prince of the church."[5] It is thus fitting that one contemporary admirer has applied this title to Schleiermacher himself, as *The Christian Faith* certainly wielded both wide-ranging theoretical and practical influence.[6]

In light of this vast influence, it is also appropriate to consider Schleiermacher a "father of modern theology," although most scholars will agree that this title must be applied equally to G. W. F. Hegel (1770–1831). What sets these two thinkers apart is their unprecedented use of a material norm to organize and evaluate every detail in a theological system.[7] As we have seen, for Schleiermacher this material norm is the feeling of absolute dependence. This feeling is the foundation of all religion and the source of all doctrine, and ultimately, it is this feeling that leads people to experience redemption through Christ the Redeemer.

Select Bibliography

Primary Sources

Schleiermacher, Friedrich, *The Christian Faith*. Edited by H. R. MacKintosh and J. S. Stewart. London and New York: T&T Clark, 1999.

Schleiermacher, Friedrich, *Der christliche Glaube nach den Grudsätzen der evangelischen Kirche im Zusammenhange dargestellt*. Edited by Rolf Schafer, 2nd ed. Berlin: Walter de Gruyter, 2008.

Other Notable Works by the Author

Schleiermacher, Friedrich, *Brief Outline of the Study of Theology*. Translated by William Farrer. Eugene: Wipf and Stock, 2007.

Schleiermacher, Friedrich, *Christmas Eve: A Dialogue on the Incarnation*. Translated and edited by Terrence N. Tice. Richmond: John Knox Press, 1967.

5 Friedrich Schleiermacher, *Brief Outline on the Study of Theology*, trans. Terrence N. Tice (Richmond: John Knox Press, 1970), 21.

6 Brian A. Gerrish, *A Prince of the Church* (London: SCM Press, 1984).

7 For an excellent introduction to this definition of modern theology, see Bruce L. McCormack, "Introduction: On 'Modernity' as a Theological Concept," in *Mapping Modern Theology: A Thematic and Historical Introduction*, eds. Kelly M. Kapic and Bruce L. McCormack (Grand Rapids: Baker, 2012), 7–9.

Schleiermacher, Friedrich, *On Religion: Speeches to Its Cultured Despisers*. Translated and edited by Richard Crouter. Cambridge: Cambridge University Press, 1996.

Secondary Sources

Dole, Andrew C., Shelli M. Poe, and Kevin M. Vander Schel, eds., *The Oxford Handbook of Friedrich Schleiermacher*. Oxford: Oxford University Press, 2024.

Kelsey, Catherine L., *Thinking about Christ with Schleiermacher*. Louisville: Westminster John Knox Press, 2003.

Mariña, Jacqueline, ed., *The Cambridge Companion to Friedrich Schleiermacher*. Cambridge: Cambridge University Press, 2005.

Niebuhr, Richard R., *Schleiermacher on Christ and Religion*. Reprint, Eugene: Wipf & Stock, 2009.

Redeker, Martin, *Schleiermacher: Life and Thought*. Philadelphia: Fortress Press, 1973.

Tice, Terrence N., *Schleiermacher*. Abingdon Pillars of Theology. Nashville: Abingdon Press, 2006.

2

Georg Wilhelm Friedrich Hegel, *Lectures on the Philosophy of Religion* (1821; 1824; 1827; 1831)[1]

Theologian of the Spirit

Georg Wilhelm Friedrich Hegel (1770–1831) is not usually considered the father of modern theology—a title more commonly applied to Schleiermacher—largely because many view him as a philosopher rather than a theologian. For Hegel, however, both philosophy and theology are oriented toward the same object: God as absolute truth and Spirit (*Geist*). Not only that, but both philosophy and religion are ways of serving God, although they do so in different ways. A more accurate portrait of Hegel, therefore, will present him as a philosopher-theologian, someone passionately concerned to know God as God knows and manifests himself as Spirit. Consequently, as a "theologian of the Spirit" who launched a theological trajectory in a radically different direction than Schleiermacher, Hegel stands next to his colleague and challenger at the University of Berlin as another father of modern theology.[2]

Born on August 27, 1770, in Stuttgart, Hegel was a bookworm from an early age, and by the time he matriculated at the Protestant Seminary (*Stift*) at Tübingen in 1788, he acquired the nickname "the old man" for his scholarly habits. Hegel had received the best of Enlightenment learning at the Gymnasium Illustre in Stuttgart, which eventually set him at odds with theological traditionalism and ministerial expectations at the Seminary. Along with his friends Friedrich Hölderlin and Friedrich Schelling, Hegel was enamored with classical Greek and Roman ideals and devoted his life to the pursuit of freedom, beauty, and philosophical grandeur.

1 Translated from *Vorlesungen über die Philosophie der Religion*; hereafter, all references to this work are taken from the English translation by Peter C. Hodgson (see notes 5 and 6 below for detailed bibliography).

2 Peter Hodgson popularized the title "Theologian of the Spirit," in *G. W. F. Hegel: Theologian of the Spirit* (Minneapolis: Fortress, 1997).

During his 7 years as a private tutor, first in Bern (1793–6) and then in Frankfurt (1797–1800), Hegel had space to articulate some of his ideals in writing. In these early writings, we observe Hegel the philosopher-theologian searching for the essence of religion, which leads him to critique "The Positivity of the Christian Religion."[3] By "positivity," Hegel means something quite negative: the eclipse of reason and freedom under the authoritarian control of institutional, dogmatic, and irrational religion. At its heart, however, Christianity is a religion of love. In his essay "The Spirit of Christianity and Its Fate," Hegel identifies love as the core of God's kingdom: the beautiful communion of humanity in God. These themes continue to pervade even Hegel's most philosophical work as he explores the dynamic relation between the finite world and an infinite God.

Hegel turned his attention more directly to philosophy after obtaining a lectureship in Jena (1801–07). During this time, he founded the *Critical Journal of Philosophy* with Schelling and wrote one of his most famous works, *The Phenomenology of Spirit* (*Die Phenomenologie des Geistes*, 1807). In this book, Hegel articulates his vision of God not as a transcendent, unknowable Being, but as the absolute Spirit constantly revealed through finite reality, human community, and the historical process. He also planted seeds for his dialectical understanding of religion, which came into full bloom in his *Lectures on the Philosophy of Religion.* Hegel did not lecture specifically on religion until several years after he filled the chair of philosophy previously occupied by Johann Gottlieb Fichte at the University of Berlin (1818). As rector of a Gymnasium in Nuremburg (1808–16), he was preoccupied with his three-volume *Science of Logic*, and as a professor in Heidelberg (1816–17), he focused on the *Encyclopedia of the Philosophical Sciences in Outline.*

In all these works and many more, religion remained at the heart of Hegel's system of thought. If Hegel is thus viewed as a philosopher-theologian, then the *Lectures on the Philosophy of Religion* represent his "summa theologica."[4] First presented in 1821, Hegel repeated these lectures three more times—1824, 1827, and 1831—each time adapting his material in response to new criticisms and to clarify previous conclusions. For example, in 1824 Hegel responded to Schleiermacher's recently published and popular *The Christian Faith,* whereas in 1827 he turned attention to August Tholuck and others charging him with pantheism and atheism.

3 G. W. F. Hegel, *Early Theological Writings*, trans. T. M. Knox (Chicago: University of Chicago Press, 1948).

4 See Hans Küng, *The Incarnation of God: An Introduction to Hegel's Theological Thought as Prolegomena to a Future Christology*, trans. J. R. Stephenson (Edinburgh: T&T Clark, 1987), 348–9.

When Hegel died suddenly in 1831 during a cholera outbreak, just a year after becoming Rector of the University of Berlin, his lectures on the philosophy of religion had not yet been published. This was quickly remedied, with an edition appearing in 1832 based on Hegel's manuscript and several student transcripts. The history of subsequent editions is complex, but in the 1980s, a team of scholars produced a new edition and translation (published concurrently in German, English, and Spanish) based on careful attention to all available sources.[5] In doing so, they kept lecture material from each year separate in order to show the development and differences between the lectures. Soon after the publication of this three-volume collection, an abridged version became available based solely on the 1827 lectures, providing a more accessible entry point to this dense material.[6] Because of this accessibility and the more mature thought represented by the 1827 lectures, this chapter relies on the one-volume edition (LPR1) while drawing attention to the complete three-volume edition (LPR3) when necessary. Before exploring the particular content of these lectures, however, it is important to grasp a few key concepts undergirding Hegel's philosophy of religion.

Holistic Perspective and Dialectic Process

Like every philosopher and theologian of his day, Hegel stood in the shadow of Immanuel Kant (1724–1804). While appreciating Kant's emphasis on mental categories that filter the sensory data of reality, Hegel felt stifled by his agnosticism toward knowing the essence of things, including the nature and being of God. Hegel bemoaned this blinding prejudice, resolving to step out from behind Kant's shadow to explore the continuity between thought and reality by the light of reason. If we deny the possibility of knowing God, Hegel explains, then philosophy of religion is restricted to our perceived relation to an unknowable God (LPR1, 89). This approach messes about in a finite cave, rather than encountering and knowing the beauty of the infinite.

5 Peter C. Hodgson, ed., *Lectures on the Philosophy of Religion*, trans. R. F. Brown, P. C. Hodgson, and J. M. Stewart, 3 vols. (Berkeley and Los Angeles: University of California Press, 1984–7). A reprint edition is available from Oxford University Press, published in 2006. Hereafter quoted as LPR3, followed by volume and page number.

6 Peter C. Hodgson, ed., *Lectures on the Philosophy of Religion: One-Volume Edition, Lectures of 1827*, trans. R. F. Brown, P. C. Hodgson, and J. M. Stewart (Berkeley and Los Angeles: University of California Press, 1988). A reprint edition is available from Oxford University Press, published in 2006. Hereafter quoted as LPR1, followed by page number.

As such, Barth astutely concludes that Hegel handled Kant as "a manikin loyally improvising his resources, however sadly limited by the cave in which he plies his handiwork."[7]

In other words, Hegel desired to replace cramped bifurcations with a spacious, holistic perspective. Faith and knowledge, objectivity and subjectivity, God and the world, transcendence and immanence: these are deadly divisions that detract from the dynamic unity of all things. At the heart of this unity is Hegel's understanding of God as the dynamic, unifying principle of reality. In contrast to more traditional, metaphysical theology, Hegel presents God not just as the infinite substance or object but also as the infinite Spirit or subject who exists in a constant state of manifestation in the world (LPR1, 118–19). The reality of God, therefore, includes his infinite Being, his manifestation in everything finite, and the reconciliation of that Being and otherness throughout history. In short, all of world history, including the history of religions, can be described as the movement of God's revelation and self-knowledge through the process of humanity knowing and relating to God.

As Hegel's holistic perspective became more popular in Berlin and beyond, some of his contemporaries accused him of promoting pantheism and even atheism.[8] In the 1827 *Lectures on the Philosophy of Religion*, Hegel denies these accusations and attempts to clarify his position. Strictly speaking, pantheism maintains that everything is God, whether a sheet of paper or the flux of history. Rather than promoting this kind of static or abstract unity, however, Hegel asserts that particular elements of reality may *participate* in the being of God, but that does not mean they *are* God. Everything is united in God, but it is still possible to maintain a distinction between God and the rest of reality (LPR1, 122–8). Other scholars have applied the label *panentheism* to Hegel's position, which acknowledges the difference as well as the inseparable unity between God and the world.[9]

7 Karl Barth, *Protestant Theology in the Nineteenth Century* (London: SCM Press, 1972), 380.

8 The accusations of pantheism began to emerge in the mid-1820s, particularly in F. A. G. Tholuck, *Die Lehre von der Sünde und vom Versöhner*, 2nd ed. (Hamburg, 1825), 231; Cf. Anonymous [Hülsemann], *Ueber die Hegelsche Lehre, oder: Absolutes Wissen und moderner Pantheismus* (Leipzig, 1829). Charges of atheism were often linked to associating Hegel's thought with Spinozism, which German philosopher Friedrich Jacobi had interpreted as atheism (*Briefe uber die Lehre Spinozas*, 1785). By contrast, Hegel interpreted Spinoza's thought as acosmism, in which everything finite is a limitation or negation of the One (LPR1, 124–5).

9 See Peter C. Hodgson, *Hegel and Christian Theology* (New York: Oxford University Press, 2005), 68; James C. Livingston, *Modern Christian Thought: The Enlightenment and the Nineteenth Century*, 2nd ed. (Minneapolis: Fortress Press, 2006), 138.

For Hegel, the deep structure of reality as the unfolding of absolute Spirit (Being, non-being, becoming) is reflected in the structure of thought itself (thesis, antithesis, synthesis, or sublation). Intrinsically linked with the dialectical movement of Spirit, rationality is the process of a universal idea being differentiated by a particular modification of this idea and then moving to a new level of truth through what Hegel calls "sublation." This dialectical pattern structures every part of Hegel's system, including his philosophy of religion. The dialectic of religion thus exists in three moments: the concept of religion, particular determinations of religion throughout history, and the consummation of religion, which Hegel identifies with Christianity. Within this holistic perspective and dialectical process, the movement of religion is the very movement of Spirit, which exists as pure concept, determines itself in history, and returns to itself in perfect reconciliation (LPR1, 100–3).

Religion and Knowledge of God

At its most basic level, Hegel defines religion as consciousness of God (LPR1, 104). It involves an immediate knowledge or certainty (*Gewißheit*) that God exists (LPR1, 133). This is part of what it means to have faith in God, but faith also includes feeling (*Gefühl*) in which this general consciousness of God becomes personal (LPR1, 138). Hegel expands on what he means by "feeling" in the 1824 lectures, where he distinguishes his position from Schleiermacher's definition of religion as "the feeling of absolute dependence." He faults Schleiermacher for several reasons: First, when we relegate religion exclusively to the realm of feeling, we lose any objective and common ground to develop knowledge of God. Second, both animals and humans possess feeling, so focusing here keeps the conversation at a base level. Third, we should view feeling as the lowest form of religion, compared to the highest form—thought—because "God *is* essentially in thought" (LPR3, 1:273).

Although Hegel misrepresented Schleiermacher's perspective on the nature of religion by aligning feeling with animal passion, his critique does highlight a critical difference between these two fathers of modern theology. As articulated above, Hegel desired to move out from under the shadow of Kant by seeking objective knowledge of God and its representation in images, narratives, and doctrine. Schleiermacher, who accepted Kant's epistemological limits, viewed doctrine merely as religious feelings fixed in language with no objective referent. To Schleiermacher, therefore, Hegel's approach was riddled with intellectual hubris; to Hegel, Schleiermacher's system was spineless and irrational.

As religion seeks its objective content, it takes the form of representation (*Vorstellung*). By this, Hegel means biblical and theological language, including images, stories, and traditional doctrines. For example, when we represent God as a Father who begets a Son, we are using images or metaphors to express our consciousness and feeling of God in a way that corresponds to divine reality (LPR1, 146). Even more directly, doctrinal language that articulates God's attributes or actions is a form of representation. For instance, to say that God created the world represents the concept of God differentiating himself, so in order to understand what this means, we need to transform these representations into thought (*Denken*). Similarly, saying God is all-wise, wholly good, and righteous represents something true about God, but it is still not wholly objective knowledge because it needs to deal with the concepts that undergird this statement, such as identity and difference (LPR1, 148–54). The highest form of knowledge is conceptual or speculative knowledge, which reaches beyond the imagistic and mythological language of theology to grasp the rationality of reality.

Within this theoretical movement of religion, there is also a practical element, which Hegel calls worship or cultus (*Kultus*). This element involves all the ways—whether implicit or explicit—that humans participate in the process of reconciliation with God (LPR1, 191). Whether expressed internally (prayer) or externally (sacraments), cultus is critical for true knowledge of God because it requires getting involved personally in this process. Cultus is not limited to what might be identified as "religious life," but includes an entire life of service to God, which Hegel calls "the most genuine cultus" (LPR1, 194). In this selfless performance of life, knowledge of God becomes real as humanity is elevated into relation with God.

Determinate and Consummate Religion

Having defined the concept of religion, Part Two of the lectures addresses the determinations of this concept in the history of religions. Hegel organized this material differently for each delivery, but what stays constant is his overarching belief that determinate religions are "necessary conditions for the emergence of true religion, for the authentic consciousness of spirit" (LPR1, 205). In the 1827 lectures, these religions are divided into three categories: immediate religion, spiritual religion, and purposive religion. In immediate or nature religion, Hegel identifies a unity of the spiritual and natural realms. This kind of religion is not nature worship, but an approach toward the spiritual element of humanity as the most natural element (LPR1, 219). Hegel deals with many religions under this category, including African traditional religions, Chinese Taoism, Buddhism, Lamaism, Hinduism, and the religions of ancient Persia and Egypt. Contemporary readers will not be satisfied by Hegel's treatment of these religions at certain points, but neither was Hegel, who continued to rearrange and adapt the material in his 1831 lectures.

The next stage includes those religions that elevate the spiritual element above the natural element by highlighting concrete individuality (Greek religion) and thought (Jewish religion). Though Hegel places Judaism at the apex of the determinate religions, in his interpretation it still does not achieve the reconciliation of divinity and humanity because of its external adherence to divine commands (LPR1, 374). Before arriving at the consummate religion, Hegel briefly discusses the purposive or Roman religion, which combines elements of Greek beauty and Jewish sublimity, but only in an expedient and external manner. Only Christianity internalizes all these determinations and unites them in a religion that does not look elsewhere for fulfillment but contains fulfillment within itself (LPR1, 391–3).[10]

As the consummate religion, Hegel also calls Christianity the revealed religion, because here the infinite God completely reveals and gives himself to what is finite: God becomes incarnate. This religion may come in external forms, such as the Bible and church doctrines, but its content must always be received spiritually. For example, even though the Bible contains Christian doctrines, it must always be subjectively appropriated "with one's innermost being, one's spirit, one's thought, one's reason, being touched by them and assenting to them" (LPR1, 399). Hegel does not believe that holding exclusively to the Bible as the source of truth is a truly scientific approach, as Charles Hodge would argue several decades later. Rather, everything represented in the Bible and in dogmatic theology needs to be transformed into a conceptual, speculative form, and Hegel seeks to achieve such transformation as he explores the content of the consummate religion.

Speculative Christianity

The three elements of consummate religion are three modes of God's being and vitality as Spirit: God existing for himself, God creating everything finite, and God reconciling all things in community. The entire religion, therefore, has a trinitarian structure, as does the very fabric of reality. God

[10] The best summary of the movement from the concept of religion to particular determinations of religion and finally to consummate religion is found toward the beginning of Part Three (LPR1, 404–10).

in and for himself—the first element of Christianity—corresponds with what traditional theologians would call the immanent Trinity, or God's eternal being. This stands in contrast to the economic Trinity, or God's triune revelation and action in history. In Hegel's perspective, however, this language, as well as describing Father, Son, and Spirit as three coequal and coeternal persons, is merely representational rather than conceptual. He describes God's trinitarian being as a speculative idea, for this is the only way to transcend the mystery of understanding (LPR1, 422). Other scholars have chosen different terms to refer to Hegel's speculative trinitarianism, such as inclusive and holistic Trinity, but even these terms fall short of the concepts he has in mind.[11]

Likewise, the doctrine of creation represents a speculative idea about God differentiating himself so that the world is "released as something free and independent" (LPR1, 434). The world is therefore other than God, but it is still included within God's being and actuality, just as the Son is distinct yet one with the Father. As a part of creation, humanity is by nature both good and evil, which creates an estrangement within each person and a longing for this rift to be reconciled. Hegel insists we should not mistake the story of the Fall for something that actually happened; rather, like the story of creation, it signifies the rational process by which humanity obtains consciousness (knowledge of good and evil) and experiences a rupture in their relationship with God and the world. In this sense, the Fall is still a tragedy, but it is a necessary tragedy that creates the possibility of reconciliation.

God himself is an eternal process of reconciliation, but this reconciliation appears concretely through the life, death, and resurrection of one human being: Jesus the Christ, the God-man. Hegel admits this is a "monstrous compound," one that contradicts understanding but nevertheless points to the concept of infinity fused with finitude, the unity of divinity and humanity (LPR1, 457). Humanly speaking, Christ dies as a criminal; but religiously speaking, he dies as God in order to achieve a new relationship with God, a consciousness and certainty of God's presence and love (LPR1, 464). The resurrection and ascension of Christ are not physical realities that point to the continuing humanity of Christ; they are spiritual realities making way for the outpouring of the Spirit within the community.

Hegel thus transitions to the third element of consummate religion: the Spirit-community. It is appropriate to hyphenate these terms because in Hegel's scheme, community *is* Spirit: "God existing as community" (LPR1, 473). Community exists as a moment in the existence of the triune God, who determines himself through creation, reconciles himself through

[11] Hodgson, *Hegel and Christian Theology*, 113.

incarnation, and becomes present to himself through community. In this final section, Hegel explains how individuals are initiated and sustained in community through baptism, faith, doctrine, repentance, and the sacrament of communion. On the surface, it may seem as if Hegel aligns himself with traditional doctrines, such as the Lutheran position on mystical communion (LPR1, 480–91). Yet to grasp what Hegel is trying to accomplish, it is important to recognize that such doctrines only represent speculative truth. In the end, Hegel hopes for Spirit-community to be realized in ethical forms of life (LPR1, 483–4). Scholars have interpreted this hope in multiple and sometimes contradictory ways, either as promoting religion's eventual resolution or complex dissonance with the modern world. The fact that Hegel's ideas have spawned opposing positions, however, reflects uncanny fittingness to the dialectical movement of his thought.

Hegelianism in Manifold Hues

Even among Hegel's immediate successors, there was no such thing as pure and simple Hegelianism. Only a few years after his death, a spectrum of scholarship had already emerged that ranged from those seeking to harmonize Hegel's thought with Protestant theology (right or old Hegelians) to those desiring to discard the theological elements and enlist Hegel's system to build humanistic agendas (left or young Hegelians). Most notable within the latter group are Ludwig Feuerbach (1804–72), who viewed theology as a projection of human imagination and experience, and Karl Marx (1818–83), who approached religion as a tool used by ruling elites to control society. These left Hegelians, therefore, while sharing Hegel's interest in the dialectical movement of history, purged this process of objective religious content and wielded it for more overtly political purposes. Situated in the middle of the left-right Hegelian spectrum are a myriad of theologians, philosophers, and biblical scholars who pursued a more balanced mediation between Christianity and modern science and society. Some of these "mediating theologians," such as Richard Rothe (1799–1867) and Isaak Dorner (1809–84), drew on Hegel's conceptual framework to a certain extent but were also significantly influenced by Schleiermacher and his emphasis on religious experience.

Outside Germany in the nineteenth century, the impact of Hegel's thought was most clearly seen in British idealism and American transcendentalism. British idealists such as Thomas Hill Green (1836–82) and Francis Herbert Bradley (1846–1924) applied Hegel's insights in a more strictly philosophical direction as an alternative to empiricism and utilitarianism.

Transcendentalism, by contrast, was a more holistic literary, political, and cultural movement, and a figure such as Ralph Waldo Emerson (1803–82), sometimes called "America's Hegel," exerted enormous sway over the rise of individualism and mystical spirituality within American Protestantism.

Although few Protestant theologians in the nineteenth and twentieth centuries adopted Hegel's system of thought wholesale, his influence can be most clearly traced through various forms of immanentism: philosophical and theological approaches that closely identify God and the world. Process theologians, for example, do not *equate* God and the world (and thus disavow pantheism as Hegel did), but place God and the world in such *dynamic interplay* that one cannot be conceived without the other. Other prominent Protestant theologians of the twentieth century, such as Wolfhart Pannenberg (1928–2014) and Jürgen Moltmann (1936–2024), leveled critiques against process theology or panentheism. Nevertheless, their theology emphasizes the immanence of God within history while seeking to maintain God's future-originated transcendence.

Another sign of Hegel's influence can be seen in Protestant theology that seeks harmonious integration of philosophy, culture, and religion. One prime example is Paul Tillich (1886–1965), who also espoused a variation of Hegel's immanentism as filtered through his fondness for existentialism. More recently, and especially since the new edition of the *Lectures on the Philosophy of Religion*, an increasing number of Protestant theologians have engaged with Hegel's thought directly and in a favorable light, viewing it as a fruitful attempt to articulate God's being and action in an anti-theological milieu.[12]

Another group of Protestant theologians, beginning with Søren Kierkegaard (1813–55), have maintained the opposite perspective by seeking to demonstrate Hegel's inherent failure to maintain God's transcendence, and by implication, the essence of Christianity. Karl Barth surmises that Hegel might have become the Thomas Aquinas of Protestant theology, but he failed by making God dependent on his creation, thus erroneously turning theology into an anthropological enterprise.[13] Similarly, Charles Taylor bemoans how Hegel's heterodox conflation of God and the world completely jettisons the gifting relationship between God and humanity.[14] Whether one

[12] A good example is Peter Hodgson's *Hegel and Christian Theology*, and the last chapter of this book provides a helpful summary of those who see either promise or failure in Hegel's theology.

[13] Barth, *Protestant Theology in the Nineteenth Century*, 370.

[14] Charles Taylor, *Hegel* (Cambridge: Cambridge University Press, 1975), 493. Another recent example of exposing Hegel's heterodoxy is William Desmond, *Hegel's God: A Counterfeit Double?* (Aldershot: Ashgate, 2003).

sides with these scathing critiques or with those who see Hegel as a fruitful conversation partner for theology, there is no doubt that he stands alongside Schleiermacher as a father of modern theology.

Select Bibliography

Primary Sources

Hegel, Georg Wilhelm Friedrich, *Lectures on the Philosophy of Religion: One-Volume Edition, The Lectures of 1827*. Edited by Peter C. Hodgson. Oxford: Oxford University Press, 2006.

Hegel, Georg Wilhelm Friedrich, *Vorlesungen über die Philosophie der Religion*. Edited by Walter Jaeschke, 3 vols. Hamburg: Meiner, 1983–5.

Other Notable Works by the Author

Hegel, Georg Wilhelm Friedrich, *Encyclopedia of the Philosophical Sciences*. Translated and edited by Klaus Brinkman and Daniel O. Dahlstrom. Cambridge: Cambridge University Press, 2015.

Hegel, Georg Wilhelm Friedrich, *The Phenomenology of Spirit*. Translated by Peter Fuss and John Dobbins. Notre Dame: University of Notre Dame Press, 2019.

Hegel, Georg Wilhelm Friedrich, *The Science of Logic*. Translated by George Di Giovanni. Cambridge: Cambridge University Press, 2015.

Secondary Sources

De Nys, Martin J., *Hegel and Theology*. London and New York: T&T Clark, 2009.

Hodgson, Peter, *Hegel and Christian Theology: A Reading of the Lectures on the Philosophy of Religion*. New York: Oxford University Press, 2005.

Küng, Hans, *The Incarnation of God: An Introduction to Hegel's Theological Thought as Prolegomena to a Future Christology*. Translated by J. R. Stephenson. Edinburgh: T&T Clark, 1987.

Pinkard, Terry, *Hegel: A Biography*. New York: Cambridge University Press, 2000.

Yerkes, James, *The Christology of Hegel*. Albany: State University of New York Press, 1983.

3

Søren Aabye Kierkegaard, *Practice in Christianity*[1] (1850)

Becoming a Christian

Many people know and appreciate Søren Kierkegaard (1813–55) for his philosophy, and some even consider him the father of existentialism. In his own perspective, however, Kierkegaard was first and foremost a religious writer and theologian. In the posthumously published *The Point of View for My Work as an Author*, he makes this point clear: "my whole authorship pertains to Christianity, to the issue: becoming a Christian, with direct and indirect polemical aim at that enormous illusion, Christendom."[2] Kierkegaard desired above all to present a vision for what it really means to become a Christian. He sought to do so by unmasking the illusion of Christendom that, in nineteenth-century Denmark, led to the blasphemous assumption that everyone was Christian.[3] His goal of waking the established church out of its nominal slumber may not have succeeded in his lifetime, but his writings have provided enduring inspiration for subsequent generations of theologians and pastors who found themselves in similar battles against the established order.

Søren Aabye Kierkegaard was born on May 5, 1813, in Copenhagen, the center of Danish government, religion, and culture. His father, Michael Pederson Kierkegaard, was a trader in the clothing business and a faithful member of the established Lutheran Church, although he was also deeply influenced by Moravian piety. Michael Kierkegaard suffered from debilitating depression, which may have influenced his decision to retire at an early age.

[1] Translated from Indøvelse i Christendom; hereafter, all references will be to Søren Kierkegaard, *Practice in Christianity*, trans. and eds. Howard V. Hong and Edna H. Hong, vol. 20, *Kierkegaard's Writings* (Princeton: Princeton University Press, 1991) and shall be noted by employing in-text parenthetical citations.

[2] Søren Kierkegaard, *The Point of View for My Work as an Author*, in *The Point of View*, trans. and eds. Howard V. Hong and Edna H. Hong (Princeton: Princeton University Press, 1998), 23.

[3] Ibid., 88, 90.

One beneficial result of his retirement is the time he devoted to entertaining friends for dinner and having lengthy discussions about philosophy and theology, which no doubt had a lasting impact on young Søren.

Following his father's wish, Søren began his studies in theology at Copenhagen University in 1830 at the age of seventeen, and he remained there until his graduation in 1840. As he began university, Kierkegaard encountered both rationalism and romanticism, and he was initially inspired by aesthetic and speculative ideals. Eventually, however, he became dissatisfied with the speculative disconnection between theory and life, which was particularly manifest in Hegelianism. As a result, he began to search for a better way to integrate the pursuit of truth with subjective experience. In 1835, Kierkegaard experienced a turning point where he realized his passion to discover a truth that actually makes a difference, "to find the idea for which I am willing to live and die."[4] Kierkegaard pursued this aim as an independent scholar and religious writer until his sudden death 20 years later at the age of 42.

At the outset of his writing career, Kierkegaard's books offered a critique of speculative idealism represented by Hegel and his followers. For example, *Either/Or* (1843) places paradox at the heart of reality as opposed to Hegel's both/and unification of the finite and infinite. Similarly, *Philosophical Fragments* (1844) contains in its title an intentional contrast with philosophy as a totalizing system. *Smulen* is the Danish word usually translated as *fragments*, and it literally means just a few bits and scraps. According to Kierkegaard, offering these mere scraps was far better than constructing a philosophical or theological system, for these systems far too easily anesthetize readers to the urgency of action and the appropriation of truth within personal existence. Kierkegaard also used pseudonymous authorship to bring readers to points of personal, decisive action rather than detached understanding. By writing under different pseudonyms, Kierkegaard was able to portray rival worldviews and modes of existence, creating a dialectical knot that readers are required to untie.[5] For example, *Philosophical Fragments* and *Concluding Unscientific Postscript to Philosophical Fragments* (1846) is written by Johannes Climacus, a pseudonym named after the sixth-century monk and author of *The Ladder of Divine Ascent*. The views of Johannes Climacus do not correspond with Kierkegaard's own perspectives; rather, they represent someone who has yet to climb the ladder of ascent to God.

Kierkegaard identifies *Concluding Unscientific Postscript* as a turning point from his first period of authorship (1836–46) to a second and more

4 Søren Kierkegaard, *Papers and Journals: A Selection*, trans. and ed. Alastair Hannay (London: Penguin Books, 1996), 32.

5 Kierkegaard hints at the purpose of pseudonymity in several places, but the language of "dialectical knot" comes from *Practice in Christianity*, 133.

thoroughly religious period (1846–55).[6] In this book, Climacus insists that true Christianity is not just a doctrine to understand, but an "existence-communication," a truth to be grasped with passionate inwardness and rigorously lived out.[7] In later books, particularly those written under the pseudonym Anti-Climacus, this passionate existence is articulated with uncompromising clarity, particularly in contrast with the contortion of Christianity within Christendom. Anti-Climacus does not represent the opposite of Climacus, but rather an extraordinarily devout Christian in contrast to someone who is barely a Christian.[8] Kierkegaard included his name as editor on every book authored by these two pseudonyms, which indicates his own placement somewhere in the middle of these dialectical poles, both of which are necessary to discover what it means to become a genuine Christian.[9]

The first work by Anti-Climacus, *The Sickness Unto Death* (written in 1848, published in 1849), presents the problem to which his second book, *Practice in Christianity* (written in 1848, published in 1850), provides the solution. In fact, Kierkegaard originally considered titling this book *The Radical Cure* as a reflection on the relationship with Christ that brings healing from the sickness of sin.[10] He also contemplated giving it a descriptive subtitle: "A Contribution to the Introduction of Christianity into Christendom."[11] In addition to presenting a vision of true Christianity, therefore, *Practice in Christianity* also proposes how to keep the established church from abolishing Christianity (36). Originally, Kierkegaard did not intend for this book to constitute an outright attack on the established church, but rather to provide a basis for its existence.[12] Particularly disheartening, however, was the flat response from Jacob Peter Mynster, Kierkegaard's childhood pastor and Primate of the Danish Church since 1834. Kierkegaard had expected either repentance or stiff opposition from Mynster, but when they met after the book was published, Mynster made a few comments, but otherwise "the conversation was just as usual."[13] This was only one disappointment in an unfortunate series of events motivating Kierkegaard to critique the established

[6] Kierkegaard, *Point of View*, 31, 94.

[7] Søren Kierkegaard, *Concluding Unscientific Postscript*, vol. 1, trans. and eds. Howard V. Hong and Edna H. Hong (Princeton: Princeton University Press, 1992), 379–80.

[8] Kierkegaard, "Selected Entries from Kierkegaard's Journals and Papers Pertaining to *Practice in Christianity*," in *Practice in Christianity*, 279–80. Kierkegaard's Journals and Papers are available in six separate volumes, but for ease of reference, I will be referencing the supplement provided for *Practice in Christianity*, hereafter cited as *Supplement*.

[9] Kierkegaard, *Supplement*, 283.

[10] Ibid., 273.

[11] Ibid., 307–8.

[12] Kierkegaard, *Point of View*, 18.

[13] Kierkegaard, *Supplement*, 357.

church more vehemently as he reached the end of his life. In 1855, a year after Mynster's death and a few months before his own, Kierkegaard prefaced the second edition of *Practice in Christianity* by asserting that Christendom was indeed indefensible.[14] Although this book did not have the impact he had hoped, Kierkegaard still considered 1848 his most fruitful year as an author and *Practice in Christianity* "the most perfect and truest thing" he had ever written. Although Kierkegaard claims authorship in his journals, this essay will continue to refer to the author of *Practice in Christianity* as Anti-Climacus, given the distinction between this pseudonym and Kierkegaard's own position.[15]

Christianity Versus Christendom

Between the authorship of *Practice in Christianity* in 1848 and its publication in 1850, great social and political changes had swept through Denmark and the rest of Europe. Following the revolution of 1848, Denmark emerged with a representative government and adopted a new constitution. Like the government, the church now belonged to the people instead of the ruling aristocrats, having been renamed The People's Church (*Folkekirke*). It maintained strong links to the state, however, and for all practical purposes it remained the established church. In light of these changes, Kierkegaard recognized this as the opportune time to call the Danish people and church leaders to embrace true Christianity and to dispel the charade of Christendom.[16]

The major calamity of Christendom, according to Anti-Climacus in *Practice in Christianity*, is that becoming a Christian is too easy, like putting on socks instead of carrying a cross (35). Becoming a Christian was no longer associated with pursuing a different way of life—a life of suffering—so people could become Christian without even noticing. With no outward manifestation of true faith, the visible distinction between Christians and non-Christians evaporates, producing a "slack universalism" (112). Anti-Climacus argues that if becoming a Christian has anything to do with Christ, then Christians should expect to come into conflict with the established

[14] Quoted in Howard V. Hong and Edna H. Hong, "Historical Introduction," in *Practice in Christianity*, xvi–xvii.

[15] Kierkegaard, *Supplement*, 287.

[16] Bruce H. Kirmmse, *Kierkegaard in Golden Age Denmark* (Bloomington and Indianapolis: Indiana University Press, 1990), 381. This book offers an excellent introduction to the social and political context of *Practice in Christianity* and all of Kierkegaard's works after 1846.

order, just like Christ came into conflict with the scribes and Pharisees (85–6). Christianity without conflict is Christianity without Christ, and in the end, it is no better than paganism (107).

Another way Anti-Climacus highlights the difference between Christianity and Christendom is by contrasting the Militant Church and the Triumphant Church. The Triumphant Church believes that all is settled because Christ reigns in his glory. The struggle is over because the victory has been won in Christ. While containing a partial truth, the Triumphant Church fails to recognize that until we are lifted up in glory like Christ, we are called to follow him in his lowliness. Ultimately, therefore, the Triumphant Church is a complete illusion (209). By contrast, the Militant Church embraces the radical call to confess and follow Christ. Rather than being content with knowing about Christ and making observations about his life, members of the Militant Church grasp the truth of Christ as a way of life (205–7). The Militant Church embraces the struggle and rigorousness of following Christ no matter how foolish this may appear to comfortable members of the establishment (228–30).

Christendom may bear the name of Christ, but in reality, it is "the secularization of everything" (91). By aligning Christianity with the established order, one's relationship with God no longer has priority over everything else, purged of its capacity to judge every other commitment and activity. Connected with this criticism is the danger Anti-Climacus perceives in viewing Christianity as the inevitable progression of world history and development of humanity. The problem with this Hegelian perspective is that it links God so closely to history and humanity that the infinite difference between God and everything he has created disappears, along with the paradox of the God-man (221–2). The ultimate antidote to the disease of Christendom is to encounter Christ: not the historical Jesus, but the contemporary Christ who is received by faith.

Contemporaneity with Christ

Anti-Climacus insists that we cannot know anything about Christ through history, precisely because we "cannot *know* anything at all about *Christ*; he is the paradox, the object of faith, exists only for faith" (25). When historians and philosophers pursue knowledge of Christ, what they fail to grasp is that there is no contact point between God and humanity that enables us to know Christ as the God-man. There is an "infinite qualitative difference" between humanity and divinity, which means that in Christ, humanity and divinity are united in a paradox that cannot be the object of historical inquiry (28–9). Anti-Climacus likewise makes the case that Christ's divinity cannot be "demonstrated," which is blasphemy, but can only be received by faith (26). For example, whereas some may claim that Christ's miracles "prove" his divinity, this would in effect make faith unnecessary. Neither miracles nor anything else can prove the paradox of Christ; instead, they lead us either to take offense or to have faith (97).

Faith is therefore the opposite of knowing historical facts about Christ. Faith is belief in the truth of Christ *for me* (64). Rather than a *historical* trust in Christ, faith is a *contemporary* trust in Christ (9). In other words, "a believer must be just as contemporary with Christ's presence as his contemporaries were" (9). We must receive Jesus's words of invitation just as his disciples who walked with him during his ministry. Christ declared and demonstrated the way of salvation in the first century, but equally he declares and demonstrates this way to us today. Faith is the process of responding to and imitating Christ in the urgency of the present moment. Thus, becoming a Christian is becoming contemporary with Christ (63). Because of this radical contrast between faith and historical knowledge, some popular works have explained the kind of faith advocated in *Practice in Christianity* and the whole Kierkegaardian corpus as a subjective leap in the dark.[17] Most scholars try to tread more carefully, however, showing how contemporaneity is not so much a leap lacking all understanding, but rather it is a leap into action from a position of personal understanding and passionate allegiance to Christ.[18] That being said, subsequent philosophers and theologians have rightly challenged Anti-Climacus's claim, which Kierkegaard also makes elsewhere, that Christ can only be believed rather than known by offering a broader concept of knowledge inclusive of its personal and relational modes.[19]

Coming into contemporaneity with Christ means encountering him in the paradox of his loftiness and lowliness. Both of these aspects of the God-man have the potential to offend, whether a human being claiming to be God (loftiness) or God claiming to be human and suffering the consequences (lowliness). Anti-Climacus traces both forms of offense as witnessed in the Gospels and presents both as options for contemporary offense. This offense does not arise when we learn a doctrine about Christ, but when we encounter Christ himself in his loftiness and lowliness (106). Members of Christendom

17 Sam Harris, *The End of Faith: Religion, Terror, and the Future of Reason* (repr., New York: W. W. Norton & Company, 2005).

18 Murray Rae, *Kierkegaard and Theology* (London: T&T Clark, 2010), 55–7. See *Practice in Christianity*, 158.

19 For example, see Karl Barth, "Faith as Knowledge," in *Dogmatics in Outline*, trans. G. T. Thomson (London: SCM Press, 1949), 22–7.

do not approach Christ in contemporaneity, and therefore they destroy the possibility of both offense and faith. They are too comfortable to entertain the radical implication of God revealing himself through the suffering of an individual human being. This implication, of course, is that the only way to become a Christian is to imitate the suffering of Christ, converting the offense into active faith.

From Admiration to Imitation

The paradox of Christ's lofty lowliness also serves as the paradigm or prototype for Christian existence. To become a Christian, it is not enough to admire the paradox of Christ; we must imitate him as a personal paradigm. To illustrate this point, Anti-Climacus refers to the tendency of young people to imagine the ideal Christian existence. This is a promising starting point, but it is not complete until that young person begins to actively will that ideal into existence. We must not just imagine the ideal; we must become the ideal (220). Living solely in the world of imagination and admiration is an adolescent error, and Anti-Climacus associated this error with many of the pastors and preachers in Denmark. They love to admire Christ and make profound observations about his life, but their own lives bear no resemblance to the beautiful form of Christ's ideal (239). True admiration does not remain at a distance from its object but seeks to move ever closer, eventually becoming what it admires. Likewise, true admiration of Christ involves active imitation of Christ (241).

Like a theater audience, admirers of Christ are content to remain detached from the play and make appropriate comments in hushed tones (244). But this is no mere metaphor. Anti-Climacus uses this opportunity to condemn Christian artists in general, because they create illusions of reality and do so with indifference to the subject matter (254). Despite this critical attitude toward Christian art, one way of understanding what Anti-Climacus is commending here is to take the theatrical metaphor one step further. In this case, the true spectator is the one who gets up off the seat and joins the other actors and Christ himself on the stage, casting off all illusions and participating in the play for real.[20] But too many people fear what would happen if they embraced the idea of this play with passionate inwardness and moved from admiration to imitation of the main character.

[20] In *Concluding Unscientific Postscript*, Climacus makes a similar observation that if a person considers himself a spectator in The Drama of Dramas, "he is simply forgetting that he himself is supposed to be the actor" (158).

The essence of imitating Christ is suffering, and it begins by leaving the audience and participating in the action. Suffering is inevitable for believers because they are contemporary with Christ in his abasement. This is the "danger of actuality" that puzzled Nicodemus when he came to question Jesus at night (Jn 3:1-15). It also caused the rich young ruler to despair, for the challenge was too great (Lk. 18:18-23). Both are examples of men who could not grasp the "infinite difference between an admirer and an imitator" (249). Similarly, the Triumphant, established church is full of admirers who refuse to be imitators, and this is the tragedy of Christendom. The challenge to move from admiration to imitation goes out to each individual, and the only way to make an appropriate response is to appropriate the truth of Christ with unconditional inwardness. For Anti-Climacus, this means focusing so intensely on Christ and being so turned inward in contemporaneity with Christ "that one is quite literally alone in the whole world, alone before God, alone with Holy Scripture as a guide, alone with the prototype before one's eyes" (225). Passages like this have led some to accuse Kierkegaard of subjectivism and individualism. While there is certainly some credence to this critique, it is important to keep Kierkegaard in his context and remember the forces and trends to which he was reacting, particularly speculative philosophy and the established church. In addition, a continuing difficulty in interpreting Kierkegaard is determining the proper relationship between his self-authored and pseudonymous works. Scholars often mention, for example, that his self-authored *Works of Love* (1847), written just a year before *Practice in Christianity*, counterbalances the individualistic strain appearing in other works. Needless to say, this debate highlights the fact that interpreting Kierkegaard is an ongoing task, and his legacy is by no means monolithic.

Kierkegaard's Diverse Kin

Kierkegaard's works did not reach a wider audience until after the First World War, partly because of delayed translation and partly because speculative approaches were still the norm for Western theology. Upon wider circulation, his work was often met with mixed reactions, although the cultural milieu after the War was more amenable to Kierkegaard's call for personal engagement and suffering witness. Overall, his influence on Protestant theology can be seen among theologians seeking to move away from rationalist speculation and toward personal engagement with Christ and radical response to his challenges. Just as Kierkegaard's perspective brought him into conflict with the established order, the same is often true of theologians who appreciated his radical perspective, particularly in his later years. No doubt one of the most prominent examples is Dietrich Bonhoeffer (1906–45), who leveled a similar critique against those who were contorting Christianity by aligning themselves with the Nazi regime. His commitment to the costly grace of Christ led him into a life of suffering and abasement, a prime example of Kierkegaard's admonition to move from admiration to imitation of Christ. For both Kierkegaard and Bonhoeffer, Christianity is a way of life focused on the concrete person and work of Christ, not detached adherence to abstract principles.

The influence of Kierkegaard on twentieth-century theology is also evident among those who emphasize the "infinite qualitative difference" between God and humanity. For example, Scottish theologian P. T. Forsyth (1848–1921) demurred from Protestant liberalism by emphasizing the problem of guilt and sin and its resolution in the atonement of Christ. Forsyth blazed the trail for Karl Barth (1886–1968), whose work represents an explosive attack against German liberalism in an effort to rehabilitate God's infinite freedom and transcendence. Despite this point of resonance with Kierkegaard, Barth later accused Kierkegaard of promoting works righteousness because of his staunch challenges in *Practice in Christianity* and other works. Many others have defended Kierkegaard against this accusation, however, hailing him as a prophet calling Christians to authentic repentance and a life of personal obedience to Christ.

Paul Tillich (1886–1965) is yet another prominent theologian influenced by Kierkegaard's dialectical method, emphasis on the infinite distinction between God and humanity, and critique of the establishment. As Tillich's theology developed, however, he placed greater emphasis than Kierkegaard would have sanctioned on correlating the gospel with contemporary culture and expressing these truths in abstract terms. A similar pattern of influence yet divergence is evident in the work of Reinhold Niebuhr (1892–1971), who drew heavily on Kierkegaard's theological anthropology and whose critique of secular and religious liberalism in America contains obvious resonance with Kierkegaard's quarrel with Christendom.

Many additional strains of Kierkegaard's influence might be explored within both theology and philosophy, but even this short survey shows his enduring impact on Protestant theology. One would be remiss, however, to seek Kierkegaard's legacy among the halls of academia alone. The most direct progeny of the vision articulated in *Practice in Christianity* are those Christians who hear Christ's invitation and actively respond by imitating him in his abasement and suffering. In sum, Kierkegaard's closest kin are those who personally confess Christ and embrace Christianity as a way of life, no matter the cost.

Select Bibliography

Primary Sources

Kierkegaard, Søren, *Indøvelse i Christendom, En opbyggelig Tale og To Taler ved Altergangen om Fredagen*. Vol. 12, *Søren Kierkegaards Skrifter*. Edited by Niels Jørgen Cappelørn, Joakim Garff, Anne Mette Hansen, and Johnny Kondrup. Copenhagen: Søren Kierkegaard Research Center and GEC Gad Publishers, 2008.

Kierkegaard, Søren, *Practice in Christianity*. Translated and edited by Howard V. Hong and Edna H. Hong. Vol. 20, *Kierkegaard's Writings*. Princeton: Princeton University Press, 1991.

Other Notable Works by the Author

Kierkegaard, Søren, *Concluding Unscientific Postscript*. Translated and edited by Alastair Hannah. Cambridge: Cambridge University Press, 2009.

Kierkegaard, Søren, *Either/Or*. Translated and edited by Howard V. Hong and Edna H. Hong. Vol. 3, *Kierkegaard's Writings*. Princeton: Princeton University Press, 1989.

Kierkegaard, Søren, *Fear and Trembling / Repetition*. Translated and edited by Howard V. Hong and Edna H. Hong. Vol. 6, *Kierkegaard's Writings*. Princeton: Princeton University Press, 1983.

Secondary Sources

Kirmmse, Bruce H., *Kierkegaard in Golden Age Denmark*. Bloomington and Indianapolis: Indiana University Press, 1990.

Pattison, George, *Kierkegaard and the Theology of the Nineteenth Century*. Cambridge: Cambridge University Press, 2012.

Rae, Murray, *Kierkegaard and Theology*. London: T&T Clark, 2010.

Walsh, Sylvia, *Kierkegaard: Thinking Christianly in an Existential Mode*. Oxford: Oxford University Press, 2009.

4

Charles Hodge, *Systematic Theology* (1871–2)

Old School Headmaster

Recent biographers of Charles Hodge (1797–1878) coined three memorable monikers to portray his vast influence as a theologian, educator, and churchman: *pride of Princeton*, *guardian of American orthodoxy*, and *pope of Presbyterianism*.[1] If Hodge deserves the third title, it is only as preeminent spokesperson for Old School Presbyterianism, not the New School variety. As a result, the extent to which one views Hodge as the custodian of orthodoxy depends on which side of the Presbyterian fence one prefers. What cannot be contested, however, is the enormous impact Hodge wielded on generations of theology students at Princeton and on the defense and propagation of confessional Reformed theology in America and around the world.

In 1797, Charles Hodge was born into a distinguished merchant family in Philadelphia. Tragically, when Charles was only 6 months old, his father died of yellow fever. His mother was more than capable of raising him, and Hodge was well prepared at age 15 to enter the classical academy in Somerville, New Jersey. He continued his studies at the College of New Jersey (later Princeton University) and then the newly formed Princeton Seminary. During this time, Hodge experienced a conversion that he described as a culmination of Christian nurture, and he eagerly received the tutelage of Archibald Alexander, a prominent professor of theology at Princeton Seminary.

As Princeton grew, an urgent need arose for a professor to teach biblical languages, and Alexander asked Hodge to fill this role, only after his roommate and best friend, John Johns, declined the invitation. Hodge readily accepted after a brief stint in Philadelphia caring for his mother and preaching in local churches, and he quickly discovered his love for teaching. In 1822, after

1 The former is from Andrew W. Hoffecker, *Charles Hodge: The Pride of Princeton* (Phillipsburg: P&R Publishing, 2012). The latter two are from Paul C. Gutjahr, *Charles Hodge: Guardian of American Orthodoxy* (Oxford and New York: Oxford University Press, 2011).

2 years of teaching and his ordination in the Presbyterian Church, he received an official appointment at Princeton Seminary as professor of oriental and biblical literature. In the same year, he married Sarah Bache, the great granddaughter of Benjamin Franklin, with whom he would enjoy the blessing of eight children.

Despite his love for teaching, Hodge became painfully aware of his inadequacies in languages and burgeoning biblical scholarship. As a result, he requested a study leave in Europe to gain proficiency in French and German as well as contemporary European scholarship. His 2 years in Paris, Halle, and Berlin (1826–8) proved enormously formative, both in terms of academic learning and the friendships he formed that would enable him to maintain connections with European centers of learning. His encounter with Schleiermacher was one among many critical encounters that solidified his distress over the "German mind," making him increasingly resolute to articulate an alternative theological vision.

His main avenue for doing so was *The Biblical Repertory and Princeton Review*, a journal Hodge started just before departing for Europe. Upon returning to Princeton, he assumed the role of editor and began a lifetime of prolific publication, the bulk of which appeared in this journal. Poor health plagued him in the 1830s and would remain with him the rest of his life, but he still managed to persist in teaching duties and wield leadership within the Presbyterian Church. Hodge was not squeamish about debates, and his resolute positions gained him notoriety as a defender of Old School Presbyterianism, typically siding with order over ardor and confessionalism over pietism. Hodge did not oppose piety and religious experience but insisted on their congruence with doctrinal orthodoxy and church order. His *Commentary on Romans* (1835) demarcated his views from Albert Barnes, Nathaniel Taylor, and other New School Presbyterians, precipitating the Old School/New School schism in 1837.

In 1840, Hodge was appointed professor of exegetical and didactic theology at Princeton Seminary. Throughout his 50-plus years of teaching, he trained more students than any other American professor in the nineteenth century. At his fiftieth anniversary as professor in 1872, thousands of people gathered to celebrate his accomplishments, including the first two volumes of his *Systematic Theology* (vols. 1–2, 1871; vol. 3, 1872), which had already replaced Francis Turretin's *Elenctic Theology* (1679–85) as the core theology textbook at Princeton. While sharing Turretin's concern to systematize and preserve confessional Reformed theology, Hodge's *Systematic Theology* engaged extensively with contemporary scholarship and is recognized by some as inaugurating a new era of comprehensive theological study.[2] Hodge distilled decades of theology lectures and hundreds of articles addressing contemporary figures and debates into these thick volumes. As such, Mark Noll rightly concludes that the *Systematic Theology* "is not so much the capstone of his life as the caboose at the end of a very long train."[3] That train reached the end of the line on June 19, 1878, but the legacy of Charles Hodge laid long tracks for the journey of Princeton Seminary and confessional Reformed theology in North America.

Just the Biblical Facts

Hodge's *Systematic Theology* spans four broad topics in the space of three volumes: theology proper or doctrine of God, anthropology, soteriology, and eschatology. In terms of general structure and several heading titles, it matches the layout of the *Westminster Confession of Faith* (1646), the confessional standard for the Presbyterian Church. A major difference, however, is that the *Systematic Theology* does not include a section on ecclesiology. Hodge did lecture extensively on the church, however, and these lectures were published soon after his death.[4] Although Hodge intended to revise this material for his *Systematic Theology*, as it stands there is more than enough substance to understand the methodology and main themes of his theology.[5]

In the Introduction, Hodge defends an inductive theological method versus a speculative, mystical, or Roman Catholic method. The essence of this method is that the Bible contains all the facts necessary for theology, and the task of systematic theology is to gather all these facts, show their relationship, and formulate principles based on them. Undergirding this method are several key presuppositions. First, Hodge presupposes that theology is a science, and just as good science begins with facts and builds a scientific theory or system based on observation, so theology moves from the facts of Scripture to a theological system. In short, "the Bible is to the

[2] Gutjahr, *Charles Hodge*, 352.

[3] Mark Noll, "Charles Hodge as Expositor of the Spiritual Life," in *Charles Hodge Revisited: A Critical Appraisal of His Life and Work*, eds. John W. Stewart and James H. Moorhead (Grand Rapids: Eerdmans, 2002), 208.

[4] Charles Hodge, *The Church and Its Polity* (Thomas Nelson and Sons, 1879). Forgotten Books published a reprint of this book in 2012, and Logos Bible Software released *The Collected Works of Charles Hodge* (29 vols.), which includes this volume.

[5] In the foreword to *The Church and Its Polity*, A. A. Hodge indicates that his father desired to write a fourth volume on ecclesiology for his systematics, but waning health prevented him from doing so. We also know this was Charles's intention because his outline of theological "departments" in the *Systematic Theology* ends with ecclesiology (32).

theologian what nature is to the man of science."[6] No fact of Scripture should be ignored. For example, the Bible contains facts about Christ knowing all things, but it also includes instances where Christ displays ignorance. The doctrinal conclusion of these disparate facts, according to Hodge, is that Christ has both a divine and human nature in one unified personality (1:12).

Second, Hodge privileges the facts of Scripture because he believes the Bible to be the inspired revelation of God containing every truth necessary for theological knowledge and personal salvation. Biblical revelation will be consistent with the facts discerned through reason and experience, because all truth comes from God. Only Scripture, however, can be the ultimate ground and guide for theology and life. Hodge recognizes a dynamic interplay between religious experience and biblical doctrine, for whereas the facts of Scripture must authenticate spiritual experience, the inward teaching of the Spirit must also interpret biblical doctrine. In fact, a "theology of the heart" as expressed in prayers and hymns was so important for Hodge that he confessed his theology would be nothing if "not sustained by the devotional writings of true Christians of every denomination" (1:17).

A third presupposition of Hodge's inductive method is the trustworthiness of our senses, mental operations, and self-evident truths. These same assumptions guide natural scientists, and when adopted by theologians, they provide guidelines for realistic doctrinal discovery. Many scholars have rightly highlighted the influence of Scottish Common Sense Realism on Hodge's theology, although this claim should be qualified. There is no doubt that since its founding by Scot-American John Witherspoon, Princeton had been a hotbed for philosophical realism in the tradition of Thomas Reid. According to this tradition, certain truths, such as the distinction between right and wrong or self-existence, should be received by common sense and not submitted to scathing skepticism. Hodge affirms the existence of these truths (1:10), but in no way asserts that they are a test for doctrine or diminish the need for supernatural revelation. When philosophers in this tradition, such as William Hamilton, began to deny the possibility of knowing a personal God, Hodge and other Princetonians readily rejected this philosophy (1:346–65).[7]

In other words, Hodge remained committed to an inductive method of moving from biblical facts to doctrinal system, in contrast to a speculative

[6] Charles Hodge, *Systematic Theology*, 3 vols. (Peabody: Hendrickson, 1999), 1:10. Hereafter, all further references to this work shall be noted by employing in-text parenthetical citations.

[7] For a thorough explanation, see Peter Hicks, *The Philosophy of Charles Hodge: A Nineteenth-Century Evangelical Approach to Reason, Knowledge and Truth* (Lewiston, Queenston, and Lampeter: The Edwin Mellen Press, 1997), 7–22. Despite his critiques of Hamilton, Hodge still held high respect for his philosophy and recommended his works for further reading (see 1:365, n.1).

method of moving from philosophical principles to doctrinal system. The supernatural revelation of Scripture needs to prove every truth of reason, and therefore Scripture is the ultimate source for theology. In general, Hodge targets Deism and Transcendentalism as theological systems that fall prey to rationalism and a speculative method (1:34–60). As his treatment of various doctrines unfolds, Hodge repeatedly remarks on speculative distortions of these doctrines. Regarding the doctrine of sin, for example, he critiques the speculative habit of identifying an external philosophical principle—sin as limitation of being, privation, sensuousness, or selfishness, and so on—that lacks congruence with biblical facts (2:132–49). He contrasts these philosophical perversions with doctrines as attested by the early church, Protestant confessions, and ultimately the Bible.

Mysticism is another erroneous method Hodge critiques, which moves from feelings to doctrinal system. Like the speculative method, mysticism displaces the authority of Scripture by recognizing feelings or experience as the ultimate source. Hodge recognizes a dangerous mystical strain running through every era of Christian tradition, but he focuses on Quietism and heterodox Quakerism as particular expressions. In his critique of the latter, Hodge distinguishes between orthodox Quakers who rightly emphasize the illumination of the Spirit and heterodox Quakers who espouse Deism, limit Christ's work to its subjective effects, and elevate the "inner light" to an authority equal to or greater than Scripture (1:92–7). Throughout the *Systematic Theology*, Schleiermacher bears the brunt of Hodge's critique as a modern mystic, particularly since Hodge sees him as representing many of the ills plaguing the modern German mind.

A third method Hodge contrasts with his inductive scheme is the Roman Catholic approach, which moves from Scripture and tradition to doctrinal system. Although tradition plays a major role in the *Systematic Theology*, Hodge opposes this method because it treats tradition as another form of revelation, and thus a standard for faith. Protestants affirm the consent of the universal Church, but only on essential matters of faith and those doctrines plainly revealed in Scripture (1:115–16). Once again, everything for Hodge goes back to the facts of Scripture, and if these are not the starting point for theology, the whole system is doomed to distort God's revelation.

The Threat of Anti-Theism

Hodge begins his "Theology Proper" by showing how it is possible to approach the Bible with confidence that God can actually be known, albeit not comprehensively. He defines theism as "the doctrine of an extramundane, personal God, the creator, preserver, and governor of the world" (1:204). Atheism, therefore, is not merely the denial of God's existence; it includes anti-theism, the denial of an extramundane, personal God (1:241). As varieties of anti-theism, Hodge deals with polytheism, hylozoism, materialism, and pantheism, but gives by far the most attention to the latter two.

Materialism is a system that reduces everything to physical forces, denying the existence of a mind or spirit. Hodge locates the seed of materialism in the philosophy of Epicurus, which germinated through Hobbes, Locke, and others, and flowered through the positivism of Auguste Comte (1798–1857). According to positivism, knowledge is restricted to physical phenomena and their observable relations. Consequently, any discipline purporting to deal with metaphysical or supernatural reality is rejected or completely revised in positivist fashion. Hodge has no patience for this worldview, arguing that it contradicts the facts of consciousness, reason, and experience (1:276–83). Whereas some forms of materialism do not explicitly deny the existence of God, Hodge claims that all forms are atheistic since their fundamental principles undermine theistic belief.

Pantheism is far more beguiling than materialism, for it often goes under the guise of Christian theology while denying fundamental truths. Most basically, it denies the distinction between God and the world, thus renouncing the unique personality of God and the finite individuality of human beings. Hodge spares no punches for pantheism, claiming that it destroys human freedom, the distinction between good and evil, and rational religion itself. In short, it is the worst form of atheism (1:333). He demonstrates its tragic rise in popularity through the work of Spinoza, Fichte, Schelling, Hegel, Schleiermacher, and others. The haste at which Hodge lumps thinkers into anti-theistic camps, however, has caused some scholars to doubt his grasp of proper distinctions. Brian Gerrish, for example, wonders whether Hodge adequately distinguished between Schleiermacher and Hegel, mistakenly viewing them both as pantheists and instances of the "modern German mind."[8]

Of these two German thinkers, Hodge extends much more effort in critiquing Schleiermacher, possibly because Hodge regarded him "as the most interesting as well as the most influential theologian of modern times" (2:440). While judging his theology a contradictory mess, Hodge held great respect for Schleiermacher's piety, conjecturing in a famous footnote that since Schleiermacher sang praises to Christ on earth, it is most likely he will be praising Christ his Savior in heaven (2:440, n. 1). Despite this underlying respect and charitable hope, Hodge was ruthless in his critique.

[8] B. A. Gerrish, "Charles Hodge and the Europeans," in *Charles Hodge Revisited*, 157.

He accuses Schleiermacher of being unbiblical, speculative, pantheistic, anti-trinitarian, and at odds with orthodox forms of anthropology, Christology, and soteriology (2:442–54). Regarding his Christology, Hodge links every problem to Schleiermacher's propensity to collapse the God-world distinction. Since anything Schleiermacher says of God is simply an expression of self-consciousness, it is impossible for him to affirm the existence of an extramundane, personal God and his incarnation as the person of Christ.

In contrast to these anti-theistic threats, Hodge articulates his doctrine of God, the Trinity, and Christ using traditional terms and meanings as articulated in the early church and Reformed confessions. The danger of pantheistic portrayals, he claims, is that they retain traditional terms (Redeemer, Mediator, Incarnation, Spirit, etc.) while changing their meaning. Such a shift in meaning is a result of pantheists embracing a principle external to Scripture rather than submitting to the facts and authority of Scripture. For example, Hodge accuses many of his contemporaries of opposing the doctrine of regeneration, which claims that God brings alive those who were spiritually dead according to his will and power. Hodge argues that such opposition is based on a variety of prejudiced philosophical principles, with no regard to clear statements in Scripture to the contrary (3:37–40). On this issue, Hodge submits everyone outside the Reformed tradition to the criticism that their theological priorities displace Scripture as the ultimate authority, including his New School Presbyterian interlocutors Nathanael Emmons, Charles Finney, and Nathaniel Taylor (3:7–14).

Given Hodge's persistent emphasis on biblical induction, it is curious to note that some sections of the *Systematic Theology* do not include any treatment of biblical material, and those that do are sometimes organized in a piecemeal fashion. For instance, while the section on regeneration just discussed contains substantial quotes from John Calvin, John Owen, Francis Turretin, the Canons of Dordt, and the Westminster Standards, only one page in this lengthy portion contains scant quotes from Scripture (3:34). Other sections include deep biblical investigation, such as his defense of the divinity of Christ (1:483–521), but the objection nevertheless remains that sometimes Hodge fails to show how his doctrinal system arises from the biblical facts. Furthermore, there are instances where Hodge's interpretation and application of these biblical facts could be contested. To pick one example, in commenting on the sixth commandment, he resolutely defends the necessity of capital punishment for murderers (3:363–4) and pronounces that those who commit suicide will lose their soul (3:367). In earlier writings, he also articulated a troubling position on slavery, arguing that while abusive slaveholding is wrong, the institution of slavery should only be phased out gradually rather than hastening emancipation.[9] Underdeveloped elements of the *Systematic Theology*, therefore, include an awareness of how social and cultural location impact interpretation of biblical facts and a more thorough defense of why these facts should be viewed through Reformed theological lenses. Without paying attention to this process, a bad habit may emerge of staring at the lenses and ignoring the facts themselves or taking them for granted.

Reading the Facts with Reformed Lenses

Hodge roots his Reformed reading of Scripture in Augustinianism. In fact, he uses "Reformed" and "Augustinian" interchangeably to distinguish his anthropology and soteriology from competing views, whether Pelagianism or semi-Pelagianism, Roman Catholicism, Remonstrant theology, Arminianism, or later varieties of Lutheranism. What sets the Augustinian-Reformed perspective apart from these other systems is a commitment to God's control over the plan of salvation and his determination of who will be saved (2:330). Hodge insists that all other systems give humans a determinative role, although they lie on a spectrum from heretical Pelagianism to the more minor errors of later Lutheranism and Wesleyan Arminianism. Whereas the former denies the corruption of human nature and affirms a natural capacity to do good works, the latter groups affirm the comprehensive depravity of human nature and deny any natural ability to cooperate with God's grace. Hodge places the Roman Catholic and Remonstrant positions in the middle of this spectrum, but to varying degrees he accuses all these systems of promoting a synergistic account of salvation. In other words, at some point they make human ability or obedience determinative of salvation, rather than ascribing every portion of this process to God alone. Hodge insists that one's entire theological system depends on whether one chooses synergism or monergism, so it is no surprise that he utilizes this distinction throughout the *Systematic Theology* to delineate his positions.

For instance, Hodge maintains a monergistic account of faith and justification in contrast to synergistic versions. This is one point where Hodge finds agreement between Reformed and Lutheran perspectives: justification is the work of God alone accomplished by grace alone through faith alone. Justification is dependent on nothing else except the righteousness of Christ graciously imputed to those who believe, which itself is a gift of God. By

9 Hodge deals most directly with slavery in a review article published in the *Biblical Repertory* in 1836. For an analysis of his perspective, see Allen C. Guelzo, "Charles Hodge's Antislavery Movement," in *Charles Hodge Revisited*, 299–326.

contrast, Hodge criticizes the Remonstrants and Arminians for making obedient faith a condition of justification. Furthermore, Romanists make a muddle of justification by believing that works done after regeneration gain merit for final justification (3:135–7). Hodge celebrates the extent to which these theological systems preserve the central truths of the Gospel—doctrines articulated in the first ecumenical creeds—but he laments the ways in which human works displace Christ as the ultimate ground of justification.

Once the human element has been introduced, Hodge observes, it begins to crop up at every point in the drama of salvation. Rather than maintaining the high standards of God's law and humanity's helpless need for God's empowering grace, Hodge argues that these synergistic systems introduce the dangerous possibility of perfection by lowering the law's demands and overemphasizing human ability. He sees the dangers of Pelagianism resurfacing among Arminians at Oberlin University, such as Charles Finney, who limit sin to voluntary actions and deny any inherent moral corruption. Less extreme but equally erroneous, Romanists and Wesleyan Arminians view perfection as attainable, but only because they think believers are bound to a milder version of the law (3:250–58). In response to these views, Hodge resolutely articulates the impossibility of perfection and launches into a lengthy exposition of the law (3:259–465). He does this to show that no amount of external obedience can fulfill God's demands, and the only possible perfection is the righteousness obtained in Christ by the Spirit.

At each point in his soteriology, Hodge distinguishes his Reformed, monergistic account of salvation with synergistic systems. This pattern continues as he deals with the sacraments and no doubt would have continued if he had managed to complete a fourth volume on ecclesiology. The result is arguably the most cogent and comprehensive summary of Reformed theology ever produced in North America. Amid the dizzying profusion of theological trends and centers of learning during the latter half of the nineteenth century, Hodge provided a solid foundation for those seeking to maintain their confessional, Reformed heritage.

Hodge's Heritage

Hodge's *Systematic Theology* accomplished more than preserving and propagating Reformed theology among nineteenth-century Presbyterians. It modeled a way of doing theology that brings a Protestant confessional tradition into conversation with modern thought and culture for the sake of the Church. His awareness of religious thought and culture in his home country, attentiveness to leading scholarship abroad, and insatiable interest in every area of knowledge is evident in the *Systematic Theology*, but it is best captured by his voluminous contributions to *The Biblical Repertory and Princeton Review*.

"Old School Headmaster" is an appropriate title for Hodge given his leadership position among Old School Presbyterians, but it also communicates his commitment to address theological debates of his day with the old answers of orthodoxy. At the end of volume two of the *Systematic Theology*, he acknowledges the great number of theological debates that surfaced in the nineteenth century, but he argues that "into these debates no new questions have entered." The form of these questions may be new, but "the principles involved in these controversies are the same as those involved in the earlier conflicts in the church" (2:732). The same rationale undergirds Hodge's controversial statement that nothing new ever originated out of the Princeton Seminary. His intention in saying this, of course, was to affirm that there is nothing new under the sun, and the best answers to seemingly new controversies are the old, tried, and true ones. This passion for countering contemporary scholarship with orthodoxy as expressed in the Reformed tradition is the heritage Hodge passed on to several generations of theologians and leaders at Princeton Seminary. It was a legacy upheld by his son, A. A. Hodge, and later by B. B. Warfield and J. Gresham Machen. When Machen left Princeton Seminary in 1929 to found Westminster Seminary, Hodge's heritage lived on through the fundamentalist battle against modernism.

Despite Hodge's vehement critique of modern theological approaches that supplant biblical authority with philosophical principles, it is possible to argue that Hodge shared one fundamental characteristic with these theologians. Like other modern theologians, Hodge used an overarching norm to structure and evaluate every detail in his theological system. As articulated above, the norm is that God is sovereign and he alone determines who is saved. This may be a theological rather than philosophical principle, but it functions in a similar way by providing a framework to interpret all the facts of revelation and experience. The extent to which this principle derives from Scripture itself has been a persistent debate in Protestant theology. Furthermore, it seems that the focus Hodge placed on this norm led him to misinterpret aspects of the biblical material by not taking into consideration other relevant sources for theology, such as the experience of slaves. It is now commonly recognized that every theologian inevitably uses lenses to interpret reality and revelation. Some are embedded in our vision by virtue of upbringing and cultural context, while others are intentional prescriptions that differ according to theological tradition. Reading Hodge's *Systematic Theology* provides a valuable reminder to discern the extent to which these lenses clarify or obscure reality and revelation.

Select Bibliography

Primary Sources

Hodge, Charles, *Systematic Theology*. 3 vols. New York: Charles Scribner and Co., 1871 [vols. 1 and 2]; New York: Scribner, Armstrong, and Co., 1872 [vol. 3].
Hodge, Charles, *Systematic Theology*. 3 vols. Peabody: Hendrickson, 1999.

Other Notable Works by the Author

Hodge, Charles, *Commentary on the Epistle to the Romans*. Grand Rapids: Eerdmans, 1950.
Hodge, Charles, *Exegetical Lectures and Sermons on Hebrews*. Edited by William VanDoodewaard. Edinburgh: Banner of Truth Trust, 2009.
Hodge, Charles, *The Way of Life*. Edinburgh: Banner of Truth Trust, 1959.

Secondary Sources

Gutjahr, Paul C., *Charles Hodge: Guardian of American Orthodoxy*. Oxford and New York: Oxford University Press, 2011.
Hicks, Peter, *The Philosophy of Charles Hodge: A Nineteenth-Century Evangelical Approach to Reason, Knowledge and Truth*. Studies in American Religion, vol. 65. Lewiston, Queenston, and Lampeter: The Edwin Mellen Press, 1997.
Hoffecker, W. Andrew, *Charles Hodge: The Pride of Princeton*. Phillipsburg: P&R Publishing, 2012.
Stewart, John W., and James H. Moorhead, eds., *Charles Hodge Revisited: A Critical Appraisal of His Life and Work*. Grand Rapids: Eerdmans, 2002.

5

Walter Rauschenbusch, *Christianity and the Social Crisis* (1907)

Doing Theology in Hell's Kitchen

Before moving to the northern border of Hell's Kitchen, a working-class and poverty-stricken neighborhood in New York City, Walter Rauschenbusch (1861–1918) had not realized the serious social crisis "beneath the glitter" of booming American cities.[1] Eleven years of pastoral ministry in this environment, however, transformed Rauschenbusch into a champion for the social gospel. Rauschenbusch steadily rose as a leader within the social gospel movement, but the stunning success of *Christianity and the Social Crisis* in 1907 launched him into the limelight. Rauschenbusch developed into the preeminent spokesperson for the social gospel, and *Christianity and the Social Crisis* was the movement's magnum opus.[2]

His father, August Rauschenbusch, was educated at Berlin University and served as a Lutheran pastor in Altena. In 1846, not long after beginning this pastoral ministry, August sensed a calling to missionary service to the United States, where he first worked as the director of the American Tract Society's program for German immigrants. After becoming a Baptist in 1850, he ministered as a church planter and pastor to German Baptist communities until his appointment as a professor at Rochester Theological Seminary in 1858.

Walter Rauschenbusch was born in Rochester, New York, in 1861. When he was 3 years old, however, the whole Rauschenbusch family moved back to Germany for 4 years, reinforcing his bicultural and bilingual upbringing. He later returned to Germany to attend Evangelische Gymnasium zu Gütersloh (1879–83), acquiring the equivalent of an American university education. After coming back to Rochester in 1883, he enrolled in Rochester Theological

1 "Beneath the Glitter" is an article Rauschenbusch published in the *Christian Inquirer* on August 2, 1886, 2 years after moving to New York as a pastor. The article narrates the economic and personal misery beneath the façade of New York's wealth and success.

2 As described in Christopher H. Evans, *The Kingdom is Always But Coming: A Life of Walter Rauschenbusch* (Grand Rapids: Eerdmans, 2004), xviii.

Seminary while finishing some courses at Rochester University. During his 3 years at seminary, Rauschenbusch became familiar with the nascent social gospel movement as represented by Washington Gladden (1836–1918), Richard Ely (1854–1943), and Josiah Strong (1847–1916). He also began to question some traditional Baptist doctrines, such as substitutionary atonement, with ideas he had first encountered in Germany. While appreciating many elements of his Baptist heritage, Rauschenbusch increasingly diverged from theological positions generally espoused at the seminary and among conservative Baptists.[3] This caused some inevitable tension, one consequence being the denial of his application for foreign missionary service in India based on a cautionary reference from an Old Testament professor.

Rather than going to India in 1886, Rauschenbusch accepted a call as pastor of Second German Baptist Church in New York City in an area known as Hell's Kitchen. Immediately confronted by the dire living conditions in the neighborhood, Rauschenbusch started forming friendships with others interested in addressing the plight of the poor in New York City. One such friend was Leighton Williams, with whom he launched *For the Right* in 1889, a small monthly newspaper seeking to reach and give a voice to the working class. This venture folded a few years later, but it had led Rauschenbusch into frequent personal encounters with the multidimensional social crisis of his day.

Plagued by partial deafness since an illness in 1888, Rauschenbusch was growing increasingly doubtful about his ability to continue pastoral ministry. As a result, in 1891, his church encouraged him to take a sabbatical to Germany. There, he studied more thoroughly the theology of Albrecht Ritschl (1822–89) and was impressed by Adolf von Harnack (1851–1930), who only a few years prior had been appointed professor of church history at the University of Berlin. Rauschenbusch also began writing a book called *Revolutionary Christianity*, which was never published but would eventually form the basis for *Christianity and the Social Crisis*. He returned to New York with renewed vigor, forming a progressive caucus within the Baptist Congress called the Brotherhood of the Kingdom. The growing interest among Protestant leaders in tackling social maladies, as well as his marriage to Pauline Rother in 1893, gave Rauschenbusch an extra boost for his final years of ministry in New York City.

In 1897, Rauschenbusch became a professor in the German department at Rochester Theological Seminary, following in his father's footsteps. This was

[3] The theology prevalent at Rochester Seminary in the late-nineteenth century is best represented by Augustus Strong's *Systematic Theology* (1886), published the same year Rauschenbusch graduated. Strong left an indelible mark on the Seminary through his long stint as president from 1872 to 1912.

the same year that Charles Sheldon published *In His Steps*, a popular novel exploring what it means to follow in Jesus's footsteps in personally confronting issues of poverty and social deprivation. While Rauschenbusch appreciated the theme of imitating Christ, he later would critique Sheldon's work for its individualism and not demanding the transformation of social institutions.[4] In 1902, Rauschenbusch was appointed professor of church history in the English department at Rochester Seminary. His years teaching church history provided him the opportunity to explore the historical roots of Christianity's social vision and why this vision had failed to bloom. This historical inquiry is the burden of *Christianity and the Social Crisis* (1907), with *Christianizing the Social Order* (1912) outlining a more positive way forward.

Christianity and the Social Crisis brought Rauschenbusch widespread recognition, not because he was attempting something entirely new, but because of its sparkling prose and the unique combination of historical, theological, political, and social perspectives. It sold 50,000 copies in the first 3 years, making it the best-selling religious book besides the Bible.[5] Throughout the next 10 years, Rauschenbusch wrote several other books, including a collection of prayers entitled *For God and the People* (1910). Such efforts demonstrate Rauschenbusch's desire to fuse personal spirituality and social action, which is also evident in the short book *Dare We Be Christians?* (1914). Most of his books have a historical orientation, but in *Theology for the Social Gospel* (1917), Rauschenbusch recognizes that "We have a social gospel. We need a systematic theology large enough to match it and vital enough to back it."[6] In this book, his overarching optimism is balanced by a new emphasis on "the kingdom of evil" and a social conception of sin, no doubt influenced by the atrocities of the First World War. Tragically, Rauschenbusch never lived to see the end of the war, but died of colon cancer on July 25, 1918. Nevertheless, his kingdom vision had inspired many Christians to pursue a new social order.

Kingdom Vision

For Rauschenbusch, the purpose of Christianity is "to transform human society into the kingdom of God by regenerating all human relations and

4 Walter Rauschenbusch, *Christianizing the Social Order* (New York: Macmillan, 1912), 46.

5 As observed by Paul Brandeis Rauschenbusch, "Foreword," in *Christianity and the Social Crisis in the 21st Century* (New York: HarperOne, 2007), xi.

6 Walter Rauschenbusch, *A Theology for the Social Gospel* (New York: Macmillan, 1917), 1.

reconstituting them in accordance with the will of God."[7] The first three chapters of *Christianity and the Social Crisis* explain how this purpose arose from the Hebrew prophets, Jesus, and the early church. The following four chapters unveil the various forces that distracted from and derailed this purpose, provide an overview of the contemporary social crisis, and suggest how the Church might realign itself with its original vision and purpose.

The Hebrew prophets addressed the major problem that has plagued God's people throughout the centuries: the eclipse of public morality by personal piety. The prophets had no patience for this, breaking down the divide between private and public religion and calling God's people to faithfulness in every sphere of life (6–8). They chided a people who had forgotten the importance of seeking justice for the oppressed and were instead "consumed in weaving the tinsel fringes for the garment of religion" (5). In calling God's people to embrace kingdom morality, the prophets were resolutely on the side of the poor, an orientation already embedded at the heart of Old Testament law (8–16). False prophets emerged who were mere purveyors of popular opinion, propagating deceptive optimism rather than the authentic realism of God's true prophets (28–9). Rauschenbusch claims that with Israel's national destruction came the demise of its social morality. In later prophets like Jeremiah, we see a turn toward personal piety, although hope remained for national restoration (19–26). Based on this prophetic heritage, Rauschenbusch argues that the burden of proof is on those who think Christianity is ritualistic, sacramental, personal, and on the side of the rich (31). It is an impressive case, despite his tenuous genealogy of Hebrew religion (natural to prophetic to personal) and his limited exploration of the Old Testament canon (similar themes permeate the Psalms and wisdom literature). He had nevertheless set a solid stage on which to explore the social aims of Jesus as a continuation of the prophetic tradition.

Jesus was a prophet in unique communion with the Father, not just a social reformer or a teacher of timeless truths (42–4). His purpose was to fulfill the prophetic hopes and usher in a kingdom even greater than they imagined. Jesus's kingdom involved the transformation of every social relation, but this would not be achieved by violence, ushered in instantaneously from heaven, or limited to the Jewish people. Jesus's kingdom is inherently peaceable and realized through organic growth of just human relationships (53–4). At the heart of this kingdom is love, which Rauschenbusch describes as a "society-

7 Walter Rauschenbusch, *Christianity and the Social Crisis in the 21st Century*, repr., ed. Paul Rauschenbusch (New York: HarperOne, 2007), xxi. This is a reprint edition of *Christianity and the Social Crisis* with reflections from contemporary theologians after each chapter. Because this is the cheapest and most widely available edition currently in print, parenthetical page numbers throughout this essay refer to this text.

making quality," since love creates and keeps people in fellowship, resisting coercion, exploitation, and inequality (55). By contrast, wealth is a divisive force that makes it difficult to sustain a society of love, service, and equality. The rich young man who encountered Jesus (Mk. 10:17-31) was not so much unfit for heaven because of his greedy spirit as he was unfit for the earthly kingdom of God (61–2). Throughout his explanation of Jesus's social aims, Rauschenbusch reflects themes and interests common within the burgeoning quest for the historical Jesus.[8] His central concern is not to demonstrate the metaphysical union of divinity and humanity in Jesus's incarnation, but to show the union of religious and social life that would provide the ultimate model for social life and existence.[9] Jesus embodied a "revolutionary consciousness" and a countercultural reversal of values, and those who call themselves Christians should be and do likewise (68–72).

The early Church (or "primitive Christianity") sought to embody a similar spirit, although there was some measure of inevitable "leakage, evaporation, and adulteration" of Jesus's kingdom vision (82). Despite persecution, they maintained hope that Jesus would soon return to consummate his kingdom, a hope that included personal victory over sin but was predominantly hope for humanity's perfect social life (90–1). Sustained by this hope, early Christians organized into "fraternal communities" that cut across lines of social division and exhibited a radical way of sharing possessions and their entire lives together. According to Rauschenbusch, these first "churches" were primarily social communities rather than worshiping communities, which is perhaps one instance where Rauschenbusch is not as careful to avoid false dichotomies (99). Overall, the early church gives a glimpse at what the kingdom of God should look like, but tragically, the Church was not able to sustain this vision and effectively work toward social transformation.

The Roots and Reality of Social Crisis

In chapter four, Rauschenbusch asks the question: Why has Christianity never undertaken the work of social reconstruction? He lists a litany of reasons,

8 Two books Rauschenbusch mentions with favor within this field of study are Francis Peabody's *Jesus Christ and the Social Question* (1900) and Shailer Matthews's *The Social Teaching of Jesus* (1897).

9 In *A Theology for the Social Gospel*, he is more explicit about these aims: "The speculative problem of christological dogma was how the divine and human natures united in the one person of Christ; the problem of the social gospel is how the divine life of Christ can get control of human society. The social gospel is concerned about a progressive social incarnation of God" (148).

beginning with the limitations of the early church, which include pervasive persecution, belief in the imminent return of Christ, general hostility toward the Roman Empire, and the gradual diminishment of an earthly kingdom vision together with the rise of an otherworldly emphasis on eternal life. Instead of focusing on a social ideal, therefore, the imagination of the Church was increasingly captured by an ascetic ideal and a longing for liberation from worldly, embodied existence. As Christianity transitioned from its marginal status to the established religion of the Empire, additional impediments to social engagement emerged. Ritual "numbed . . . ethical passion" (148) and dogma acted "as a narcotic on the intellect of the people" (149). As the Church rose in power and prominence, the distinct goal of Christ-likeness was eclipsed by "churchly correctness" (150) and the "all-absorbing and all-dominating ecclesiastical organization" (154). Not only that, but the Church's subservience to the state deformed socially active, fraternal communities into an institution inundated by "bureaucratic despotism" (158). The picture of church history Rauschenbusch paints is grim. He claims, though, that his point is not so much to condemn the Church as simply to highlight its shortcomings (164). The Reformation was one high point in this history, but Rauschenbusch sees the modern socialist movement as the fulcrum in the kingdom drama. In a phrase reminiscent of Kierkegaard, he holds out hope that "Christianity itself is being converted to Christ" (171).[10] If this conversion is to occur, however, the Church must collectively confront the comprehensive social crisis.

Rauschenbusch is writing in the midst of the Industrial Revolution. At the center of his critique is the power of the machine. Machines created the promise of modern cities, but within this promise lies a tragic paradox: "The instrument by which all humanity could rise from want and the fear of want actually submerged a large part of the people in perpetual want and fear" (181). Rauschenbusch wrestles with many aspects of this tragedy, but most prominent is the gaping divide between wealthy employers and poor wage earners. With profit as the bottom line, workers become a means to an end, diminishing proper concern for their morale, physical health, living conditions, and family life. He identifies rampant diseases such as tuberculosis and alcoholism as inherently social diseases, rooted in the unjust chasm between rich and poor (198–9). Rauschenbusch likens unequal wealth distribution to manure: if it's spread evenly over the soil it will enrich

[10] A similar appeal later in the book to "re-Christianize the Church" (271) sounds similar to Kierkegaard's concern, particularly evident in *Practice in Christianity* (1850), to introduce Christianity into Christendom. The major difference, of course, is that while Kierkegaard's ideal was the Militant Church suffering within society, Rauschenbusch's ideal was closer to what Kierkegaard called the Triumphant Church in which Christianity and society become synonymous.

the land, but if left in heaps most of the land will be impoverished while suffocating vegetation under the heaps (227). Since those with the wealth control both the industrial and political machines, democracy crumbles when economic equality does (207–14). What will the Church do in the face of such a crisis? Will it simply stand by and watch civilization fall? Or will it hear the "Spirit of the First Century" (177–8) and rise to the challenge by standing for justice and love? In short, Rauschenbusch calls the Church to choose between "a revival of social religion or the deluge" (230).

Social Reconstruction and the Church

Although the bulk of *Christianity and the Social Crisis* charts the crisis, the final two chapters hint at some solutions that Rauschenbusch develops more fully in *Christianizing the Social Order*. Before offering particular suggestions, however, Rauschenbusch explains why the Church has a critical stake in the social movement. While some may argue that the Church should simply deal with healing wounds caused by the social crisis, much like the Good Samaritan cares for the injured man, Rauschenbusch takes this parable one step further. Of course, the Samaritan should not go after the robbers with a weapon, but if other Samaritans continued to find injured people along the road, it would be their responsibility to figure out the cause and source of their woundedness (248). In other words, the Church should not abandon relief work and caring for individuals, but it should be equally committed to addressing systemic injustice. If the Church does not confront unjust systems, these systems will conquer the Church. For instance, Rauschenbusch remarks: "If the Church cannot Christianize commerce, commerce will commercialize the Church" (255). Although some church leaders disagreed with this optimistic proposal for "Christianization," his prophetic diatribe spurred many to action. For many in the social gospel movement, another persuasive element in Rauschenbusch's warning was that, if society decays and disintegrates, so will the Church (274). The very survival of the Church is wrapped up in effectively addressing the social crisis. But what can be done?

To begin, Rauschenbusch deals with what the Church should *not* do. The church should not revert to older stages of economic development, base its social action on outdated biblical models, retreat into communistic colonies, or tackle the process of social transformation on its own. The first thing the Church *should* do is repent and believe the gospel. Rauschenbusch's overt emphasis on repentance and faith reflects his goal to fuse personal religion with social action. He was adamant that the greatest contribution to social transformation is a "regenerated personality" (287). It is also critical to observe, however, that when Rauschenbusch refers to repentance and faith, he primarily means repentance of *social* sins and faith in the possibility of *social* transformation (287). His conception of salvation is similarly social: the transformation of all human relations and the redemption of everyday life (288–91). Preaching can play a critical role in this social evangelization, and it should do so by displaying the mind rather than being a platform for political lobbying (295). Ministers will be most effective in addressing the social crisis if they mingle with both rich and poor, thereby understanding both worlds and mediating between them. In all its ministries and activities, Rauschenbusch views the Church's task as opposing "materialism and mammonism" by living out a theology that puts God before self and by supporting a political economy that puts the human person before wealth (300–1).

Ultimately, this means the Church and state should work together toward the same goal: to "transform humanity into the kingdom of God" (308). Rauschenbusch uses the word "communism" to describe this goal, but for him, this word was synonymous with "communalism" or "socialism" and did not have any associations with totalitarian regimes. Specifically, he identifies the home, school, Church, and state as all "communistic institutions," simply because they exist to serve the common good (314–17). The church shares the same goal as these other institutions to the extent that it supports social solidarity more than individualism and its concomitant selfishness (320). In other words, Rauschenbusch envisions the transformation of society through the influence of Christian socialism. This socialism is based on "the brotherhood of men and solidarity of interests" (322), and it shares with the modern labor movement a commitment to the upward mobility of the working class (322–30).

Rauschenbusch insists that this dream is not a "utopian delusion" but rather a realistic hope that a new social order can emerge from the wreckage of the social crisis (237). There is no such thing as a perfect social order, but the possibility remains for achieving a close approximation. In his famous words, "the kingdom is always but coming" (338). Although the past is riddled with roadblocks to the kingdom's emergence, Rauschenbusch interprets the present as the opportune time to resist the forces of evil and to participate in social transformation.

Rauschenbusch and the Rise of Social Theology

Many rose to Rauschenbusch's challenge. The peak of the social gospel movement is often associated with the period from 1907—the year *Christianity and the Social Crisis* was published—to 1914 and the beginning of the First World War. Although the movement inspired by Rauschenbusch lost some of its resilience and optimism after the war, it is possible to trace the influence of his kingdom vision on subsequent champions of social and political liberation. For example, Martin Luther King, Jr., (1929–68) praised Rauschenbusch for "insisting that the gospel deals with the whole man" rather than restricting the gospel to spiritual matters. He continues: "It has been my conviction ever since reading Rauschenbusch that any religion which professes to be concerned about the souls of men and is not concerned about the social and economic conditions that scar the soul, is a spiritually moribund religion only waiting for the day to be buried."[11] Rauschenbusch's involvement with women's liberation, however, was ambiguous. While he addressed the cruelty shown to women within the industrial economic system (223–5), his support of women's suffrage was tepid, causing some to criticize his "Anglo-Saxonist chauvinism."[12]

Rauschenbusch's influence was also felt as his vision for the social gospel united theologians and church leaders from various traditions, both within and beyond Protestantism. In 1882, Rauschenbusch and Leighton Williams founded the Brotherhood of the Kingdom, which initially showed the potential for ecumenical collaboration among social gospel advocates. The most prominent example, however, was the Federal Council of Churches (FCC), which Rauschenbusch helped launch in 1908. In fact, most of the key leaders in the FCC were also leaders of the social gospel movement, which found its way into the Council's constitution. Its fourth point proposed "to secure a larger combined influence for the churches of Christ in all matters affecting the moral and social condition of the people, so as to promote the application of the law of Christ in every relation of human life." This was a lofty goal, and prominent among those theologians who doubted its optimism was Reinhold Niebuhr (1892–1971). In Niebuhr's preface to the 1956 edition of *An Interpretation of Christian Ethics*, delivered as the Rauschenbusch Memorial Lectures at Colgate Rochester Divinity School in 1934, he hailed Rauschenbusch as "the most celebrated exponent" of the social gospel and placed himself within this movement. Nevertheless, he was critical of its conflation of justice and love, a problem stemming from a denial of original sin and obliviousness to individual and collective self-regard.[13] Niebuhr's ethical realism became one major alternative to the theological and social optimism of Rauschenbusch's legacy.

11 Martin Luther King, Jr., *Stride Toward Freedom* (New York: Harper & Row, 1958), 91.

12 Gary Dorrien, *The Making of American Liberal Theology: Idealism, Realism, and Modernity, 1900–1950* (Louisville: Westminster John Knox, 2003), 154.

13 Reinhold Niebuhr, *An Interpretation of Christian Ethics*, Library of Theological Ethics (Louisville: Westminster John Knox Press, 2013), xxxi.

Even though, as Gary Dorrien notes, the biblical exegesis, cultural conservatism, and optimism of Rauschenbusch are dated and have been challenged by convincing alternatives, his enduring legacy is the recognition that theology must not be done in a vacuum and the church cannot ignore the social and political dimensions of existence.[14] Liberation theology, Black theology, feminist theology, political theology, and many other forms of social theology all have links to *Christianity and the Social Crisis*. Although primarily a pastor and a church historian, the work of Walter Rauschenbusch was pivotal in placing Protestant theology on a trajectory toward greater social awareness and engagement.

Select Bibliography

Primary Sources

Rauschenbusch, Walter, *Christianity and the Social Crisis*. New York: Macmillan, 1907.

Rauschenbusch, Walter, *Christianity and the Social Crisis*. Reprint, Library of Theological Ethics. Louisville: Westminster John Knox Press, 1992.

Rauschenbusch, Walter, *Christianity and the Social Crisis in the 21st Century*. Reprint, edited by Paul Rauschenbusch. New York: HarperOne, 2007.

Other Notable Works by the Author

Rauschenbusch, Walter, *Christianizing the Social Order*. Waco: Baylor University Press, 2010.

Rauschenbusch, Walter, *For God and the People: Prayers of the Social Awakening*. Miami: HardPress Publishing, 2014.

Rauschenbusch, Walter, *A Theology for the Social Gospel*. Eastford: Martino Fine Books, 2011.

Secondary Sources

Dorrien, Gary, "Thy Kingdom Come: Walter Rauschenbusch, Vida Scudder, and the Social(ist) Gospel." In *The Making of American Liberal Theology: Idealism, Realism, and Modernity, 1900–1950*, 73–150. Louisville: Westminster John Knox, 2003.

[14] Gary J. Dorrien, *Reconstructing the Common Good: Theology and the Social Order* (Maryknoll: Orbis Books, 1990), 47.

Evans, Christopher H., *The Kingdom is Always But Coming: A Life of Walter Rauschenbusch.* Grand Rapids: Eerdmans, 2004.
Handy, Robert T., ed., *The Social Gospel in America, 1870–1920.* New York: Oxford University Press, 1966.
Smucker, Donovan E., *The Origins of Walter Rauschenbusch's Social Ethics.* Montreal and Kingston: McGill-Queen's University Press, 1994.

6

Dorothy L. Sayers, *The Mind of the Maker* (1941)

The Making of Sayers

From the beginning of her upbringing in Oxford (1883–7) and the Fens of eastern England (1887–1912), Dorothy L. Sayers was captivated by beauty, stories, and the arts. One of her earliest memories was the ringing of university bells in Oxford when her father, Reverend Henry Sayers, was the headmaster of University Cathedral Choir School. For most of her childhood, however, Sayers lived in the small village of Bluntisham, where her father became the Church of England parish priest. As an only child, she found company with the ample books scattered throughout the home and began writing her own poems and plays at an early age in addition to playing violin and singing in the church choir.

Sayers was educated at home until her parents, recognizing her remarkable talent, sent her to St. Goldolphin boarding school in preparation for university. Despite battling a horrible sickness that forced her to finish her schooling at home, Sayers won the Gilchrist Scholarship in 1912 to enroll in Somerville College, a women's college at the University of Oxford, where she studied Modern Languages and specialized in French. At Somerville, Sayers participated in the Mutual Admiration Society, a literary group with whom Sayers shared poems and other writings, some of which were published in her first collection in 1916 entitled *Op. 1*. After finishing her studies at Oxford, Sayers tried various teaching and editing jobs, but she found these positions too demanding to leave room for her true passion—writing—although she continued to publish volumes of poetry.

In 1922, Sayers settled into a job with S. H. Bensen in London as an advertising copywriter, which helped her hone her craft and afforded enough time to complete her first novel, *Whose Body?*, featuring detective Lord Peter Whimsey. Sayers would go on to write eleven more detective novels in the 1920s and 1930s, earning her a place among the Queens of Crime along with Agatha Christie, Margery Allingham, and Ngaio

Marsh. The success of these novels propelled Sayers into the public eye, and upon the suggestion of her friend Charles Williams, she was invited to write a play for the prestigious Canterbury Festival. At this point, she had only published one play, *Busman's Honeymoon: A Detective Comedy in Three Acts*, in collaboration with her friend Muriel St. Clare Bryne, and had not attempted any theological or ecclesial writing. But Sayers accepted the invitation and finished *The Zeal of Thy House* in 1937, which was an enormous success and "created a new Dorothy Sayers."[1] From that time on, Sayers dedicated much of her energy toward writing theological plays, essays, editorials, and translations, and became one of the most recognized Christian writers and thinkers in wartime and postwar England alongside her friend C. S. Lewis.[2]

Soon after the staging *The Zeal of Thy House*, Sayers began writing about Christianity as "the greatest drama ever staged"[3] and completed more plays, including another for the Canterbury Festival (*The Devil to Pay*, 1939) as well as a comedy (*Love All*, 1940), an adaptation of Alexander Pushkin's *The Golden Cockrel* (1941), and two sacred radio plays, *He That Should Come* (1938) and *The Man Born to Be King* (1941). The latter solidified Sayers's reputation as a creative and subversive theological voice, willing to explore new expressions and implications of the drama of Christian dogma.[4]

With war brewing in Europe, Sayers was also intensely concerned with social decay, and she conceived of a series of books on social reconstruction called *Bridgeheads*. Inspired in part by T. S. Eliot's *The Idea of a Christian Society*, originally given as lectures at the University of Cambridge in 1939, Sayers wanted to write books "to quicken the creative spirit which enables man to build . . . systems in the light of his spiritual, intellectual, and social needs."[5] She had already tested some of these ideas in her book *Begin Here: A War-Time Essay* (1940), but it was written in haste, and Sayers poured her energy into writing the first volume of the *Bridgeheads* series, *The Mind of*

[1] Barbara Reynolds, *Dorothy L. Sayers: Her Life and Soul. A Biography* (New York: St. Martin's Griffin, 1997), 283.

[2] For more on the friendship between Sayers and Lewis, see Gina Dalfonzo, *Dorothy and Jack: The Transforming Friendship of Dorothy L. Sayers and C. S. Lewis* (Grand Rapids: Baker Books, 2020).

[3] Originally published as "The Greatest Drama Ever Staged is the Official Creed of Christendom," *The Sunday Times*, April 3, 1938; later published as an essay in *The Greatest Drama Ever Staged* (London: Hodder & Stoughton, 1938).

[4] For the subversive nature of Sayers's work in her context, see Crystal Downing, *Subversive: Christ, Culture, and the Shocking Dorothy Sayers* (Minneapolis: Broadleaf Books, 2020). "The Dogma is the Drama" is the title of an essay in Dorothy L. Sayers, *Creed or Chaos? and Other Essays in Popular Theology* (London: Hodder & Stoughton, 1940).

[5] From the Aims of the Series, quoted in Reynolds, *Sayers*, 308.

the Maker (1941). The seed for this book, which would turn out to be Sayers's most extensive theological investigation, was planted in the closing scene of *The Zeal of Thy House*, where the archangel states:

> Praise Him that He hath made man in His own
> image, a maker and a craftsman like Himself, a
> little mirror of His triune majesty.
> For every work of creation is threefold, an
> earthly trinity to match the heavenly.[6]

The Mind of the Maker explores this idea that the earthly trinity of creativity—Idea, Energy, and Power—mirrors God's triune nature and creative activity. Sayers is aware that she is building off a long theological tradition of the *vestigia trinitatis*, the vestiges of the Trinity in human life and society, but her own investigation begins with the experience of human artistry as a revelation of God's triune action. While Sayers did not receive any formal theological training, she gained awareness of the Christian theological tradition through voracious reading—G. K. Chesterton was one of her favorites—formative friendships with scholars and writers such as Charles Williams and C. S. Lewis, and active participation in Anglican church life. Other influences include the philosophers Jaques Maritain (*Art and Scholasticism*, 1930) and R. S. Collingswood (*The Principles of Art*, 1938), which Sayers acknowledges more fully in "Toward a Christian Esthetic," which builds on the trinitarian dynamics of *The Mind of the Maker*.[7]

Sayers continued writing, including more plays, nonfiction, and translations, until her sudden death in 1957 at the age of 64. She received an honorary Doctor of Literature from Durham in 1950 and devoted much of her later years to translating Dante's The Divine Comedy. For these contributions and many more, it is fitting to acknowledge Sayers not only as a craftswoman of great literature, but as a premier lay theologian, and as C. S. Lewis wrote in "A Panegyric for Dorothy L. Sayers," we can "thank the Author who invented her."[8]

[6] Dorothy L. Sayers, *The Zeal of Thy House* (repr., Eugene: Wipf and Stock, 2011), 130.

[7] "Toward a Christian Esthetic" was originally delivered as one of the Edward Alleyn Lectures in 1944, first published in V. A. Demant, ed., *Our Culture, Its Christian Roots and Crisis* (London: SPCK, 1947), and later included in Dorothy L. Sayers, *Christian Letters to a Post-Christian World: A Selection of Essays* (Grand Rapids: Eerdmans, 1969) and other subsequent volumes of her collected essays.

[8] C. S. Lewis, *On Stories: And Other Essays on Literature* (New York: HarperOne, 2017), 148.

The Maker and His Makers

The Mind of the Maker opens with a defense of Christian creeds, which Sayers declares are not arbitrary constructs but rather statements of fact about the universe. To say that God is triune, that the triune God is Maker of all, and that God's creation reflects his triune nature is not mere conjecture or flimsy opinion, but an observation about how the world works. It is akin to saying that you need to break eggs to make an omelette: a necessary and universal truth (16–17). If God is the Maker, and humans are created in God's image, then to be human is to be a maker. Both God and humanity share "the desire and the ability to make things" (22). To speak of God as a Maker and God's creation as an artistic project, of course, is to speak analogically. All speech about the infinite God is by nature analogical, so in a way proper for all theological endeavors, Sayers encourages a healthy dose of humility and caution, aware of the danger of overextending the analogy "to extrude itself outside its terms of reference" (97).

Nevertheless, she insists that the analogy between human and divine making is generative and underdeveloped in the Christian tradition, which has been plagued by an "analytic bias" (31). The more we learn about artists and the creative process, the more we can learn about God, and vice versa. *The Mind of the Maker* does just that, guiding us through an interdisciplinary conversation between theology and the arts, which Sayers hopes will produce "a synthesis of experience" that produces theologically informed artistry and artistically informed theology (31).

Threefold Creativity: Idea, Energy, and Power

When Sayers reflects on the process of her own creative writing and the artistic task more generally, she identifies a threefold dynamic of Idea, Energy, and Power.[9] Like three sides of a triangle, these are distinct elements of the creative process while forming a unified whole. Comparatively, the three Persons of the Trinity are distinct yet share one being, with the Father (Idea), Son (Energy), and Spirit (Power) all contributing to God's creative mission.

In the writer's experience, which Sayers knows best, the Idea refers to the overall concept for a book or writing project. This Idea is separate from the Energy (or Activity, an alternate term Sayers uses) of writing the book,

[9] These are capitalized in the original.

but it can only be known and revealed in the process of writing. Thus, the relationship between creative Idea and Energy sheds light on the relationship between the Father and the Son, who is eternally begotten by the Father as his unique revelation (38–9). The Idea ensures a unity of purpose and theme in the creative Energy, and it cannot merely be reduced to the sum of all the parts. The Idea is timeless and holds the whole creative project at once, which is then revealed through the Energy and incarnation of each word.

The Energy is the actual work of making, like when a writer fleshes out characters, settings, scenes, and plot. Good writers pour all their Energy into each character and scene, but they do so with attentiveness to the uniqueness and diversity of each while maintaining fittingness with the overarching Idea. Without this investment of Energy, the work will lack Power, boring those who read it with stock characters and overly predictable plot development (53–4). In this creative process, the author and her Idea remain distinct from the creation, but there is also complete investment—pouring oneself out—in the Energy. Sayers observes how "nobody but a god can pass unscathed through the searching ordeal of incarnation" (92). This, of course, confronts us with the core mystery of Christianity: that God not only incarnated his Idea in characters other than himself but also became one of the characters and suffered the full brunt of incarnation. For writers as well as for God: "the writing of autobiography is dangerous business," but it can also be a mark of "supernatural courage" (92) as well as energetic love (129).

If the Idea is the book as thought and the Energy is the book as written, then the Power is the book as read and its effects upon the readers and the author (115). If created in congruence with a powerful Idea, the Energy and incarnation of any creative work has inherent Power, but that Power grows when others encounter the work and respond. Similarly, the Spirit "is thus a social power, working to bring all minds into its own unity" through a diversity of experiences and reactions. This Power is already in the author's mind as a part of the Idea, but only through the energetic incarnation can Power become manifest (111). Again, we see the threefold pattern in which Idea, Energy, Power (and by analogy Father, Son, and Spirit) are distinct expressions of the same creative essence.

In exploring this threefold dynamic of the creative process and the life of God, Sayers deals with various objections and common conundrums. First, there is the issue of free will, and Sayers believes the best analogy for understanding the relationship between God and free creatures is to look at the relationship between a playwright and actors. A good, non-egotistical playwright does not operate with strict determinism but rather welcomes the free and imaginative performances of the cast, as long as they remain faithful to the original Idea (64–5). This is based on the playwright's love for the play's medium and willingness to submit to its nature and limitations. By analogy, God delights to unleash the freedom of his characters, who like actors on a stage develop according to their own nature yet within the will of their Maker. Whether in the story of God or one created by human authors, authorial interventions are possible, but they should serve the story and be an integral part of the Idea (82). In addition, miracles in God's story fulfill rather than circumvent natural laws (83). Sayers concludes that ultimately it is love that drives God's involvement in his own creation, that allows for freedom rather than possessiveness, and the need to edit and judge the work (129–32). "Love is the Energy of creation" (136).

A second conundrum Sayers addresses is the nature and problem of evil in the making of all things. When a human author creates a work like *Hamlet*, it naturally introduces the possibility of Not-Hamlet, just as the creation of light introduces the possibility of darkness. The absence of a creative work does not have reality on its own but only as a deprivation of creativity. But "if Not-Hamlet becomes associated with consciousness and will . . . we get Anti-Hamlet" (102). Likewise, in the drama of life, the Not-Being that emerged from God's creation of Being became Evil when free creatures became conscious of this possibility (103). The only way to redeem the nothingness of Evil is by another creative act, by an incarnation or new creation that is fully in keeping with the original Idea. Thus, Sayers draws the connection between God's creative, redemption mission and the call of human makers to keep creating.

Scalene Creativity

Given the fact that there are no perfect artists, we should not expect the Idea, Energy, and Power of a creative project to be either equally balanced or completely perfect. Sayers explains, "All writers (being human, however good) tend to have their trinities permanently a little out of true—slightly scalene," so that one of the sides either dominates or atrophies (155).

The dominance of the Idea in a writing project, for example, means that there is an oppressively strong tone and theme that run roughshod over the particularities of a work, if the work even manages to be written. These "father-ridden" writers are trying to get their message across "without the full mediation of the son," or the real work of incarnation and expression (151). The atrophy of the Idea, by contrast, produces a rambling disunity of tone and theme that leaves the work without a compelling throughline, as if the author is making it up as she goes. Theological ideas can suffer similar imbalances, where the role of the Father-Idea is either too dominant, as in Docetism and a denial of full incarnation, or where the Father is drawn too deeply into the creative activity, as in Patripassianism, which embraces the suffering of the Father alongside the Son (174). For the writer, when the Idea is properly balanced with the other sides, it does not dominate or get lost in the Energy and Power but propels both and provides an integrated wholeness and direction for the work.

If the Energy is too dominant, a creative work may display impressive craftsmanship but lack a compelling idea. It becomes a "mechanical contrivance" that is all technique and no vision (153). On the other hand, if the Energy is too weak, an artist may have good ideas but fail to bring them to fitting expression with the materials or medium. Sayers uses the examples of a play that is good on the page but not on the stage because it may have a good idea but has not considered the actual medium of live actors, physical scenery, and a real audience (165). Similarly, scalene theologies arise when the Son-side is either too prominent (various forms of Christomorphism that neglect the roles of Father and Spirit) or does not embrace the full reality of incarnation (as in Gnosticism). True balance arises in both artistry and theology when there is "perpetual community" between the threefold dimensions, not letting the incarnate Activity—whether human or divine—be disproportionately related to the Idea and Power (166).

Finally, Sayers contends that when the Power is too dominant, the artist relies on emotion to carry the work without appropriate attention to its material expression or conceptual consistency. A Power-dominant work can easily become sentimental, indulging in emotions for their own sake in a way that does not require thoughtfulness or craft, like a shoddy romance novel. On the other hand, the atrophy of Power stems from lack of inspiration, wisdom, and passion, which produces a lifeless piece of work that is soon forgotten. This kind of "unghosted" artist is not only uninspired but also uncritical, since "creative criticism is the Spirit's continual response to its own creation" (176–7). Just as the Spirit of God is the animating force of the divine drama, so the Power of a creative work brings it alive and sets it apart from dead (and deadening) attempts to communicate, whether the communicator is an artist, a pastor, or a politician.

Sayers concludes her argument by extending the pattern of threefold creativity from the work of artists to include every form of human work and making. Since every human being is made in God's image, everyone operates out of this creative mind that follows "the grain of the spiritual universe" (185). This brings a new perspective to bear on all human activity, which does not merely operate within a mechanistic, problem-solution framework, but entails bringing something new into the world. Indeed, part of the modern malaise pertaining to work is that they approach "life problems" like detective problems that are inevitably and completely solvable on their own terms and according to a predictable timeline (196–206). But life does not unfold that way, and its problems require improvisation and attentiveness to threefold creativity, which enable us to live according to the pattern of a universe created by the triune God. The creative process of artists is a witness to the way the world works, and that threefold creativity is a form of prayer.

Theology and the Arts in a Protestant Key

The Mind of the Maker was immediately praised by literary critics, clergy, philosophers, and theologians alike.[10] Sayers was keenly aware of the perilous nature of doing lay theology,[11] yet she persisted in her efforts, believing in the importance of relating theology to every sphere of life. Her way of doing lay theology and integrating theology and the arts was influential on C. S. Lewis, whose own wartime radio broadcasts, later published as *Mere Christianity* (1952), became enormously popular. What Sayers accomplished in *The Mind of the Maker*, however, was a more sustained dialogue between Christian doctrine and the arts than Lewis or other Protestant writers had attempted. Many Protestant theologians have reflected positively on the arts before and after Sayers, such as Abraham Kuyper's *Stone Lectures* (1888–9), P. T. Forsyth's *Christ on Parnassus* lectures (1911), Karl Barth's book on Mozart (1956), and Paul Tillich's *On Art and Architecture* (1987), but Sayers's contribution is unique, not only reflecting theologically on the arts but also letting the arts shape theology.

In this way, Sayers initiated a new way of integrating theology and the arts from a Protestant perspective, showing the fruitfulness of this mutual dialogue. Inheritors of Sayers's wisdom include Madeleine L'Engle (1918–2007), who wrote the introduction to the 1987 edition of *The Mind of the Maker*, as well as a whole new generation of Protestant theologians, pastors, and writers engaging with the arts such as Rowan Williams, Jeremy Begbie, Patrick Sherry, Natalie Carnes, Trevor Hart, William Dyrness, David Brown,

[10] For example, Canon John Thurmer said that *The Mind of the Maker* is "of overwhelming importance for the analogy of the Trinity." Quoted in Reynolds, *Sayers*, 315.

[11] In a 1937 letter to Herbert Kelly, Sayers wrote: "It's always perilous for laymen to meddle with expounding theology." Quoted in Laura K. Simmons, *Creed without Chaos: Exploring Theology in the Writings of Dorothy L. Sayers* (Grand Rapids: Baker Academic, 2005).

Judith Wolfe, and many others.[12] While the theology of threefold creativity Sayers developed is not without critique,[13] it laid the groundwork for heuristic theological engagement with the arts and the formulation of a Christian aesthetic grounded in God's nature and revelation. The mind of Dorothy L. Sayers deserves to be placed among the greatest minds of modern Protestant theology, and her work stands as a testimony to the mind of the Maker.

Select Bibliography

Primary Sources

Sayers, Dorothy L., *The Mind of the Maker*. New York: Harcourt, 1941.

Sayers, Dorothy L., *The Mind of the Maker*. Reprint, San Francisco: HarperCollins, 1987.

Other Notable Works by the Author

Sayers, Dorothy L., *Letters to a Diminished Church: Passionate Arguments for the Relevance of Christian Doctrine*. Nashville: W Publishing Group, 2004.

Sayers, Dorothy L., *Whose Body?* Garden City: Dover Publications, 2009.

Sayers, Dorothy L., *The Zeal of Thy House*. Eugene: Wipf and Stock, 2011.

Secondary Sources

Dalfonzo, Gina, *Dorothy and Jack: The Transforming Friendship of Dorothy L. Sayers and C. S. Lewis*. Grand Rapids: Baker Books, 2020.

[12] Prominent works from these authors in the field of theology and the arts include Madeleine L'Engle, *Walking on Water: Reflections on Faith and Art* (New York: Convergent Books, 2016); Rowan Williams, *Grace and Necessity: Reflections on Art and Love* (London: Bloomsbury Academic, 2006); Jeremy Begbie, *Voicing Creation's Praise: Toward a Theology of the Arts* (Edinburgh: T&T Clark, 2000); Patrick Sherry, *Spirit and Beauty* (Oxford: SCM Press, 1992); Natalie Carnes, *Beauty: Theological Engagements with Gregory of Nyssa* (Eugene: Wipf & Stock, 2014); Trevor Hart, *Making Good: Creation, Creativity, and Artistry* (Waco: Baylor University Press, 2014); William Dyrness, *Visual Faith: Art, Theology, and Worship in Dialogue* (Grand Rapids: Baker, 2001); David Brown, *Gospel as Work of Art: Imaginative Truth and Open Text* (Grand Rapids: Eerdmans, 2024); Judith Wolfe, *The Theological Imagination: Perception and Interpretation in Life, Art, and Faith* (Cambridge: Cambridge University Press, 2024).

[13] For example, see Hart, *Making Good*, 268. He argues that Sayers flirts with a form of neo-Platonism in which the Idea can exist independently of the Energy or Incarnation.

Downing, Crystal, *Subversive: Christ, Culture, and the Shocking Dorothy Sayers*. Minneapolis: Broadleaf Books, 2020.

Reynolds, Barbara, *Dorothy L. Sayers: Her Life and Soul. A Biography*. New York: St Martin's Griffin, 1997.

Simmons, Laura K., *Creed without Chaos: Exploring Theology in the Writings of Dorothy L. Sayers*. Grand Rapids: Baker Academic, 2005.

7

Paul Tillich, *Dynamics of Faith* (1957)

Boundary Theologian

Paul Tillich (1886–1965) was a theologian who lived on the boundary between many different worlds. In an autobiographical work written a few years after his move to America, Tillich identified several dimensions of his boundary existence. Partly because of circumstance and partly out of choice, Tillich found himself living between personal temperaments, city and country, social classes, reality and imagination, theory and practice, heteronomy and autonomy, church and society, religion and culture, Lutheranism and socialism, idealism and Marxism, native and alien land, and philosophy and theology.[1] Tillich's correlation between religion and culture and between philosophy and theology is perhaps most well-known, but each facet of his boundary existence shaped his identity and method as a theologian. Wherever he taught and lectured, Tillich encountered both gushing praise and goring opposition, which confirms both the originality and difficulty of his passion to mediate between different disciplines and worlds.

Paul Tillich was born on August 20, 1886, in the town of Starzeddel, just outside of Berlin. His father, Johannes Tillich, was a Lutheran pastor, and so naturally Paul was confirmed in the Lutheran Church in 1902. In fact, despite his eventual departure from Lutheran orthodoxy, Tillich always considered himself a Lutheran theologian. He studied theology in Berlin, Tübingen, and Halle, identifying with the analysis of human existence offered by Karl Barth in opposition to liberal theology, while also adopting the historical-critical approach of Rudolf Bultmann and Ernst Troeltsch. He was also a voracious reader of philosophy from an early age and developed a particular appreciation for Friedrich Schelling, who was the subject of his Doctor of Philosophy awarded in 1911. In 1912, Tillich completed his theology degree and was ordained in the Lutheran Church,

1 These are the chapter titles of Paul Tillich, *On the Boundary* (New York: Charles Scribner's Sons, 1966). "On the Boundary" was originally Part One of Tillich's *The Interpretation of History* (New York: Charles Scribner's Sons, 1936).

becoming an assistant minister in Moabit, the workers section of Berlin. He married Margarethe "Grethi" Wever in September 1914. Four days later, however, Tillich volunteered for military service and served as a chaplain in the German army until January 1919.

The war had a deep and lasting impact on Tillich, not least because of the emotional and physical anguish experienced on the front lines. Tillich also returned to a wife who had been unfaithful, and they were eventually divorced in 1921. He was remarried to the artist Hannah Werner in 1924, but this was a notoriously unconventional and often strained marriage, which Hannah documented in her own autobiography.[2] These tragedies led Tillich to believe that theology and philosophy must somehow do justice to the abyss in our lives.[3] Upon returning from the war, Tillich started teaching theology at the University of Berlin (1919–24) and then for three semesters at Marburg (1924–5), where he was meant to replace Rudolf Otto. At Marburg, Tillich encountered "the strong but tight-fitting armor of Barthian supranaturalism," which he believed led to an anti-humanistic attitude.[4] Because of this, he gladly accepted an offer as Professor of Religious Studies at the Dresden Institute of Technology, which at that time did not have a theology department.

In Dresden, Tillich began to find his own unique style, both in life and in scholarship. He adopted a Bohemian lifestyle, pursuing his love for expressionism and modern dance and often using his home as a place to practice and reflect on the arts. His voracious interest in culture was expressed in *The Religious Situation* (1925), which also articulated his perspective of "belief-ful realism" in contrast to pessimistic realism and utopian idealism. From 1929 to 1933, Tillich was professor of philosophy at the University of Frankfurt, where he lectured and wrote widely on social ethics and political philosophy. He also put his beliefs into action, joining the Social Democratic Party and writing *The Socialist Decision* (1932). Because of his outspoken position and critique of the Nazis, Tillich was dismissed from his university position in 1933, and on the invitation of Reinhold Niebuhr he came to America as visiting professor of religion and systematic theology at Union Theological Seminary in New York. While also lecturing in philosophy at Columbia University, Tillich struggled to find his niche at Union, not only because of cultural and linguistic barriers, but also because of his unique blend of philosophy and theology. Nevertheless, he stayed at Union for a total

2 Hannah Tillich, *From Time to Time* (New York: Stein and Day, 1973).
3 Tillich, *On the Boundary*, 52.
4 Ibid., 41.

of 22 years, becoming assistant professor of philosophical theology (1937–45) and then full professor (1940–55).

The much-anticipated first volume of Tillich's *Systematic Theology* was published in 1951, which outlined his theological form (apologetic), method (correlation), and norm (New Being in Jesus as the Christ). In contrast to the kerygmatic theology of Barth and others, Tillich insisted that the message of Christianity is always inherently related to the questions arising out of cultural situations. As such, theology is always apologetic theology or "answering theology," implying a common ground with culture that Barth denied.[5] Tillich's method, therefore, involved correlating "questions and answers, situation and message, human existence and divine manifestation."[6] Tillich invokes the opening sentence of John Calvin's *Institutes of the Christian Religion* in support of his position that existential questions and theological answers are interdependent.[7] This method departed from Calvin and Protestant orthodoxy, however, by asserting a plethora of sources for theology, rather than privileging historical and biblical revelation.[8]

Just a year after Tillich launched his *Systematic Theology*, he also published *Courage to Be* (1952), which, together with *Dynamics of Faith* (1957), would be his most popular books. The goal and appeal of these slim volumes was their revision of traditional religious language in a way that was informed by and connected to contemporary culture. In particular, Tillich was keen to build a connection with experiences of doubt and despair as represented by existentialism.[9] *Dynamics of Faith* appeared the same year as the second volume of Tillich's *Systematic Theology*, while he was university professor at Harvard (1955–62). Tillich finished his career as professor of theology at the University of Chicago Divinity School (1962–5), where he released his third volume of the *Systematic Theology* (1963). In these last years, he also wrote and lectured extensively on morality and world religions. His illustrious career was cut short, however, after he suffered a heart attack, dying several days later on October 22, 1965.

5 Paul Tillich, *Systematic Theology*, vol. 1 (Chicago: University of Chicago Press, 1951), 6.
6 Ibid., 8.
7 Ibid., 63.
8 More specifically, Tillich contrasted his correlationist method with supranaturalism (theology derived from revealed truths), naturalism (theology derived from human truths), and dualism (a supranatural structure on a natural basis). Ibid., 64–6.
9 This was also Tillich's goal in his *Systematic Theology*, although in a more academic fashion. The terms he uses throughout his corpus, however, remain the same: sin is *estrangement*, grace is *reunion*, God is the *ground and aim of Being*, faith is *ultimate concern*, Holy Spirit is *Spiritual Presence*, and Christ is *New Being*.

Reinterpreting Faith

The premise of *Dynamics of Faith* is that the concept of faith has been distorted, and it needs reinterpretation, reinvention, and healing (xxi).[10] Rather than being a term that divides and confuses people, faith should be an idea that empowers unified, clarified existence. Tillich defines faith as "ultimate concern." By this, he means giving total surrender to what one considers ultimate in hope of experiencing total fulfillment (1). As ultimate concern, faith includes both an objective referent (the Ultimate) and subjective involvement (concern). It is a passionately human act oriented toward an ultimate reality (9–14).[11] In Hebrew religion, that ultimate reality is Yahweh and his justice; in Christianity, it is New Being in Jesus as the Christ. But faith is not a "sacred" phenomenon divorced from the "secular" world. Everyone has faith because everyone has an object of ultimate concern, whether that is God, the nation, or economic success (2–4). The problem with these "faiths" just mentioned, according to Tillich, is that they contain "false ultimacy" by deeming a finite object (e.g., the nation) as something ultimate (13). Only an infinite or absolute object is worthy of our ultimate concern; everything else is idolatry.

Another distortion of faith is identifying it with only one aspect of human personality. True faith, on the contrary, is an act of "total personality," involving our minds, wills, emotions, and bodies. It is conscious and unconscious, rational and nonrational. As such, faith is an act of integration, a "centered act" that keeps each aspect of personality in dynamic interplay (4–9). Tillich addresses three distortions of faith that focus on merely one aspect of personality. The intellectual distortion defines faith as belief, a cognitive assent to the Bible or some kind of authority (35–41). The voluntaristic distortion defines faith as action, which is manifest either as the Catholic "will to believe" or the Protestant "obedience of faith" (41–4). The emotional distortion sees feelings as the source of faith, a position represented by Schleiermacher. Tillich objects to this approach because it avoids orienting ultimate concern toward truth and ignores the brokenness of human experience (46).[12] When the act of faith involves every element of personality, however, it possesses an integrative, healing power. Yet this healing can never be complete, as disintegration is always present (125–7).

Part of this inevitable disintegration is the presence of doubt. Since faith is a matter of finite being relating to the infinite, it always involves a measure

[10] Page numbers are taken from the reprint edition: Paul Tillich, *Dynamics of Faith* (New York: HarperCollins, 2009).

[11] Cf. Tillich, *Systematic Theology*, vol. 1, 12–14; 214–15.

[12] In the *Systematic Theology*, Tillich explains that experience is the medium rather than the source of theology (Ibid., 42).

of uncertainty (18). In a phrase reminiscent of Kierkegaard, Tillich claims the only absolute certainty is our complete inability "to bridge the infinite distance between the infinite and the finite from the side of the finite" (122). Doubt is not an enemy of faith; it is faith's necessary companion. In this sense, doubt is the dialectical opposite of faith as ultimate concern. The way to deal with this doubt is not to deny it, but to accept the risk of faith and respond to it with courage (115–22). The "courage to be" is to persevere in faith in the midst of despair and in the face of inevitable idolatry.[13] Every human being—let alone every theologian—is simultaneously a person of faith and a doubter.[14]

Comprehending Faith

If faith is the ultimate concern, then to what extent is this concern reasonable? How is the truth of faith comprehended, and how does it relate to scientific, historical, and philosophical truth? First, it is important to remember that Tillich views faith as an act of total personality, so the mind is inevitably involved. If faith and reason were at odds, then faith would be a dehumanizing act. There is a degree of conflict between faith and reason, however, because we experience estrangement from our true nature as integrated beings.[15] Yet Tillich affirms the inseparable relationship between faith and reason (85–91). In sum, "reason is the presupposition of faith, and faith is the fulfillment of reason" (88).[16]

No inherent tension exists, therefore, between science and faith (92–8). Conflict arises only when science becomes the object of ultimate concern, thus becoming faith rather than science. Tillich observes this problem with the theory of evolution and with naturalism more generally, both of which exemplify going beyond the limits of scientific analysis and thus coming into conflict with the truth of faith. When the boundaries between faith and science remain intact, however, then faith has nothing to fear or gain from science.

Tillich maintains a similar distinction between the truth of faith and historical truth (98–102). He presupposes that we have no access to the historical events on which the biblical accounts are based. Something has happened that transformed history, but finding out exactly what happened is

13 Tillich addresses this concept in *The Courage to Be* (New Haven: Yale University Press, 1952).

14 As this applies to theologians, see Tillich, *Systematic Theology*, vol. 1, 10.

15 For an extensive discussion of the estrangement of existence, see Tillich, *Systematic Theology*, vol. 2, 44–75.

16 Elsewhere, Tillich unpacks the semantic, logical, and methodological rationality of faith. Tillich, *Systematic Theology*, vol. 1, 54–9.

not the responsibility of faith. It is the task of historical research to determine what parts of the Bible are historically verifiable. This is separate from the task of faith, which is simply to utilize biblical stories as symbols for ultimate concern. For example, the Fall of Adam and Eve may not be a historical event, but it can be interpreted as a symbol for humanity's estrangement. Jesus of Nazareth may not have risen from the dead in actual history, but the biblical testimony to Jesus as the risen Christ is a powerful symbol for New Being. In this way, the truth of faith and historical truth remain independent, liberating both to pursue their separate tasks.

Of all the different spheres of truth, Tillich recognizes the greatest degree of overlap between the truth of faith and philosophical truth, although there are important distinctions (104–9). Both faith and philosophy are oriented toward ultimate reality, but philosophy articulates this reality in concepts, whereas faith articulates it in symbols. As an intellectual discipline, philosophy is detached from its object of contemplation, but faith is inherently participatory. At the same time, genuine philosophy is carried out with passionate faith, and faith naturally leads one to ask philosophical questions. Tillich observes no conflict between faith and philosophy, but neither does he seek a synthesis.[17]

If scientific, historical, and philosophical truths do not constitute criteria for judging the truth of faith, then what does? For Tillich, faith contains truth to the extent that "it adequately expresses an ultimate concern" (110). By "adequate," Tillich means an expression of ultimate concern that creates an active response within a community, whether in the form of morality, ritual, art, or other modes. These modes of expression change throughout time, however, so we cannot make them absolute. Every affirmation of truth must be accompanied by a negation, which is why Tillich considers Christ the most powerful symbol, since affirming this symbol also means accepting its negation: Christ crucified (112).

Expressing Faith

As already observed, Tillich views the truth of faith as something expressed in symbols. Since the ultimate cannot be expressed directly, it must be expressed symbolically. Tillich explains several functions of a symbol, including signifying a reality beyond itself, participating in this reality, opening up new levels of reality, and unlocking new dimensions of the soul (47–50). God is

[17] For more on the relationship between philosophy and theology, see Ibid., 18–28.

the most fundamental symbol, since this symbol is always present within our ultimate concern. Tillich anticipates the criticism that this makes God *merely* a symbol by reminding his readers that symbols participate in the reality they signify. Tillich cryptically remarks: "God is a symbol for God" (53).[18]

Faith is expressed in symbols, and symbols are organized into stories. This is what Tillich refers to as myth: "symbols of faith combined in stories about divine-human encounter" (56). On the one hand, Tillich is adamantly opposed to demythologizing myths by giving them scientific interpretations because the power of myths is precisely their existence as myths. But on the other hand, Tillich warns against the error of literalism, which links symbols with historical or scientific truth. In Tillich's perspective, the danger of literalism is its fixation on temporary and conditional expressions of truth, rather than focusing on the eternal truth signified by concrete symbols. For example, he asserts that viewing the Messiah's virgin birth as a literal, biological event robs faith of its ultimacy by chaining it to the finite (59–60). Christianity is an expression of ultimate concern, says Tillich, and therefore it is and must remain a myth.

Faith is expressed through symbols and myths, but it is also expressed through forms of life. In this regard, Tillich identifies two main types of faith: ontological and moral. The ontological type seeks to experience the holiness of being itself, whereas the moral type responds to the holiness of being by seeking what ought to be (64–5). For the former, Tillich addresses sacramental, mystical, and humanist faith (66–74). For the latter, he discusses juristic (Talmudic Judaism and Islam), conventional (Confucianism), and ethical (Jewish prophets) faith (74–80). While distinguishing between different types of faith, Tillich also recognizes their underlying unity. The cause of conflict between types of faith is not divergent beliefs, but the extent to which they express ultimate concern most adequately (76). Dialogue between faiths should entail neither "tolerance without criteria" nor "intolerance without self-criticism" (143). Tillich believes that Protestantism has the potential to unify the types of faith and express ultimate concern most adequately (at least better than Catholicism or fundamentalism), but he claims it must first deal with its aversion to the sacramental (83, cf. 140). Ultimately, he points to the New Testament—and Paul's Spirit-centered faith in particular—as a unification of the sacramental and mystical elements of faith with the moral and rational elements (82–3).

When Tillich discusses the expression of faith, he clarifies that this is not merely an individual expression; it takes place within the community. On a fundamental level, this is because faith is dependent on language, and

[18] For more on the meaning of "God," see Ibid., 211–18.

language arises within community (27). It is the community of faith that provides the content for ultimate concern, although this content—such as the creeds or liturgies—should never be the object of ultimate concern. In Tillich's opinion, this would violate the precious "Protestant principle"—that criticism and doubt are embedded within the act of faith—and so annihilate the risk of faith (33). In addition to providing the language of faith, the community is also the context for the active expression of faith as it works itself out in love. Tillich defines love as the desire to be united with the object of ultimate concern (130). Faith implies love, and love determines action. In several respects, therefore, Tillich insists that "the state of ultimate concern is actual only within a community of action" (136).[19] Even more profoundly, where there is no community of faith, true community does not exist, because faith is the force that truly binds people together (137–8).

Tillich and the Correlationists

Paul Tillich made a massive contribution to twentieth-century Protestant theology, but his legacy pertains more to his unique method and mood of doing theology rather than the content of his theological claims. Tillich was responsible for popularizing a correlationist theological method and a mood of "self-transcending realism." His correlationist method explored the dynamic interplay between cultural questions and biblical-theological answers, while his self-transcending realism grew out of his concern to cultivate a kind of realism infused with faith-driven idealism.[20] Several other theologians before and during Tillich's career leveled realistic critiques against the social gospel and idealistic liberalism, including Karl Barth in Germany and H. Richard Niebuhr and Reinhold Niebuhr in America. But in contrast with Barth in particular, Tillich responded by finding a new way to engage culture, while Barth responded by forging a new way to engage with the Word of God. In fact, Reinhold Niebuhr observed that if Barth was the Tertullian of his day, then Tillich was the Origen of his day, at least in terms of relating the Gospel to culture.[21]

[19] For Tillich's full explanation of the Spiritual Community as a community of faith and love, see Tillich, *Systematic Theology*, vol. 3, 172–82.

[20] For more on the phrase "self-transcending realism," see Tillich, *The Protestant Era* (Chicago: Chicago University Press, 1948), 75f.

[21] Reinhold Niebuhr, "Biblical Thought and Ontological Speculation in Tillich's Theology," in *The Theology of Paul Tillich*, edited by Charles W. Kegley (New York: The Pilgrim Press, 1982), 216–27.

Indeed, Barth and Tillich are often linked with two distinct ways of doing Protestant theology today, a distinction represented by Yale-school theologians in contrast to Chicago-school theologians. Generally speaking, Yale-school or postliberal theologians promote postfoundational theology performed in and for the church, whereas Chicago-school or correlationist theologians advance public theology that correlates revelation with human reason and experience.[22] Although he only taught at the University of Chicago for 3 years, Tillich's theology had a notable influence on several Chicago-school theologians, including Langdon Brown Gilkey (1919–2004) and David Tracy (1939–2025). Gilkey, who studied under Tillich at Union, developed a similar dialogue to Tillich's between philosophy and theology, addressing in particular the "death of God" movement and its impact on religious language.[23] David Tracy shared Tillich's commitment to orient theology toward the human situation, but he critiques Tillich for not listening to the cultural answers together with the cultural questions, thus offering his own method of "critical correlation."[24]

The influence of Tillich's theology and method of correlation, of course, extends beyond theologians who have taught at the University of Chicago, including prominent Protestant theologians John Macquarrie (1919–2001) and Gordon Kaufmann (1925–2011), Catholic theologians Karl Rahner (1904–84) and Bernard Lonergan (1904–84), and many liberation and feminist theologians. One example of the latter is Mary Daly (1928–2010), who attended Tillich's lectures at Harvard. Daly explains how Tillich's *Courage to Be* was particularly motivating for her feminist agenda as the courage to be liberated from patriarchy.[25] She also criticized Tillich, however, for his own personal and theoretical blindness to patriarchal oppression, which she saw as stemming from his abstract symbolization of the cross.[26]

[22] These are broad generalizations, especially given the fact that the Chicago school is technically much older, beginning with the founding of the University of Chicago Divinity School in 1890. The Yale school did not emerge until the 1970s with the work of Hans Frei and George Lindbeck. In the 1960s, roughly corresponding to the time when Tillich was professor of theology at the University of Chicago, a new phase of the Chicago school emerged that could be appropriately called correlationist or revisionist in contrast with the more modernist, scientific liberalism of the previous phases.

[23] Langdon Brown Gilkey, *Naming the Whirlwind: The Renewal of God-Language* (Indianapolis: Bobbs-Merrill, 1969). See also *Gilkey on Tillich* (New York: Crossroad, 1990).

[24] David Tracy, *Blessed Rage for Order* (New York: Seabury Press, 1975), 46.

[25] Mary Daly, *Beyond God the Father: Toward a Philosophy of Women's Liberation* (Boston: Beacon Press, 1973), 23.

[26] Mary Daly, *Gyn/Ecology: The Metaethics of Radical Feminism* (Boston: Beacon Press, 1978), 94f.

In addition to these wide-ranging influences, Tillich's theological engagement with science, politics, psychology, literature, painting, and many other areas of culture impacted the rise of interdisciplinary dialogue between theology and nontheological disciplines. Tillich's voracious interest in culture corresponded with his passion for theology and religion, for he believed that "as religion is the substance of culture, so culture is the form of religion."[27] Although it is difficult to categorize Tillich given his existence on the boundary, "cultural theologian" is perhaps the most fitting description and a theology of culture his most lasting legacy.

Select Bibliography

Primary Sources

Tillich, Paul, *Dynamics of Faith*. New York: Harper & Row, 1957.
Tillich, Paul, *Dynamics of Faith*. Reprint, New York: HarperCollins, 2009.

Other Notable Works by the Author

Tillich, Paul, *The Courage to Be*. 3rd ed. New Haven: Yale University Press, 2014.
Tillich, Paul, *On the Boundary*. New York: Charles Scribner's Sons, 1966.
Tillich, Paul, *Systematic Theology*. 3 vols. Chicago: University of Chicago Press, 1951–3.

Secondary Sources

Kegley, Charles W., ed., *The Theology of Paul Tillich*. Rev. ed. New York: The Pilgrim Press, 1982.
Manning, Russell Re, *The Cambridge Companion to Paul Tillich*. Cambridge: Cambridge University Press, 2009.
O'Neill, Andrews, *Tillich: A Guide for the Perplexed*. London: T&T Clark, 2008.
Pauck, Wilhelm, and Marion Pauck, *Paul Tillich: His Life and Thought*, vol. 1: *Life*. New York: Harper & Row, 1976.

[27] Tillich, *On the Boundary*, 69–70.

8

Karl Barth, *Church Dogmatics* (1932–67)[1]

Barth's Theological Bombshell

Karl Barth (1886–1968) is often hailed as one of the greatest theologians of the twentieth century. Whatever judgment one makes on Barth's theological proposals, it is difficult to contest this acclaim, especially when considering his voluminous *Church Dogmatics*. More than a decade before he began this vast work, however, Barth had dropped "a bombshell onto the playground of the theologians."[2] The bombshell was his Romans commentary, and the playground was the liberal establishment in which Barth received his education. In subsequent years, Barth was called a theologian of crisis, a dialectical theologian, and the founder of neoorthodoxy, but none of these labels adequately describe the breadth of Barth's theological endeavors and achievements.

Born in Basel, Switzerland, on May 10, 1886, Karl was the oldest son of Fritz and Anna Barth. Three years after his birth, his father was appointed lecturer of New Testament and Early Church History at the University of Bern, eventually succeeding Adolf Schlatter as full professor. Karl received an excellent education in Bern, which is also where he began his theological studies before moving on to Berlin, Tübingen, and Marburg. In Berlin, Barth attended lectures by Adolf von Harnack and was thoroughly impressed. Even more impressive for Barth, however, was Wilhelm Hermann, with whom he studied in Marburg. Hermann was an avid appreciator of Schleiermacher, and Barth admits that he "absorbed Hermann [and by implication Schleiermacher] through every pore."[3]

[1] The English version is translated from *Die Kirchliche Dogmatik*. Karl Barth, *Church Dogmatics*, eds. G. W. Bromiley and T. F. Torrance, trans. G. W. Bromiley et al., 13 vols. (Edinburgh: T&T Clark, 1936–69.) Hereafter, all references to this work shall be noted by employing in-text citations.

[2] Karl Adam, "Theologie der Krisis," *Das Hochland* 23 (1926): 276–7.

[3] In the autobiographical sketch *Fakultätsalbum der Evangelisch-theologischen Fakultät Münster* (1927), quoted in Eberhard Busch, *Karl Barth: His Life from Letters and Autobiographical Texts*, trans. John Bowden (London: SCM Press, 1976), 45.

When Barth finished his theological education at Marburg, he served as a part-time pastor in Geneva from 1909 to 1911. There he devoted his time to preaching and studying John Calvin's *Institutes of the Christian Religion*.[4] After this short stint, he became a pastor of a Reformed Church in the agricultural and industrial parish of Safenwil in Aargau, Switzerland. Here Barth encountered the plight of industrial workers while beginning to wrestle with the predicament of religion conceived as a human project. These years were a mix of happiness and sadness, as he married Nelly Hoffman in 1913 yet experienced the outbreak of the First World War in 1914. Barth became increasingly distressed by support for Kaiser Wilhelm's war policy among his former teachers, most notably Adolf von Harnack. This distress, combined with his study of Romans, brought Barth to the point of a *krisis*, a German term that includes the meaning of the English transliteration "crisis" while carrying overtones of judgment, trial, and separation. In the second edition of his Romans commentary (1922), Barth identified the core of this *krisis* as submission to what Kierkegaard called the "infinite qualitative distinction" between time and eternity or between God and humanity.[5]

This perspective gained Barth an audience, and when he became professor of dogmatic theology in Göttingen in 1921, a movement called "dialectical theology" was gaining momentum around him. Together with theologians such as Rudolf Bultmann, Friedrich Gogarten, and Emil Brunner, Barth started to chart an alternative to the popular liberal theology of Schleiermacher, Harnack, and Ritschl. Dialectical theology began with divine revelation rather than religious experience or philosophy, and it emphasized the dialectical movement between the "Yes" and "No" of God, or between God's revelation and hiddenness. While in Göttingen, Barth cofounded a new journal, *Between the Times*, and lectured extensively on Reformed confessions and theologians, various portions of Scripture, and dogmatic theology (1924–5, eventually published as *Göttingen Dogmatics*). In 1925, he transferred to Münster, where he also lectured on dogmatics.[6] Barth later considered this a failed attempt to begin his dogmatics, although some of this material is reworked and expanded in his definitive *Church Dogmatics*.

[4] John Calvin published different versions of *The Institutes of the Christian Religion*, with a Latin version released in 1536 and a French version in 1541. Expanded and definitive editions were published in Latin in 1559 and French in 1560.

[5] Karl Barth, *Epistle to the Romans*, trans. Edwyn C. Hoskyns (London: Oxford University Press, 1933), 10.

[6] These lectures were published as Karl Barth, *Die christliche Domatik im Entwurf* (Munich: München, 1927).

By the time Barth became a professor of theology at Bonn in 1930, he had charted his own theological path and parted ways with Bultmann, Brunner, and other early enthusiasts of dialectical theology.[7] Barth identified his study of Anselm of Canterbury as a critical stage in his development and a catalyst for his *Church Dogmatics*. He resolved to build his dogmatic theology on Jesus Christ rather than on "the eggshells of a philosophical system."[8] He called this a "Christological concentration" of theological tradition, particularly Reformed theology.[9] In 1932, Barth published the first volume of the *Church Dogmatics*, which he so titled because dogmatics finds its life and structure within the church (I/1, xiii). Furthermore, Barth distinguishes dogmatics from systematic theology, since the former bears progressive witness to the truth rather than codifying truth into a closed system.

Barth labored over the *Church Dogmatics* for the rest of his life, the result being four "volumes"—Doctrine of the Word of God, Doctrine of God, Doctrine of Creation, and Doctrine of Reconciliation—each containing several books. The last volume was never finished, and the planned fifth volume on the Doctrine of Redemption or eschatology remains unwritten. Debates persist regarding the unity and development of thought within these volumes, with many identifying a shift between the two books in the Doctrine of God (II/1 and II/2) because of Barth's Christological revision of election. Barth maintained, however, that "no important breaks or contradictions [exist] in the presentation" (IV/2, xi), so it is important not to overplay this supposed shift. Reading through these volumes is an enormous yet rewarding task, and Barth tried to assist readers by keeping his main argument in normal print while setting apart biblical exegesis and historical theology with small print. Barth admits that "at a pinch," the main text can be understood without the small print, but certainly not vice versa (I/1, xii).[10]

While in Bonn, Barth wrote the Barmen Declaration in 1934 as a spokesman for the Confessing Church, opposing Hitler and the Third Reich by asserting the lordship of Jesus Christ and the separation of church and state. Because of this position, Barth lost his chair in Bonn and was deported to Basel, Switzerland, in 1936, where he remained until his death in 1968. During these years, he worked tirelessly on the *Church Dogmatics* and other writings, supported ecumenical efforts, and lectured throughout Europe and

7 Barth resisted himself identifying with any theological school or movement, including the label "dialectical theology" (*CD* I/1, xv).

8 Karl Barth, *How I Changed My Mind* (Edinburgh: Saint Andrew Press, 1969), 43.

9 Ibid.

10 Another accessible way into the *Church Dogmatics* is to pick up a reader that selects key sections, such as R. Michael Allen, *Karl Barth's Church Dogmatics: An Introduction and Reader* (London: T&T Clark, 2012).

around the world. Before he retired from his teaching post in 1962, Barth gave his "swan song" lectures on the topic of evangelical theology, which he also delivered throughout the United States. In his foreword to the American edition of *Evangelical Theology*, Barth affirmed that his *Church Dogmatics* is in no way a conclusion, but rather the initiation of a new theological conversation centered on the God of freedom revealed in Jesus Christ.[11]

Symphonic Theology

George Hunsinger compares the experience of reading the *Church Dogmatics* to entering a magnificent cathedral: once one's eyes are adjusted to the light, the spectacle is awe-inspiring and unparalleled.[12] This is an apt aesthetic metaphor, except for the fact that Barth objected to viewing the *Church Dogmatics* as a house to enter, since houses are static. He preferred to see this work as an introduction to a dynamic way of life.[13] Better, therefore, is Hans Urs von Balthasar's suggestion to read Barth's magnum opus as one would listen to a Mozart symphony.[14] This is especially fitting given Barth's love for Mozart, whose music he enjoyed every morning before beginning his work. Barth even wrote a book on Mozart, appreciating most of all how Mozart broke free from the "snail shell of his own subjectivity" into the "free objectivity" of the aural universe.[15] Barth viewed the purpose of theology in similar terms, and so admired Mozart that he resolved to seek him out first upon arrival in heaven.[16]

Other features of the *Church Dogmatics* lend themselves to a musical, even symphonic, description. First, Barth's perspective on any given topic cannot be summarized in a single statement but, as John Webster notes, "only in the interplay of a range of articulations of a theme."[17] Like a symphony, the *Church Dogmatics* contains four "movements," which are connected

11 Karl Barth, *Evangelical Theology: An Introduction* (Grand Rapids: Eerdmans, 1963), xi–xii.

12 George Hunsinger, *How to Read Karl Barth: The Shape of His Theology* (New York: Oxford University Press, 1991), 27–8.

13 A conversation with youth chaplains of the Rhineland in 1963, quoted in Busch, *Karl Barth*, 375.

14 Hans Urs von Balthasar, *The Theology of Karl Barth: Exposition and Interpretation*, trans. Edward T. Oakes (San Francisco: Ignatius Press, 1992), 28–9.

15 Karl Barth, *Wolfgang Amadeus Mozart*, trans. Clarence K. Pott (Grand Rapids: Eerdmans, 1986), 49–51.

16 Ibid., 16.

17 John Webster, "Introducing Barth," in *Cambridge Companion to Karl Barth*, ed. John Webster (Cambridge: Cambridge University Press, 2000), 9.

not by a neat, linear argument but by a complex intermingling of melodies and countermelodies. Consequently, Barth's logic follows a sonata form—exposition, development, recapitulation—more than a syllogistic one.[18] Most of the time, this musical logic is not stated overtly, but at one point Barth does describe how the polyphony of creation is harmonized in the symphony of the covenant (IV/3.1, 159).

Second, Barth's admiration for the beautiful, objective form of Mozart's music matches his preference for theological objectivism instead of expressivism or emotivism. Theology is not merely anthropological projection, but exists as a response to the authoritative voice of Jesus Christ. As such, faith and knowledge are not inherent human capabilities, but depend entirely on hearing Jesus in the present moment (I/1, 41). The Church is inherently a hearing Church before it is a teaching Church (I/2, 797). Symphonic theology is only an echo of the objective music of revelation.

Third, identifying the *Church Dogmatics* as symphonic theology is appropriate given the overall tone of triumph and joy rather than despair, the same tone of resolution that Barth appreciated in Mozart.[19] In Barth's understanding, evil has no real existence; it is nothingness, much like the pauses in music (III/3, 163). Although dissonance does exist in Barth's theology, it is a dialectical dissonance that enters into darkness for the sake of hearing God's "Yes" in Christ even more clearly. Fourth and finally, Barth's symphonic theology, which focuses on the beauty of Christ, is a fitting contrast to what he calls the "utterly unmusical" form of natural theology (II/1, 666). According to Barth, while natural theology embarks on the joyless and futile task of seeking truth apart from the Word of God, dogmatic theology is a "particularly beautiful science" that bears witness to the glory of God in Christ (II/1, 662).

Encountering the Word of God

Church Dogmatics commences with the doctrine of the Word of God, but this doctrine also permeates every volume, leading T. F. Torrance to call Barth a "theologian of the Word."[20] For Barth, the Word of God exists in threefold form as the Word of God preached, written, and revealed (I/1, §4). The

[18] Theodore A. Gill, "Barth and Mozart," *Theology Today* 43 (1986): 409.
[19] Barth, *Mozart*, 34.
[20] Thomas F. Torrance, *Karl Barth: Biblical and Evangelical Theologian* (Edinburgh: T&T Clark, 1990), ch. 3.

former two manifestations—church proclamation and the Bible—are only indirectly the Word of God, since the only direct form of God's Word is God himself. In his act of revelation, God always remains a mystery, infinitely free and beyond human grasp (I/1, 321). If God's Word could be identified with something static, like words on a page, then God could be domesticated and controlled. Consequently, the Bible itself is not revelation, but a *witness* to revelation (I/1, 111) that becomes God's Word as God addresses us through the biblical words (I/2, 109).

The Word of God is the free speech and action of God addressed to humanity; it is God as he reveals himself for us and for our salvation. Since God speaks and acts as Father, Son, and Spirit, God's revelation is inherently triune. "*God* reveals himself. He reveals Himself *through Himself*. He reveals *Himself*" (I/1, 296; emphasis original). In other words, the triune God is Revealer (Father), Revealed (Son), and Revealedness (Spirit). Consequently, through the prism of revelation, it is possible to see how God exists in a threefold mode of being (I/1, 299), with each mode dynamically participating in the other modes (I/1, 370). In contrast with Schleiermacher, therefore, Barth demonstrates how the Trinity prefaces, structures, and controls the entire project of Christian theology, rather than being tacked on at the end (I/1, 301).

The triune God does not reveal himself generally but does so particularly and concretely in the person and work of Jesus Christ. In fact, Barth contends that the revealed Word is identical with Jesus Christ, and as such, any theology that seeks to take its bearing from divine revelation is "fundamentally Christology" (I/2, 123).[21] This insight leads to what are perhaps the most radical reformulations of Reformed theology throughout the *Church Dogmatics*, whether in connection with doctrines of creation, election, anthropology, ethics, or reconciliation. Some have labeled these reformulations, usually with critical intent, Barth's "Christomonism," although Barth abhorred this "unlovely term" (IV/3, 713). In keeping with his Reformational heritage, Barth desires to take the *solus Christus* (in Christ alone) principle seriously, but he never endorses Christomonism in the sense that Christ's history obliterates responsible human action (IV/4, 23).

Humans are responsible actors in the drama of redemption, yet God's Word and action in Christ by the Spirit always takes primacy in this drama. In fact, Barth believes that divine revelation is a drama rather than mere data

[21] Elsewhere Barth likewise affirms that Christology "is the touchstone of all knowledge of God in the Christian sense, the touchstone of all theology." Karl Barth, *Dogmatics in Outline*, trans. G. T. Thomson (New York: Harper & Row, 1959), 66. This short book is another way of getting a sense for the themes and perspectives of the *Church Dogmatics*, but it should not be considered a substitute.

because revelation is always an act, a personal event involving particular people at particular times. Because the "being, activity, and speech of Jesus Christ" is a particular history unfolding through particular events, Christology is essentially "the unfolding of a drama" rather than an "obscure metaphysics" (IV/3, 137). We are not just spectators of the dramatic revelation of Christ, however, because this drama is also our drama (I/2, 498). We do not watch the drama of Christ unfold from a distance; we encounter Christ as fellow-performers who must respond to this event (III/1, 387). In sum, Christ is the principal performer of this drama, and the Church exists as a real yet completely dependent participant in the theater of the Word (I/2, 690; III/3, 332).

Receiving the Grace of God

For Barth, humanity's complete dependence on God is rooted in our natural antagonism toward God and our incapacity to know and relate to him (I/1, 168). Consequently, any receptivity to the Word of God and active participation in the drama of salvation is an act of grace. Faith itself is created by the Word and received as a gift of the Holy Spirit (I/1, 244). This is the crux of Barth's objection to liberal theology and the notion of "religion" in general, arguing that it represents a futile attempt to achieve self-salvation rather than relying entirely on the grace of God (I/2, §17). God's grace is his free decision to be for us rather than against us. It is the overflowing of God's love, which is the very being of God. As such, it is unconstrained and unconditional (II/2, 9–10).

The grace of God is not limited to his loving and covenantal interaction with humanity but includes the acts of creation and providence. The Creator God is the same God who freely gives himself in Christ by the Spirit, so Barth views the doctrine of creation through the lens of Christology. Both creation and providence, therefore, are bound up with the gracious acts of the triune God for us and for our salvation (III/1, 42). To return to Barth's dramatic metaphor—which he draws in large part from John Calvin—creation is a theater or a stage for the drama of the covenant of grace (III/1, 44). The relationship between creation and covenant is not one of nature and grace, since everything is under the grace revealed in Jesus Christ. The doctrine of creation, therefore, is a statement of faith not accessible in a *natural* way (III/1, 3). This helps explain why Barth was so vehemently opposed to the natural theology promoted by Brunner and several of his contemporaries.[22]

22 Brunner's pamphlet on natural theology was published as *Natur und Gnade: Zum Gespräch mit Karl Barth* (Tübingen: J. C. B. Mohr, 1934). Barth's response was *Nien! Antwort an Emil Brunner* (Munich: Chr. Kaiser Verlag, 1934). They were combined

At the heart of God's free decision to be gracious is his election (II/2, 121). Barth is even so bold as to say that divine election is the whole of the Gospel (II/2, 13). What he means by election, however, is very different than normally articulated within the Protestant theological tradition. In short, God elects himself in Jesus Christ, the one who is both reprobate and elect for the sake of humanity. In other words, Jesus is "the original and all-inclusive election" (II/2, 117). Because the electing God is also the Elect one, Barth places the doctrine of election within the doctrine of God. He critiques those theologians who discuss the eternal decree or will of God in an abstract or static manner, arguing that this decree is dynamically and concretely revealed in Jesus Christ. In talking about the election of individuals, Barth distinguishes between the elect who are witnesses to the truth and the rejected as those who choose godlessness and who isolate themselves from God. As the Elect one, however, Christ represents both classes of people, and as such embodies the "Yes" of God's mercy and the "No" of God's judgment for all humanity. This unique position on the election has led some theologians to accuse him of universalism.[23] In reality, Barth claims that we cannot make the salvation of all people either inevitable or impossible, since God is free to accomplish whatever he chooses (II/2, 417–18). All is dependent on the mysterious grace of God.

This emphasis on the free and boundless grace of God permeates the *Church Dogmatics*. As we have already seen, *general* grace is already present within the doctrine of creation, and redemptive or *special* grace is a ubiquitous theme in the doctrine of reconciliation (III/1, §58.1). At every turn, Barth reminds his readers that the Christian life—and indeed all creaturely life—is an existence of grace. Some scholars have objected that grace "triumphs" so resolutely in Barth's theology that it blunts the reality of evil and undercuts the necessity of human action.[24] Yet Barth demurred, asserting that if anything is central in his theology, it is the freedom of Jesus Christ, the very freedom that liberates the responsibility of human persons.[25]

in an English translation by Peter Fraenkel under the title *Natural Theology* (London: Centenary Press, 1946). Some scholars have pointed out how this disagreement was based on some critical misunderstandings. See Trevor Hart, "The Capacity for Ambiguity: Revisiting the Barth-Brunner Debate," in *Regarding Karl Barth: Essays Toward the Reading of His Theology* (Carlisle: Paternoster Press, 1999), 139–72.

23 One of the first and most scathing critiques in this regard came from Emil Brunner in *Dogmatics, Vol. 1: The Christian Doctrine of God*, trans. Olive Wyon (London: Lutterworth Press, 1949), 349. For an excellent summary of Barth's position, see Hunsinger, *How to Read Karl Barth*, 128–35.

24 Most famously, see G. C. Berkouwer, *The Triumph of Grace in the Theology of Karl Barth*, trans. Hans R. Boer (London: Paternoster, 1956).

25 See Barth's letter to Berkouwer on December 30, 1954, in which he suggests replacing "freedom" with "triumph" and "Jesus Christ" with "grace." Quoted in Busch, *Karl Barth*, 381.

Responding to the Command of God

According to Barth, human action in the drama of redemption serves to give an account of God's grace as we respond to the existence of Jesus Christ (II/2, 576). Because human action takes place as a response to God's action, Barth places ethics within the doctrine of God (II/2, §36–9). Encountering God means encountering his demands, which God gives us the grace to fulfill (II/2, 512). Barth also views ethics as a critical component that concludes every volume of the *Church Dogmatics* (I/2, §22.3; III/4, §52–7; *The Christian Life*, §74–8).[26] Ethics is dogmatics and dogmatics is ethics, held together by the command of God in Jesus Christ. Jesus is the answer to the question "what is good?" (II/2, 516), and our actions witness to the rightness of his action (II/2, 543).

In addition to linking ethics to Christology, Barth also connects ethics to anthropology (III/2, §45). To be a created human being is to exist in relational and responsive encounter with God and other people. In short, response-ability is inherent to personhood. Because of God's grace, we relate to him not merely as creatures but as covenant partners through the mediation of Christ. We are not on equal footing in this partnership, since God is infinitely distinct from his covenant partners. It is, however, a real partnership in which we encounter God, hear his command, and respond within our creaturely limits (III/4, §56).[27]

When Barth writes of the command of God, he means God's direct command to us in the present, not the commands recorded in Scripture. Like God's revelation, his command is always a concrete and personal event (II/2, 548). By implication, ethics is concrete or "special," given the concrete responses of the Christian community to the concrete Word of God (III/4, §52.1). Just like Barth's aversion to natural theology, he opposes philosophical ethics in favor of theological ethics that takes its bearing from a responsive relationship to Jesus Christ (II/2, 543–4).

[26] *The Christian Life* is the "ethics of reconciliation" with which Barth intended to conclude volume 4 of the *Church Dogmatics*. He was only able to complete the section on baptism before his death, however, so this volume is a posthumously published collection of Barth's lecture manuscripts. *The Christian Life: Church Dogmatics IV/4: Lecture Fragment*, trans. Geoffrey W. Bromiley (Grand Rapids: Eerdmans, 1981).

[27] For an excellent exploration of the nature of human responsibility in Barth's theology, see John Webster, *Barth's Moral Theology: Human Action in Barth's Thought* (Edinburgh: T&T Clark, 1998).

Barth's New Melody

Although Barth's early commentary on Romans was considered an explosive bombshell, this violent metaphor is not the most appropriate way to describe Barth's theology. It seems more fitting to describe the *Church Dogmatics* as a mature work of symphonic theology that introduced a new theological melody into what Barth perceived as the cacophony of anthropological projection in Protestant theology. Other theological melodies emerged in reaction to Protestant liberalism in the twentieth century that improvised off Barth's and provided countermelodies with varying levels of consonance and dissonance. A theologian like Reinhold Niebuhr, for example, resonated with Barth's themes of human inability and divine grace in constructing his political theology, but his approach clashed with Barth's in other ways, both theologically and politically.[28] Another example is postliberal theology, also called the Yale school, which shares Barth's conception of the task of theology and his critique of correlationist theological method, as in the work of Paul Tillich. George Lindbeck, for example, resonates with Barth's emphasis on biblical narrative and the community of faith.[29] What he does not share, however, is the rational, reality-referential nature of Barth's theology and his placement of Scripture as an authority over tradition.[30] Dissonance also exists among those who enlist Barth for the construction of non-foundational, postmodern theology.[31] Most notably, these theologians fail to appreciate the particularity of Barth's doctrine of revelation, both in its objective reality and its absolute claims.[32]

If some theologians think Barth is too biblical and theologically traditional, others think he is not enough so. The latter is often the case with evangelical theologians, who have experienced a conflicted relationship with Barth's theology. Some, like Cornelius Van Til, condemned "Barthianism" as unorthodox, while others, such as Bernard Ramm, saw Barth's theology as

[28] See the fascinating and fictional conversation between Barth, Niebuhr, a feminist, and a liberationist in Daniel L. Migliore, *Faith Seeking Understanding: An Introduction to Christian Theology*, 4th ed. (Grand Rapids: Eerdmans, 2023), 494–511.

[29] George Lindbeck, *The Nature of Doctrine: Religion and Theology in a Postliberal Age* (Louisville: Westminster John Knox, 1984).

[30] See George Hunsinger, "Truth as Self-Involving: Barth and Lindbeck," in *Disruptive Grace: Studies in the Theology of Karl Barth* (Grand Rapids: Eerdmans, 2000), 305–18.

[31] For example, see Walter Lowe, *Theology and Difference: The World of Reason* (Bloomington: Indiana University Press, 1993); Graham Ward, *Barth, Derrida, and the Language of Theology* (Cambridge: Cambridge University Press, 1995); William Stacy Johnson, *The Mystery of God: Karl Barth and the Postmodern Foundations of Theology* (Louisville: Westminster John Knox Press, 1997).

[32] For a similar assessment, see Bruce L. McCormack, *Orthodox and Modern: Studies in the Theology of Karl Barth* (Grand Rapids: Baker, 2008), 113–37.

a means for moving beyond fundamentalism.[33] Overall, Barth continues to receive this mixed reaction among evangelicals, who appreciate his emphasis on salvation by grace alone through faith alone in Christ alone, while often critiquing Barth's views on revelation, Scripture, and election.[34] Of course, "evangelical" is a slippery term with a usage further complicated by its diverse meanings throughout history and within different cultures. Many Reformed theologians who are students and lifelong appreciators of Barth would identify with this label to varying extents, which is a fitting move to the extent that Barth understood himself as a theologian committed to the gospel (*euangelion*) of Jesus Christ. It is no doubt testimony to the significance and sheer scope of Barth's theological melody that it has been replayed and reworked by such a diverse range of theologians and ethicists.[35] Given his resounding influence, it is appropriate to speak of Protestant theology before and after Karl Barth.

Select Bibliography

Primary Sources

Barth, Karl, *Church Dogmatics*. 13 vols. Edited by G. W. Bromiley and T. F. Torrance. Translated by G. W. Bromiley, et al. Edinburgh: T&T Clark, 1936–69.

Barth, Karl, *Die Kirchliche Dogmatik*. Munich: Christian Kaiser Verlag, 1932 [I/1]; Zurich: Evanglischer Verlag, 1938–67 [I/2–IV/4].

Other Notable Works by the Author

Barth, Karl, *Epistle to the Romans*. Translated by Edwyn C. Hoskyns. London: Oxford University Press, 1933.

[33] Cornelius Van Til, *Christianity and Barthianism* (Philadelphia: Presbyterian and Reformed Publishing, 1962); Bernard Ramm, *After Fundamentalism: The Future of Evangelical Theology* (San Francisco: Harper & Row, 1983).

[34] For a range of reactions, see Bruce L. McCormack and Clifford B. Anderson, eds., *Karl Barth and American Evangelicalism* (Grand Rapids: Eerdmans, 2011); Sung Wook Chung, ed., *Karl Barth and Evangelical Theology: Convergences and Divergences* (Grand Rapids: Baker, 2008); David Gibson and Daniel Strange, eds., *Engaging with Barth: Contemporary Evangelical Critiques* (London: T&T Clark, 2009).

[35] Space does not allow us to trace out Barth's unique impact on theological ethics, but those who stand in his trajectory yet critique him at various points include Stanley Hauerwas, John Howard Yoder, Oliver O'Donovan, and Nigal Biggar.

Barth, Karl, *Evangelical Theology: An Introduction*. Translated by Grover Foley. Grand Rapids: Eerdmans, 1963.
Barth, Karl, *The Göttingen Dogmatics: Instruction in the Christian Religion*. Translated by Geoffrey Bromiley. Edited by Hannelotte Reiffen. Vol. 1. Grand Rapids: Eerdmans, 1991.

Secondary Sources

Bromiley, Geoffrey W., *Introduction to the Theology of Karl Barth*. Edinburgh: T&T Clark, 1979.
Busch, Eberhard, *Karl Barth: His Life from Letters and Autobiographical Texts*. Translated by John Bowden. London: SCM Press, 1976.
Hart, Trevor A., *Regarding Karl Barth: Essays Toward a Reading of His Theology*. Carlisle: Paternoster Press, 1991.
Hunsinger, George, *How to Read Karl Barth: The Shape of His Theology*. New York: Oxford University Press, 1991.
Webster, John, ed., *Cambridge Companion to Karl Barth*. Cambridge: Cambridge University Press, 2000.

9

James H. Cone, *Black Theology and Black Power* (1969)

Embracing Blackness

In the 1960s, the United States was a cauldron of social struggle and protest. At the heart of this struggle was the Civil Rights Movement, seeking equal rights and opportunities for African Americans. As this movement progressed, however, some African Americans became increasingly critical of desegregation, celebrated distinctly Black culture, and began to rally under the banner of "black power." All of this was happening as James Cone finished his PhD in theology and began his teaching career. Despite all his education, the Civil Rights and Black Power movements awakened Cone from his theological slumber.[1] Driven by a desire to relate theology to the struggle of Black people, Cone's first writing project was *Black Theology and Black Power*. Nothing like it had ever been written, and it set Cone on a trajectory to be the father of Black liberation theology.

James Cone (1938–2018) was born during the age of Jim Crow. In his hometown of Bearden, Arkansas, segregation was a daily reality, whether at schools, water fountains, movie theaters, or churches. In his own church—the Macedonia African Methodist Church—Cone had a real and lasting encounter with Jesus, but he also encountered an uncritical faith embedded in an otherworldly mentality. This mentality was incapable of dealing with the harsh realities of life, which led to a divide between "churchpeople" and "bluespeople," the latter finding "the Sunday religion of Jesus inadequate for coping with their personal problems and the social contradictions they experienced during the week."[2] Needless to say, Cone was not content with the anti-intellectual and socially evasive culture of his upbringing.

[1] James H. Cone, "Looking Back, Going Forward: Black Theology as Public Theology," in *Black Faith and Public Talk: Critical Essays on James H. Cone's* Black Theology and Black Power, ed. Dwight N. Hopkins (MaryKnoll: Orbis Books, 1999), 250.

[2] Ibid., 247.

While attending Shorter College (1954–6) and Philander Smith College (1957–8), Cone was involved in leading several small churches, and his desire to be well-grounded theologically compelled him to enroll in the Master of Divinity program at Garrett Theological Seminary. At Garrett, he discovered his love for theology, and instead of pursuing a permanent church ministry position, Cone chose postgraduate study at Northwestern University. He completed his PhD in systematic theology in 1965, writing his dissertation on the anthropology of Karl Barth. During brief stints teaching theology and religion at Philander Smith College and then Adrian College, he realized that the Western theology he had come to love—exemplified by Bultmann, Barth, and Tillich—was not adequate to address the situation of Black oppression. Inspired by the March Against Fear in 1966, Stokely Carmichael's articulation of Black power, the Newark and Detroit riots of 1967, and finally by the assassination of Martin Luther King, Jr., in 1968, Cone was convinced that theology must embrace Blackness, and he devoted himself to writing *Black Theology and Black Power*.

Cone identifies his "turn to blackness" as an even deeper conversion experience than his turn to Jesus.[3] Because of this conversion, he now saw himself as a *Black* theologian addressing *Black* existence. In his Preface to the 1989 edition of *Black Theology and Black Power*, Cone explains how this book was his first attempt to fuse the visions of Martin Luther King, Jr., and Malcolm X.[4] On the one hand, Martin stood up against injustice while calling Blacks to love their enemies nonviolently. On the other hand, Malcolm asserted that Blacks must first and foremost love themselves—love Blackness—and then must defend Blackness by any means necessary. In bringing together Martin and Malcolm as "the yin and yang in the black attack on racism,"[5] Cone was the first theologian to articulate "liberation as the heart of the gospel and blackness as the primary mode of God's presence" (vii).

Black Theology and Black Power unleashed a torrent of responses, both energetically supportive and indignantly critical. To address these responses and to flesh out his original thesis, Cone wrote *A Black Theology of Liberation* (1970), which confirmed his status as a leading liberation theologian. In the same year, he became the first Black systematic theologian at Union Theological Seminary in New York City. One of the common critiques of Cone's early work was his propensity to rely on white theological concepts rather than Black experience. However accurate this critique, in subsequent

3 Ibid., 251.

4 James H. Cone, *Black Theology and Black Power* (Maryknoll: Orbis Books, 1997), viii. Hereafter, all references to this work shall be noted by employing in-text parenthetical citations.

5 Cone, "Looking Back, Going Forward," 256.

works—such as *The Spirituals and the Blues* (1972) and *God of the Oppressed* (1975)—Cone expanded his sources and drew more consistently on Black concepts and culture. In these books and his subsequent work, including *The Cross and the Lynching Tree* (2011), Cone clearly articulates the preeminence of Blackness in his personal experience and theological reflection: "I am *black* first—and everything else comes after that."[6]

Blackness and the Gospel

Because of his commitment to being Black before everything else, Cone begins *Black Theology and Black Power* by addressing what it means to be Black in the United States. Given the history of white oppression, Cone recognizes that being Black should inevitably lead to a commitment to Black power. He defines Black power as the "complete emancipation of black people from white oppression by whatever means black people deem necessary" (6). In blunter terms, Cone concurs with Stokely Carmichael that Black power means "taking care of business" the Black way, not the white way.[7]

Cone compares the concerns of Black power to existential themes arising in Tillich's theology and the philosophy of Camus. Riffing off Tillich's *The Courage to Be*, he views Black power as the way forward because it enables Black people to affirm their being and humanity (6–7). Black people say "yes" to their being by rebelling and fighting back, rather than wallowing in despair or plodding forward in weak neutrality. Black power is essentially a complete and consistent "affirmation of the humanity of black people in the face of white racism" (16).

Integration into a white system is not an option, because this ignores the root problem, giving the appearance of victory while hiding ongoing oppression. In radical language taken from *The Rebel* by Albert Camus, Cone asserts that it would be better to die than to capitulate to white oppression, because life without freedom is worse than death. This marks the absurdity of the Black situation, which only Black power can adequately address. To stand up against white oppression is not a form of racism; it is humanity-affirming rebellion. In fact, Cone maintains that the problem of race in

[6] James H. Cone, *God of the Oppressed*, rev. ed. (Maryknoll: Orbis Books, 1997), xi.

[7] Similar to the terms "Black" and "Blackness," Cone intends both a literal and figurative-theological meaning for the terms "white" and "whiteness." Whiteness is being on the side of oppressors—whether intentionally or through supposed neutrality—and Blackness is being on the side of the oppressed. According to Cone, these groups can be generally distinguished by skin color, although both white and black come in different shades.

America is a white problem, and merely lending Black people a helping hand cannot remove this guilt (22). White and Black people are simply deluded if they fail to realize that an extreme, oppressive situation requires extreme, revolutionary action. As Cone presents it, this is a matter of life and death; everyone must be willing to die in order to secure life for all.

If the task of theology is to show how God's revelation applies to particular situations, then, in Cone's perspective, most theologians have failed to do good theology because they have been silent regarding the oppression of Black people (31). Black theology, by contrast, not only speaks out against this oppression; it aligns God and his gospel with this struggle. According to Cone, the gospel must be emancipated from its "whiteness" and should be identified with Black liberation from white oppression (32). Black power *is* the gospel because it is the contemporary expression of Jesus's liberating mission. Echoing the words of Kierkegaard, Cone claims that Jesus is our contemporary, and that he is present in the ghetto and in the Black rebellion against white oppression (37–8).

To be a Christian is to embrace the liberating work of Christ that leads to true freedom. In one sense, Christ won the battle against oppression on the cross, but bringing God's freedom and justice to bear in the present is a continual campaign (40). Drawing on insights from Jürgen Moltmann and Karl Barth, Cone emphasizes that justification by faith inevitably leads to political responsibility. Justified by God, we are liberated to fight for justice, joining with the work of God in history (47).

At this point, Cone addresses a major objection against identifying Christianity with Black power, namely, that it contradicts Jesus's command to love our enemies. For Cone, this supposed contradiction dissolves when we recognize, as Tillich did, the inseparability of love, power, and justice.[8] When these are intertwined, love resists sentimentality and justice transcends legalism (51). True love does not just accept the current situation, but it instead works to destroy anything that opposes love. In other words, love is truncated if limited to random acts of kindness, but it flourishes by "working for political, social, and economic justice, which always means a redistribution of power" (55). Moreover, Cone explains that love may require violence if it is necessary to achieve lasting justice (55–6). In sum, for Cone, embracing the gospel means nothing less than embracing Black power. If people are filled with the Holy Spirit, they will be committed to justice for oppressed Black people (58). Similarly, a mark of the true church is caring for and identifying with the poor and needy, which means identifying with

[8] Paul Tillich, *Love, Power, and Justice* (New York: Oxford University Press, 1960).

Christ. Cone argues therefore that the church that opposes Black power opposes Christ himself.

Blackness and the Church

Putting his discussion in the context of the biblical narrative, Cone defines the church as God's suffering people, "that people called into being by the power and love of God to share in his revolutionary activity for the liberation of man" (63). The church is no doubt a people committed to God's Word, to service, and to fellowship, but the church only exists where it identifies with and fights for the liberation of the oppressed. The white church has actively oppressed Black people rather than fighting for their liberation, and therefore it cannot be the true church. Cone minces no words for describing the failure of the white church, identifying its accommodation to "sick, middle class egos" (80) and "chaplaincy to the forces of oppression" (90). The white racist church is no more orthodox than the portion of the church that supported Arius and his denial of Christ's incarnation in the fourth century. Like the Arians, the white church denies the incarnation because it refuses to see Christ among Black people (73).

In contrast to this heresy, Cone articulates a new kind of orthodoxy: "*Christ is black baby*, with all of the features which are so detestable to white society" (68). The affirmation that Christ is Black, Cone contends, is just as important in the twentieth century as understanding him as Jewish in the first century (69).[9] Christ is Black because he always identifies with the oppressed, and the church will be Black to the extent that it does the same. Unless the white church converts and embraces liberating action, it will continue to be the anti-Christ. In short, Cone calls the white church to repent and believe the gospel. What this means practically is "a radical reorientation of their style in the world toward blacks," not claiming "lofty neutrality," but "tasting the sting of oppression themselves" (81).

Cone's critique of the white church is unflinchingly harsh, but the Black church hardly fares any better. Because the Black church was born out of slavery and protest, it initially grasped the gospel and its liberating hope and power. Although some in the Black church capitulated to the worldview of

[9] Elsewhere, Cone explains that the literal color of Jesus's skin is irrelevant, just as "blackness" comes in different shades. Christ is Black simply because he was against oppression and for liberation as the incarnate suffering servant. Nevertheless, Cone also points out that Christ was not *white* "in any sense of the word, literally or theologically." James H. Cone, *A Black Theology of Liberation* (New York: J. B. Lippincott Company, 1970), 218.

white slave owners, a vision of an oppression-free future inspired protest against slavery in the present, as expressed in the best of Black preaching and spirituals. After the Civil War, however, the Black church started losing its resolve to pursue comprehensive liberation, capitulating to Jim Crow laws and the agenda of white churches. In this way, Black ministers began perpetuating white oppression, which was only partly caused by their fear of opposing segregation and discrimination (106–7). This is why Martin Luther King, Jr., stood out: he refused to accept the current state of existence for Black people. He rekindled the dream for an authentically Black church (108).

King's dream was cut short, but he paved the way for the emergence of Black power, which Cone recognizes as "the only hope of the black church in America" (109). Black power is not only the sole hope for the Black church but for organized Christianity as a whole. If the essence of Christianity is liberating the oppressed and defending the needy, then Black power shows the way forward. The church is the body of Christ in the world, "and in twentieth-century America, *Christ means Black Power*!" (112). Cone thus challenges both the white church and the Black church: will we join the revolution, or will we retreat into comfortable havens? Cone recognizes no neutral or easy option for renewal; the church will choose either "costly obedience" or "confirmed apostasy." And costly obedience will be fueled by a thoroughly worldly theology.

Blackness and Theology

By worldly theology, Cone means theology that refuses abstractions and addresses concrete realities of oppression. This is the kind of theology that will lead to words and deeds that are "harmonious with Jesus Christ" (84). Understood in this way, theology is not primarily an intellectual exercise but a risky, creative, and prophetic response to life and society. This response is genuinely Christian when it flows from identification with the disinherited. Cone commends Barth as a prime proponent of this kind of theology, given his stance against Nazi oppression of the Jews (86–8).

Black theology is a prime example of worldly theology. Its task is "to analyze the black man's condition in light of God's revelation in Jesus Christ with the purpose of creating a new understanding of black dignity among black people, and providing the necessary soul in that people to destroy white racism" (117). The point of departure for Black theology, therefore, is the predicament of Black people and the problem of oppression. Since Black people only know Christ through oppression, says Cone, this reality and the struggle for freedom is the only binding authority for Black theology (120). Every Christian doctrine should therefore relate to and support Blackness and emancipation for Black people. Despite Cone's criticism of theoretical modern theology, his vision for Black theology places him firmly within the trajectory of modern theology, given its characteristic use of a material norm to organize and evaluate doctrines.[10]

One example of how Cone reconstructs doctrine from the perspective of the Black predicament is his approach to eschatology. He bluntly observes how an otherworldly ethos is a "white lie" that has corrupted many Black churches (122). Hope in Jesus, in this sense, is merely a ploy to avoid the harsh realities of injustice. By contrast, Black theology maintains an earthly focus, more concerned with overturning white oppression in the present than adjudicating between different views of the end times. Drawing on Moltmann, Cone maintains that eschatology is more about this world being transformed than the hope of a distant, heavenly reward. "Our future expectations must be turned into present realities": justice and Black self-determination (126).

It is perhaps even more evident that Cone uses the Black predicament as his point of departure and binding authority when it comes to his understanding of reconciliation. First, reconciliation with God "means that white people are prepared to deny themselves (whiteness), take up the cross (blackness) and follow Christ (black ghetto)" (150). Justification happens by becoming Black, not literally, but figuratively, by aligning one's heart, soul, mind, and body with the dispossessed (151). Unless white people become "black," reconciliation will not be possible. In fact, reconciliation cannot happen until Black people have experienced emancipation, because otherwise the white oppressors will determine the terms of reconciliation. Until then, violence may be the means necessary for Black people to obtain freedom. Cone is clear that unless white racists repent and overturn their systemic violence against Black people, a violent revolution may be necessary to make Blackness beautiful once again (138–43).

According to Cone, Black theology is not just one way among many to think and live as a Christian. Black theology makes Christianity "*really* Christian" and exists "to destroy heretical white American Christianity" (130–1). Cone ends his book with an invitation and a challenge. Anyone—

[10] For a nuanced conception of how "modern" might best be understood in a distinctly theological context, see Bruce L. McCormack, "Introduction: On 'Modernity' as a Theological Concept," in *Mapping Modern Theology: A Thematic and Historical Introduction*, eds. Kelly M. Kapic and Bruce L. McCormack (Grand Rapids: Baker, 2012), 1–20.

Black or white—can take up the mission of Black theology. What matters is not Black skin but a black heart, which is evident through a resolute stance with oppressed Black and against white oppressors. Everything rests on how one answers and lives out the questions, "Where is your identity? Where is your being?" (152)

Cone and the Birth of Black Theology

Most scholars identify the 1966 statement by the National Committee of Negro Churchmen as the first expression of Black theology in conjunction with Black power. Cone's *Black Theology and Black Power*, however, represents the first book-length exposition of these themes and the first extended effort to locate the liberation of oppressed Black at the heart of the gospel. Soon after its publication in 1969, others added their voices to the growing chorus of Black theologians, including Vincent Harding, Jacquelyn Grant, Gayraud Wilmore, Albert Cleage, William R. Jones, Charles Long, C. Eric Lincoln, J. Deotis Roberts, Joseph Washington, and Preston Williams. This first generation of Black theologians labored to legitimize their theological interpretation of the Black situation as they continued to battle against marginalization and discrimination.

In the Preface to the 1989 edition of *Black Theology and Black Power*, Cone rearticulates why Black theology was necessary in the 1960s, but he also admits to several shortcomings in his inaugural attempt. First, he acknowledges his blindness to sexism. In reviewing his book 20 years later, Cone is "embarrassed by its sexist language and patriarchal perspective" (x). Instead of changing this language in the revised edition, however, he decided to leave the original "as a reminder of how sexist I once was and also that I might be encouraged never to forget it" (x). He insists on remembering his insensitivity to the oppression of women, because "amnesia is the enemy of justice" (xi). As such, Cone expresses gratitude for how his sexism was challenged by the rise of womanist theology, led by theologians like Jacquelyn Grant, Katie Cannon, and Delores Williams. These theologians exposed the inconsistency of Black liberation theology that remained blind and silent to the oppression of Black women, revealing vast theological and practical consequences of ingrained misogyny. For example, Delores Williams, who was a student of Cone's and later his colleague at Union Theological Seminary, criticizes Cone for using the Exodus as a paradigm for liberation, when this liberation did not apply to non-Hebrew female slaves.[11] As it developed in the 1990s, womanist theology thoroughly revised Christian theology through the lens of the Black female experience, including traditional theories of the atonement.[12]

The second shortcoming Cone identifies in his first book is the failure to link the Black struggle for liberation with parallel experiences in the Majority World. He recognizes that both Martin Luther King, Jr., and Malcolm X maintained a global perspective, which was necessary for understanding oppression at home. Cone links his blindness to non-Western oppression to his overreliance on Western theology, particularly his dependence on Karl Barth.[13] Cone still appreciates the centrality of Christ championed by Barth, but he views Barth's aversion to natural theology as a hindrance to Black theology. Finally, and directly related to the second shortcoming, Cone laments how *Black Theology and Black Power* disregards classism. He recognizes how greater awareness of global economic realities would have enabled him to view the Black struggle as more than a racial one, and how class privilege is pervasive in both white and Black communities in the United States.

Beginning in the early 1980s, a second generation of theologians joined Cone in his passionate pursuit of Black theology. In general, these theologians worked on "strengthening ties between scholarship, ministry, and social activism."[14] Dwight Hopkins and Cornel West are two notable theologians in this second generation, although they pursue divergent methodologies. Dwight Hopkins follows in Cone's footsteps by advancing the "black hermeneutic school," which remains committed to Christian faith as expressed within Black communities and affirms the Blackness of Jesus. Cornel West, by contrast, participates in the "black philosophical school," which pursues "humanocentric theism" allied with philosophical investigation.[15] Despite their different norms, methods, and goals, both

[11] Delores S. Williams, *Sisters in the Wilderness: The Challenges of Womanist God-Talk* (Maryknoll: Orbis Books, 1993), 147.

[12] Not all womanist theologians are equally critical of traditional Protestant theology, as represented by the fascinating essays in Amy Plantinga Pauw and Serene Jones, eds., *Feminist and Womanist Essays in Reformed Dogmatics* (Louisville: Westminster John Knox Press, 2006). While in his 1997 preface to *God of the Oppressed*, Cone voices agreement with womanist rejection of patriarchal doctrines and acknowledges that their insights have been personally transformative, he still maintains that the cross of Christ can be a source of liberation and empowerment. Cone, *God of the Oppressed*, xv–xviii.

[13] Cone, *God of the Oppressed*, xi–xiii.

[14] Frederick L. Ware, "Black Theology," in *Global Dictionary of Theology*, eds. William A. Dryness and Veli-Matti Kärkkäinen (Downers Grove: IVP Academic, 2008), 113.

[15] Frederick Ware delineates these categories in his article on Black theology in *Global Dictionary of Theology*, but more fully in *Methodologies of Black Theology* (Cascade:

approaches are indebted to Cone's vanguard expression of Black theology. Cone was not only the father of Black theology in all its contemporary forms, but remains an influential voice shaping social, contextual, and political theology in the Protestant tradition.

Select Bibliography

Primary Sources

Cone, James H., *Black Theology and Black Power*. New York: Harper & Row, 1969.

Cone, James H., *Black Theology and Black Power*. Rev. ed. Maryknoll: Orbis Books, 1997.

Other Notable Works by the Author

Cone, James H., *A Black Theology of Liberation*. 50th anniversary ed. Maryknoll: Orbis Books, 2020.

Cone, James H., *The Cross and the Lynching Tree*. Maryknoll: Orbis Books, 2011.

Cone, James H., *God of the Oppressed*. Rev. ed. Maryknoll: Orbis Books, 1977.

Secondary Sources

Burrow, Rufus, Jr., *James H. Cone and Black Liberation Theology*. Jefferson: McFarland & Company, 1994.

Hopkins, Dwight N., ed., *Black Faith and Public Talk: Critical Essays on James H. Cone's* Black Theology and Black Power. Maryknoll: Orbis Books, 1999.

Hopkins, Dwight N., and Edward P. Antonio, *The Cambridge Companion to Black Theology*. Cambridge: Cambridge University Press, 2012.

Ware, Frederick L., "Black Theology." In *Global Dictionary of Theology*, edited by William A. Dryness and Veli-Matti Kärkkäinen. Downers Grove: IVP Academic, 2008.

Wipf & Stock, 2008). In addition to the hermeneutic and philosophical school, he also identifies a human sciences school of Black theology.

10

Kosuke Koyama, *Water Buffalo Theology* (1974)

Stammering About God with a Crucified Mind

Kosuke Koyama (1929–2009) grew up in war-torn Tokyo. He received Christian baptism in 1942, the same year American planes began raiding Japanese cities. As the bombs intensified, Koyama hunkered down with John Bunyan's *Pilgrim's Progress*. The experience of reading Bunyan while enduring the bombing of Tokyo was pivotal for Koyama's initial growth as a Christian and his later formation as a theologian. He realized the journey of a Christian toward God is riddled with danger, most notably the reality of violence and the peril of idolatry.[1] The Christian resists idolatry and endures violence by cultivating a crucified mind and rejecting a crusading mind. The crucified mind is the mind of the crucified Christ, which desires to serve others in all their complexity. By contrast, the crusading mind "bulldozes people and history without appreciation of their complexities" (159).

Koyama's training as a theologian began in 1946 with a preparatory course at Tokyo Union Theological Seminary, where he graduated in 1952 with a thesis on Francis of Assisi. From there, he studied in the United States for the rest of his twenties, earning a BA at Drew University and a PhD from Princeton Theological Seminary on Martin Luther's interpretation of the Psalms. Thirty years old and a newly minted PhD, the United Church of Christ in Japan commissioned Koyama, now with a young family, as a missionary to Thailand. He dove headlong into studying the Thai language, which he described as "my second spiritual baptism, a baptism into the unfamiliar sounds and symbols of a different culture and religion" (173).

Despite his rudimentary grasp of the Thai language, in 1961 Koyama began lecturing at Thailand Theological Seminary in Chiengmai. As he worked out

1 Kosuke Koyama, *Water Buffalo Theology*, 25th anniversary ed. (Maryknoll: Orbis Books, 1999), 171–2. All parenthetical page numbers refer to this revised anniversary edition. Koyama's book *Mount Fuji and Mount Sinai* (1985) is an extended critique of idolatry within a Japanese context.

how to do theology with and for the Thai people, Koyama wrestled with the influence of his Japanese upbringing and American theological training. He realized he needed to start with the local culture and context, but this required a "triple accommodation process with Tokyo, New Jersey, and Chengmai" (174). His pioneering effort to construct a local, intercultural, and ecumenical theology led to an invitation, in 1968, to join South East Asia Graduate School of Theology in Singapore as their dean. In 1974, after 6 years in Singapore, he became Senior Lecturer in Religious Studies at the University of Otago in New Zealand.

That same year, a collection of Koyama's essays was published as *Water Buffalo Theology*, which was recognized as a groundbreaking work in local or contextual theology. Some of the essays express theology firmly grounded in the Thai context, while others are oriented to the broader Asian context. Koyama wrote several other books in English while in New Zealand, including *Fifty Meditations* (1975), *No Handle on the Cross: An Asian Meditation on the Crucified Mind* (1976), and *Three Mile an Hour God* (1979). In 1980, Koyama joined the faculty of Union Theological Seminary in New York City as professor of ecumenics and world Christianity, where he taught until his retirement in 1996. While in New York, Koyama deepened his intercultural and ecumenical approach to theology through dialogue with Judaism and other world religions. In addition, he became increasingly interested in the topic of violence, which was a major theme in *Mount Fiji and Mount Sinai: A Critique of Idols* (1984). According to Koyama, the ultimate test of Christian theology and mission is the removal of violence. Overall, Koyama wrote thirteen books, many of which have not been translated from his native Japanese, including a three-volume study on the Christian life.

Of all Koyama's books, *Water Buffalo Theology* is perhaps his most poetic and raw. There is no thesis or argument that builds neatly from beginning to end, but each essay is riveting, insightful, and often surprising. Koyama reveals his desire to keep his contextual methodology open for that very reason: so that doing theology can be "a journey full of surprises" (xi). If he adopted any methodology while doing theology in Thailand, it was "to see the face of God in the faces of people" (x). In that sense, it was a "theology from below," with the audience guiding the theological process. For *Water Buffalo Theology*, that audience was Thai farmers, the ones familiar with water buffaloes roaming in the rice fields. Koyama gave these farmers priority instead of any one theologian or theological system. Koyama claimed that as a missionary in Thailand, true understanding of great works such as Thomas Aquinas's *Summa Theologiae* or Karl Barth's *Church Dogmatics* occurs only out of relating them to the lives of Thai farmers (xv–xvi).

As a theology that arises out of and orients itself toward a particular place, *Water Buffalo Theology* takes steps toward ecological theology, but does so more experientially than substantively (xiii). Nevertheless, Koyama demonstrated that local theology inevitably incorporates and addresses the ecological dimension of life. The main concern and focus of *Water Buffalo Theology*, however, is people. For Koyama, theology is the process of engaging with local people in their local language in order to offer a "stammering description" of God whose historical action culminates in a local crucifixion and resurrection (135). That stammering comes from a crucified mind, which Koyama characterizes elsewhere as a mind theologically inspired, honest and careful, weak yet strong, and foolish yet wise, but not a sickly, mutilated, paternalistic mind.[2] It is a shaken mind, "which has decided to live by the power of the crucified Lord."[3]

Local People

Koyama views theology and life as the collision of particular people with a particular God. Theology is "neighborology," and neighborology is theology (64–7). God's reality must be viewed in light of the reality of our real neighbors and vice versa. If this does not happen, we misjudge the reality of both. In short, Christological exegesis and neighborly exegesis are inextricable. This is the heart of what Koyama identifies as missionary existence: a life lodged between the real Christ and real neighbors (65). He advocates a form of correlationism, but not in the vein of Paul Tillich who saw philosophy and culture providing the questions and theology the answers.[4] Rather, it is neighbors who ask the questions and Christ that we seek for answers. For Koyama, this brings theology to the ground where it belongs. "Philosophy neither sweats nor hungers nor feeds water buffaloes. But his neighbor does! Theology can become a religious crossword puzzle. But his Christ cannot be reduced to a game" (66).

If theologians have sometimes been guilty of reducing theology to a game, missionaries have been guilty of using Christianity as a gun. To the extent that the missionary enterprise was linked with militaristic colonialism, it was a gun (wounding) together with ointment (healing). As the West brought modernization to the East, it was a similar mix of gun and ointment,

2 Kosuke Koyama, *No Handle on the Cross: An Asian Mediation on the Crucified Mind* (Eugene: Wipf and Stock, 2011), 12.

3 Ibid., 8.

4 Paul Tillich, *Systematic Theology*, vol. 1 (London: SCM Press, 1978), 63.

or ointment with a sting. Since the missionary story is linked with the modernization story, Koyama admits the lamentable "entanglements between mission ointment and the conquest-expansion gun" (42). If missionary existence is to bring more ointment than gun, it needs to be oriented toward real neighbors and the real Christ. Moreover, missionaries must recognize the inherent ointments within Asian culture while bringing the healing message of Christ. Identifying these indigenous ointments requires paying attention to real people, to neighbors that bear the image of God.

Paying attention to these particular people takes precedence over understanding their system of belief. That means interacting with Buddh*ists* before trying to understand Buddh*ism*. Christian theology and mission misses the mark to the extent that it pays more attention to "isms" (ideas) than it does to "ists" (people). Koyama admits that when he moved to Thailand, he held a negative impression of Theravada Buddhism. He witnessed other missionaries writing off Buddhism as demonic, and this influenced his initial cautionary—even fearful—approach. But the more he got to know actual Buddhists, the more he was intrigued and humbled by their way of life. He began to see their mutual human faults and desires, and realized his need to live the doctrine of the *imago dei*. Through this experience, Koyama saw more clearly the dangerous "tyranny of doctrines," where *ism* matters more than *ist* (95). The most critical interaction and dialogue happens between Christians and Buddhists, not between Christianity and Buddhism.

Koyama discusses this with brutal honesty. He regrets his seminary education that drove him to understand ideas more than people. "They did not teach me that it is more interesting to know a Hindu than to know Hinduism; it is more rewarding to know a Buddhist than Buddhism, a Marxist than Marxism, a revolutionary than revolution, a missionary than missiology, a wife than the 'marriage and the family' course, Jesus Christ than Christology" (150). Giving priority to interactions with living persons makes life and theology far more satisfying but also more complex. A person is irreducibly complex; consequently, interacting with a Buddhist produces much greater nuance and creativity than interacting with Buddhism. "Library-Buddhism" can provide a framework for relationships with "street-Buddhists," but it's the relationships that matter (151). Only when real relationships take precedence is genuine communication of the gospel possible. In encounters between particular people, "communication" is not merely the delivery of a message, but the sharing of a life. In a word, it is incarnational. Mission is to participate in "God's concrete drama of dead-alive—lost-found" while interacting with concrete neighbors (157). It is to adopt the crucified mind and to decrease before Christ and our neighbors so that their stories can increase. When missionaries decrease, "the local people increase," in hope that they might encounter Christ and let him increase. The pattern of decrease-increase is "the wave of salvation-history, the beginning and end of which is Jesus Christ" (159).

Local Language

If local theology seeks attentiveness to local people, it must know and use their language. Koyama recounts how many Thai Buddhists have rejected Christianity simply because the language seems strange, because Western terms invoke "cultural resistance, psychological antipathy, and emotional reaction" (59). To do theology in Thailand, one has to ask: How should I talk about Christ in a Thai kitchen? What language would really connect with Thai people? Koyama uses the kitchen analogy to propose that local theology should also be "kitchen theology." In the case of theology in Thailand, this kitchen theology should be seasoned with a variety of spices, both "Aristotelian pepper and Buddhist salt" (56–63). There is no such thing as unseasoned theology, theology that has not taken on the language and flavors of a particular place and culture. Consequently, "imagining an unseasoned and raw Christ is as absurd and impossible as a de-Hebraized Yahweh" (63). Cultural and linguistic seasoning should be used sparingly, however, since not every spice complements the fragrance of Christ. Likewise, theology in Thailand should not throw out all the Aristotelian pepper from the West, but the theology will lack flavor to the locals if it is not seasoned with some local Buddhist salt.

Koyama practices what he preaches, for *Water Buffalo Theology* is thoroughly sprinkled with Buddhist concepts and language. For example, in the chapter "Cool *Arhat* and Hot God," Koyama shows how *dukkha*, *anicca*, *anatta*, and *arhat* can spice up the story of Israel to Thai taste while also revealing the distinct ingredients of a Hebrew worldview. Within Buddhism, *dukkha* is existence in all its unsatisfactoriness, suffering, and stress. The goal is to escape *dukkha* and move along *sotas* (the stream of emancipation) toward *nirvana* and the transcendence over *dukkha*. Moving along *sotas* involves embracing *anicca* (impermanence) and *anatta* (self-elimination) in order to reach the final state of *arhat*, or complete detachment.

When these terms are used to describe the story of Israel, they are historicized and brought into covenantal perspective. In this story, it is Israel—and indeed, all of humanity—who is *dukkha*, *anica*, and *anatta*, not just inwardly but in relation to the covenant God. *Dukkha*, *anica*, and *anatta* are marks of covenant unfaithfulness, and the solution is not further detachment, but greater covenant attachment between God and his people. Instead of moving toward "cool *arhat*," the biblical story is about a "hot God" attaching himself to an unsatisfactory, impermanent, self-destructive people (114–15).[5] In Christ, God embodied the opposite of *arhat*, embracing *dukkha*, *anica*, and *anatta* not for the sake of eliminating the self, but for the resurrection of self: new creation.

This is Koyama at his best: adding Buddhist salt and Hebrew pepper into a fragrant theological pot. He calls this particular attempt to "kitchenize theology" a process of "Hebraization" or "covenantization," which injects "the covenant concept into the Thai indigenous spiritual and religious concepts" (115). The result is a theological dish that Thai people will actually eat and maybe even enjoy and decide to integrate into their lives. Koyama insists that this method is not syncretistic; rather, it is the way to engage with local people in their local language so that they can taste the goodness of a hot God in a culture of cool tranquility. According to Koyama, some parts of the Bible are already poised to do this effectively in the Thai context. He identifies the letter of James, for example, as a book that connects with a "cool" mindset while introducing "hot" elements of covenantal existence (118–24). Several aspects of James radiate coolness—the transience of life, the trap of evil desires, the virtue of patience—and yet its hotness is undeniable. It draws the audience into more involvement with neighbors and attachment to history, not less. What is true religion? It is precisely to pursue greater attachment to needy and marginal people, to embrace suffering with joy, and to do the Word. It is through these "hot" attachments that the Christian way of life offers detachment, "a detachment not from the world, but from the corrupting influence of the world" (124).

Engaging with local people in their local language is something Koyama had to learn to do by trial and error, but he acknowledges that Japanese theologian Kazoh Kitamori provided a compelling model in his *Theology of the Pain of God*.[6] In this book, Kitamori fused two Japanese words—*tsutsumu* (to embrace what is good and bad) and *tsurasa* (to suffer so others can live)—to express the heart of the gospel within Japanese culture. Kitamori shows how both *tsutsumu* and *tsurasa* are present in the action of Christ, and this insight was pivotal for "re-rooting" the gospel in postwar Japan. By theological re-rooting, Koyama means "a thoughtful attempt to translate the inner meaning of the message of Jesus Christ from one culture milieu

[5] When Koyama uses the adjectives "hot" to describe God, therefore, he's referring to God's passionate, covenantal involvement with his people, which is scandalous in a culture that prizes "cool" detachment.

[6] Kazoh Kitamori, *Theology of the Pain of God* (Eugene: Wipf and Stock, 2005). Originally published in Japanese in 1946.

and root it in another" (86). Re-rooting is a hermeneutical task, since both the message of Jesus Christ and the cultural milieu need to be interpreted. Within this interpretive process of re-rooting, Koyama contends, the gospel is discovered in its radiant fullness (87). Thus, the gospel permeates a culture, but also the culture and its language illuminate the gospel in new ways. Engaging with local people in their local language, in other words, enables us to stammer a bit more poetically about the local God.

Local God

Koyama never specifically refers to God as "local," but his method of contextualization is overtly grounded in the person of Christ, who "indigenized the message of God through his life of suffering" (17). The God of Israel and the Church is a historical God, and while his action is global and even universal, it is also always local. The Creator interacts at the level of his creation. The once-for-all, beyond-nature God engages with the many-times world of monsoons, mosquitoes, and the people that get wet and bitten. Yet, Koyama hopes the question of chapter two is rhetorical: Will the monsoon rain make God wet? Of course not, because "God is the Lord of the monsoon rain" (31). Yet God is involved in the cycles of nature just as he is involved in the linear progression of history toward its goal of new creation. Doing theology in Thailand means combining the biblical, linear view of history with the cycles of nature into a unified "history-and-nature" (20): an ascending spiral over which the Lord God gets locally involved.

Because God is involved in history, he is inherently passionate, both in promoting righteousness and opposing unrighteousness. With Lactantius, the early Christian apologist, and Martin Luther, the Protestant reformer, Koyama rejects the apatheia of God and affirms the capacity for God to be "perturbed" (68). In Thai culture, largely influenced by Buddhism, tranquility and detachment are the epitome of virtue, and the notion of a perturbed God causes confusion and offense. Nevertheless, Koyama insists that God is moved to wrath and joy because he is involved in history, and therefore Christian theology must wrestle with the "strange work of God" (73). This is one example where the Buddhist salt should not be added to the theological pot, since anti-historical, perturbance-averse Buddhism is fundamentally at odds with the impassioned God of history. For the Thai people, the greatest stumbling block, as well as the reality most capable of transforming hearts and lives, is the historical incarnation of God in the person of Jesus. In the ultimate act of involvement, this God-man experienced every aspect of *dukkha* in order to provide not just salvation from *dukkha,* but salvation for new life within *dukkha*.

God's local, historical action also challenges the technological mindset spreading across the globe. Koyama is not against technology and technological efficiency, but he does believe it presents greater challenges for hearing God's Word and appreciating the way God works. God's primary mode of operation is love, and love is supremely inefficient and inconvenient (46). One of the aggravating and awe-inspiring aspects of the biblical story is how long things take. Forty years in the wilderness? "Wasn't there a more efficient way?" In the Internet age, we expect things to move at the speed of light, but God moves at the speed of love.[7] The action of God, therefore, has its own efficiency; it is efficiency of the Crucified One (48–9). What could be less efficient than being nailed down? And yet what could be more efficient in revealing God and the depth of his love? Those who bear the name of the Crucified and Risen One will have a distinct mode of presence in our increasingly technological world: a stumbling, discomforted, unfree presence (163–70). It is in this "strange mode of life" that Christians are able to participate in "God's *pathos* toward all scattered things which are held together in the *glory* of the *crucified* Lord" (170).

Locally Ecumenical Theology

In the preface to the twenty-fifth anniversary edition of *Water Buffalo Theology*, Koyama describes his work as "distinctively local and openly ecumenical," in that it was rooted in northern Thailand while aware of its "global webbedness" and connection to the universal Church (x). In the first chapter, Koyama outlines the "raw situations" in several Asian countries ripe for theological engagement. Doing theology in these various contexts should look different because the situations are unique, but each situation calls for a similar cultivation of a crucified mind. According to Koyama, theology—whether theology in Asia, America, or anywhere else—should be a theology of the cross. This is the core of his ecumenical theology.

As the church and its theology develop in particular places, they inevitably take on local color. While it is appropriate to speak of the church in Thailand or any other locality, Koyama maintains that the local church is first and foremost the "church of Christ." There is only one church: the church of Christ in various localities (142). Likewise, although it is appropriate to speak

[7] Koyama unpacks this metaphor in *Three Mile an Hour God* (London: SCM Press, 1979), 7.

of Thai theology, the underlying continuity between this and other local theologies is Christ and him crucified. Therefore, while Koyama believes denominations and confessions contain much value, he contends they must never morph into a "dominating theological insight." In fact, theological domination is the very definition of denominationalism, which Koyama describes as deadly and demonic, for it "monopolizes Christ theologically" (145). Christians who identify with a denomination are called to great humility and must identify preeminently with Christ himself. In Koyama's perspective, being a Methodist, Baptist, Lutheran, or Presbyterian is helpful only to the extent that it helps you make much of Christ and adopt his form of life: self-denial. Lamentably, denominational identification and promotion is often shot through with pride, which divides Christ. Denominations and their theological contributions will remain fruitful if they are willing to be "mocked, spat upon, scourged, killed, and cast out," just like Christ (149).

To relate this back to "kitchen theology," each local theological dish will have different flavors, but each one should emit the fragrance of the crucified Christ. Subsequent attempts to trace out a methodology for local theology have drawn upon Koyama's culinary metaphor,[8] but few have communicated with equal force that any theological dish that cares about Christ will be a "spat-upon" dish.[9] In doing so, Koyama was both a pioneer of local theology and a champion of ecumenical theology centered on the cross. Although Koyama never traced out a detailed methodology for doing local theology, others have helpfully plotted his work among the rapidly increasing body of local, indigenous, inculturated, and contextual theologies.[10] Within Asian contextual theology, Moonjang Lee suggests three primary strands. The first strand engages with the social, political, and economic reality in Asia, such as Minjung theology, the Korean version of liberation theology. The second strand interacts with the cultural reality of Asia. The third strand focuses on interreligious or interfaith dialogue.[11] Although Lee places Koyama within the second strand of Asian contextual theology, Koyama's writing combines

[8] For example, see Clemens Sedmak, *Doing Local Theology: A Guide for Artisans of a New Humanity* (Maryknoll: Orbis Books, 2002), 17–20.

[9] This is a common theme throughout Koyama's writing, and in *No Handle on the Cross*, he writes that the reality of a spat-upon Jesus requires "spat-upon theology" and "spat-upon churches" (93).

[10] Robert Schreiter explains how these terms are generally interchangeable, although "contextual theology" and "contextualization" have become the standard terms in Protestant circles. Robert Schreiter, "Local Theologies," in *Global Dictionary of Theology*, eds. William A. Dyrness and Veli-Matti Kärkkäinen (Downers Grove: IVP Academic, 2008), 500.

[11] Moonjang Lee, "Asian Theology," in *Global Dictionary of Theology*, 74–7.

elements of all three strands. Overall, Koyama's theology does not fit neatly into any "strand," and is simultaneously local, intercultural, and ecumenical.

In the Afterword to a collection of essays commemorating Koyama's retirement from Union Theological Seminary in 1996, former president Donald Shriver remarks not only on Koyama's groundbreaking work in contextual theology, but ranks him among the twentieth century's greatest biblical theologians.[12] Of course, Koyama did not pursue biblical studies according to the strictures of the Western academic guild. According to Shriver, however, that is precisely what makes him so great. He had the courage to take his neighbors seriously, bringing the world of the Bible to bear on their concrete lives. As a result, he made that strange world come alive, not just for those neighbors but also for everyone who has the pleasure of sitting in Koyama's theological kitchen.

Select Bibliography

Primary Sources

Koyama, Kosuke, *Water Buffalo Theology*. Maryknoll: Orbis Books, 1974.

Koyama, Kosuke, *Water Buffalo Theology*. Reprint, Maryknoll: Orbis Books, 1999.

Other Notable Works by the Author

Koyama, Kosuke, *Mount Fuji and Mount Sinai: A Critique of Idols*. Maryknoll: Orbis Books, 1985.

Koyama, Kosuke, *No Handle on the Cross: An Asian Meditation on the Crucified Mind*. Maryknoll: Orbis Books, 1976.

Koyama, Kosuke, *Three Mile an Hour God*. London: SCM Press, 1979.

Secondary Sources

Irvin, Dale T., and Akintunde E. Akinade, eds., *The Agitated Mind of God: The Theology of Kosuke Koyama*. Maryknoll: Orbis Books, 1996.

[12] Donald W. Shriver, Jr., "An Afterword," in *The Agitated Mind of God: The Theology of Kosuke Koyama*, eds. Dale T. Irvin and Akintunde E. Akinade (Maryknoll: Orbis Books, 1996), 228.

Lee, Moonjang, "Asian Theology." In *Global Dictionary of Theology*, edited by William A. Dyrness and Veli-Matti Kärkkäinen. Downers Grove: IVP Academic, 2008.

Sedmak, Clemens, *Doing Local Theology: A Guide for Artisans of a New Humanity*. Maryknoll: Orbis Books, 2002.

Sugirtharajah, R. S., ed., *Asian Faces of Jesus*. Maryknoll: Orbis Books, 1993.

11

José Míguez Bonino, *Doing Theology in a Revolutionary Situation* (1975)

Theologian Seeking Effectiveness

José Míguez Bonino (1924–2012) was a pioneer of Protestant liberation theology in Latin America. Born in 1924 in Santa Fe, Argentina, Bonino's parents were Italian immigrants and active participants in the Methodist Church. After 2 years of medical school, Bonino completed an undergraduate degree in theology at the Evangelical School of Theology in Buenos Aires, graduating in 1948. Following graduation, he served churches in Bolivia and Argentina before pursuing a masters in theology at Candler School of Theology in Atlanta. Bonino came back to Argentina to teach dogmatic theology but then returned to the United States to complete a PhD in ecumenism at Union Theological Seminary.

These formative years of ministry and education equipped Bonino for his role, beginning in 1961, as director of the Evangelical School of Theology (later the Evangelical Institute of Theological Studies, or ISEDET) in Buenos Aires. Meanwhile, he continued serving as a Methodist pastor and launched a lifelong involvement with the World Council of Churches (WCC). At first, he participated in the WCC's Commission on Faith and Doctrine (1961–75), but he eventually served as the Council's president (1975–83). In addition to this ecumenical leadership, Bonino was the only Latin American Protestant invited to observe the Second Vatican Council, and he also attended the 1968 Conference of Latin American Bishops in Medellin, Columbia.

Although Bonino engaged widely in ecumenical efforts and taught at several international seminaries as a visiting professor, he remained rooted in Argentina and committed to the Latin American context. Bonino's first major publication in English was *Doing Theology in a Revolutionary Situation* (1975). Later, he translated this book into his native Spanish as *Fe en Busca de Eficacia* (1977), or *Faith Seeking Effectiveness*. In doing so, Bonino proposed a way of doing Protestant theology that diverged from European theology influenced by Saint Anselm's methodology of "faith seeking understanding." In Bonino's perspective, theology arises out of and is oriented toward effective—even revolutionary—action. Following this original manifesto on liberation theology, Bonino continued his account of faith in action in *Christians and Marxists: The Mutual Challenge to Revolution* (1976) and *Toward a Christian Political Ethics* (1983).

Through his publications, pastoral ministry, theological education, and leadership within the WCC, Bonino emerged as a widely respected leader, not just of liberation theology but also of Protestantism in Latin America. In 1993, Bonino was invited to deliver the Carnahan Lectures, which were published as *Faces of Latin American Protestantism* (1997). In these lectures, he traced the four main faces of Latin American Protestantism: mainline, evangelical, Pentecostal, and immigrant. Bonino believed that the revolutionary situation that arose in mid-twentieth-century Latin America created potential for a common goal among Protestants, if indeed each "face" would open its eyes to see and respond to their common reality.

Bonino confesses that when he looks at the Latin American situation, he does so as an "*evangélico*," someone who "belongs to the grace of God."[1] This dependence on grace motivated and strengthened Bonino's resolute commitment to theology that constantly moves toward practical and political effectiveness. The revolutionary theologian, just like any Christian, has nothing to fear, because "a Christian can offer his praxis to the fire of criticism totally and unreservedly on the trust of free grace just as he can offer his body totally and unreservedly in the hope of resurrection." This freedom is "the very center of the gospel," and the foundation of revolutionary action.[2]

Emergence of a Revolutionary Situation

To understand the revolutionary situation, Bonino begins *Doing Theology in a Revolutionary Situation* by urging his readers to grapple with the colonial legacy in Latin America (5–7). Intertwined with the economic and political purposes of the sixteenth-century European colonization of Latin America was a theological mission: Christianizing the known world. In contrast to this utopian dream, however, colonizers constructed a social and political order that legitimized genocide, class stratification, and subservience of

1 José Míguez Bonino, *Faces of Latin American Protestantism*, trans. Eugene L. Stockwell (Grand Rapids: Eerdmans, 1997), viii.

2 José Míguez Bonino, *Doing Theology in a Revolutionary Situation* (Philadelphia: Fortress Press, 1975), 100. Hereafter, all references to this work shall by noted by employing in-text parenthetical citations.

church to state. Consequently, rather than transforming the new world into the kingdom of God, conquest and colonization merely made this world an extension of the European empire. Except for a few lone figures, the church did not question this colonial project but rather baptized the social and economic order as God's eternal order. The legacy of colonization is the dependence of the working class on a dominating ruling class.

As political structures began to change at the turn of the nineteenth century, Latin America experienced an era of disorganization and chaos, which set the stage for a new project of modernization beginning in 1870. Development was the mantra of modernization, but Bonino argues that this "development" simply represented a new form of dependence. Instead of depending on the dominant class in their own country, the Latin American people simply shifted their dependence to those who controlled the free market system, whether in their country or abroad (10–13). Modernization was linked with Protestantism from the beginning, since both share a commitment to freedom and democracy. In reality, however, Protestantism promoted and supported the rise of neocolonialism, which also gained Catholic support after Vatican II.

Neocolonialism continues the pattern of dependence and domination, with northern countries benefiting from Latin American dependence and underdevelopment. In this new era, "Latin America has discovered the basic fact of its dependence," along with the "hoax of democracy" (15). If dependent nations refuse to be used as factories for northern development, northern countries train and fund repressive police states to protect production. Ruling elites in Latin America become more dependent on foreign interests and less interested in the plight of their own people. This whole system, claims Bonino, is perpetuated by mass media, which coaxes everyone to consume and encourages escapism from the harsh realities created by this very consumption (30–1).

This neocolonial system—domination and dependence, capitalist production and consumption, northern development conjoined with southern underdevelopment—created the revolutionary situation with its postcolonial possibilities. As dreams of development deteriorated, the response of churches and Christian leaders covered a wide spectrum, from traditional to progressive to revolutionary. The most faithful response, according to Bonino, is to move away from development and to join with the socialist project of liberation. Bonino identifies various methods and allegiances among those promoting a project of liberation in Latin America. Nevertheless, he highlights seven common elements: rejecting developmentalism, promoting social revolution, viewing the political dimension of life as determinate, working toward a strong centralized state, encouraging citizen participation, supporting an authentically Latin American brand of socialism, and pursuing holistic transformation (38–9).

It should come as no surprise, Bonino notes, that Christians are among the most ardent participants in the project of liberation, since its global, historical, and human dimensions are inherently theological. The struggle for liberation is not a bandwagon Christians jumped on in order to be culturally relevant; liberation is inherently Christian. As Camilo Torres, the Columbian priest and prominent forerunner of liberation theology, once stated: "I am a revolutionary because I am a priest" (43). Latin American Christians began to develop a theology of liberation because, as human beings and as Latin Americans, they were inextricably involved in the struggle for liberation. While the church as a whole was slow to take a stance—whether for its desire to protect church unity or because of its implicit fear of revolution (57)—several Christian leaders forged ahead in practicing and understanding revolutionary action.

Bonino highlights five theologians committed to this new way of doing theology in Latin America. Juan Segundo, a Uruguayan Jesuit, maintained deep connections with European theology (particularly Rahner's anthropology and Chardin's eschatology), but was also deeply committed to contextual socio-historical analysis that fosters fitting action (62–5).[3] Following the Second Vatican Council, Argentinean priest Lucio Gera emerged as a leader of the Movement of Priests for the Third World, championing the mission of the church among the poor (65–8).[4] Dominican priest Gustavo Gutiérrez was the first to popularize the language of liberation in his widely acclaimed *A Theology of Liberation* (1971), which asserts that sociopolitical struggle, human development, and reconciliation with God are a unified reality (69–71).[5] Hugo Assmann, a Brazilian priest, demonstrated how theology is action and action is theology, seeking to unmask the ideology of praxis (72–3).[6] Finally, Brazilian Protestant theologian Rubem Alves courageously took European theology to task, criticizing Barth's transcendentalism, Bultmann's existentialism, and

[3] Bonino references several of Segundo's books, most notably *Teología Abierta para el Laico Adulto*, 5 vols. (Buenos Aires: Ediciones Carlos Lohlé, 1968–72). A reprint of the English translation is still available as *A Theology for Artisans of a New Humanity*, 5 vols. (Eugene: Wipf and Stock, 2011).

[4] Bonino notes how "Gera's theological production consists mostly of unpublished theological documents, frequently of great depth and scholarship, related to the concrete problems faced by the Church in the Argentine situation" (*Doing Theological in a Revolutionary Situation*, 65 n. 3).

[5] Gustavo Gutiérrez, *A Theology of Liberation* (Maryknoll: Orbis Books, 1973). Original Spanish: *Teología de la Liberación* (Lima: Editorial Universitaria, 1971).

[6] Assmann's most notable early work was *Teología desde la praxis de liberación* (Salamanca: Sígeueme, 1973), translated into English as *Theology for a Nomad Church*, trans. Paul Burns (Maryknoll: Orbis Books, 1975).

Moltmann's futurism alike for failing to embrace "messianic humanism," which entails real political action on behalf of the oppressed (74–7).[7]

Reflection in the Revolutionary Situation

Liberation theology in Latin America—whether Protestant or Catholic—shares a shift in theological method from metaphysical speculation to anthropological reflection, from the inner-personal realm to the public-historical, and from abstract concepts to political and historical concreteness (78). Bonino claims that some European and American theologians—most notably Jürgen Moltmann, Johann Baptist Metz, and Harvey Cox—align with the first two shifts but have not embraced the third.

In particular, Bonino spends time engaging with Moltmann, specifically his discussion of political liberation in *The Crucified God*.[8] Bonino appreciates the fact that the German theologian identifies "demonic circles of death" (poverty, violence, racial and cultural deprivation, industrial destruction of nature, meaninglessness), but laments that he does not delve into their socio-analytic roots. What dismays Bonino even more is that Moltmann describes the crucified God as the God of the poor while claiming this God is classless and without country.[9] "But," Bonino retorts, "the poor, the oppressed, the humiliated *are a class* and *live in countries*" (148, emphasis original). To be for the poor, argues Bonino, is to be for them in their concrete, historical situations, which means refusing to remain ideologically neutral. If you claim to remain neutral, as Moltmann does, you just end up aligning with the "liberal, social-democratic project" in opposition to socialism (150).

Moltmann took Bonino's criticism seriously, writing what has been deemed the first significant response to liberation theology from a prominent Western and Protestant theologian.[10] He is disturbed by Bonino's position while also being "deeply moved" by his passion for liberation, celebrating that both European political theology and Latin American liberation theology share a turn toward real people in real situations. The major difference, Moltmann explains, is their divergent assessments of the situation. Whereas

7 Rubem Alves completed his PhD at Princeton Theological Seminary in 1968, and his thesis was published in English as *A Theology of Human Hope* (Washington, DC: Corpus Books, 1969).

8 Jürgen Moltmann, *The Crucified God* (London: SMC Press, 1974). Original German: *Der gekreuzigte Gott* (Munich: Christian Kaiser Verlag, 1972).

9 Ibid., 305.

10 Jürgen Moltmann, "An Open Letter to José Míguez Bonino," *Christianity and Crisis* 36, no. 5 (March 29, 1976): 57–63.

Bonino sees the need for revolution, Moltmann believes liberation can be achieved through a democratic process. He concludes: "However we analyze our situation, hope is faithfulness to the resurrection and therefore perseverance in the cross."[11]

Moltmann represents the most common response to liberation theology among the critical crowd, namely, accusing it of ideologization. But is there an alternative, wonders Bonino, for those who suffer oppression and live in such a reality? According to Bonino, there is no other option in this situation than for theology to be political and partisan. The task of theology is not to formulate abstract concepts and then apply them to particular situations. Rather, theology is reflection in the midst of action (89–90). Truth and action are fused to the extent that understanding arises out of doing, and doing informs understanding. This radical synthesis of thought and practice, explains Bonino, is the new way of doing theology in Latin America, in which orthopraxy takes precedence over orthodoxy.

In other words, the task of theology is to understand and live faithfully within history, rather than seeking to understand and then apply metaphysical concepts. The latter approach is not possible, since we have "no direct access from words and meaning to a theological reality outside time and history" (81). As such, theology's main tools are socio-analytic rather than philosophical. Bonino explains that Marxism is theologically helpful to the extent that it is used as a historical tool rather than a philosophical one. Received in this way, Marxism is "the best instrument available for an effective and rational realization of human possibilities in historical life" (97).[12] Theologians who fail to see Marxism as a profitable instrument do so as a result of a historical dualism: dividing world history from salvation history. Bonino believes, "with due reserve," that this dualism can be traced back to Augustine's *City of God*, where the city of man, or world history, is a "mere stage" for the city of God, or salvation history (136). By contrast, faith does not introduce "a different history, but a dynamic, a motivation, and in its eschatological horizon, a transforming invitation" (138). In other words, while the kingdom of God is not completely coterminous with history as its natural development, it does grow and come to fruition within real history.

If Marxism structures Christian obedience, then how is Christian obedience distinct from Marxist action? How are the actions of God and Jesus determinate in understanding history and forming Christian obedience? Bonino responds to these questions by identifying the death and resurrection

[11] Ibid., 63.

[12] For more on how Bonino relates Christianity and Marxism, see his *Christians and Marxists: The Mutual Challenge to Revolution* (Grand Rapids: Eerdmans, 1976).

of Jesus as "intrinsic tests" for Christian obedience (100). In other words, these are real events that occurred in real history, and therefore—contrary to the existentializing perspective of Rudolf Bultmann—they have a tangible bearing on our history. Of course, the death and resurrection of Jesus are inevitably approached from a subjective perspective, but Bonino still asserts their objective historicity, bolstered by his belief that the Bible faithfully witnesses to these events. There is a "hermeneutical circulation," rather than a circle, between these germinal events and Christian interpretation and obedience in the present context (102). Because these historical events and actions of God provide the ultimate framework for Christian obedience, it moves Christian praxis away from mere feeling and toward relevant, and, if necessary, revolutionary action. This is a dangerous path, but then, "obedience is always a risk" (104).

Acting in a Revolutionary Situation

Christian obedience is a risk because it involves forging solidarity with the poor and resisting the oppressor. True solidarity involves recognizing that poverty robs people of their humanity because it takes away the dignity, creativity, and joy of work. Bonino appreciates Marxism for its understanding of human beings as workers, and he insists that if Christian theology ignores this dimension of life, it will "falsify both the gospel and man's most authentic experience." If that happens, Christian talk of redemption becomes "a parody lived out in the realm of ideas (doctrine) or of subjectivity (intention or feeling) instead of the real world of creation," thus becoming, as Marx claimed, the "opiate of the people" (110). Christians must therefore confront the alienated nature of work and the inevitability of class struggle, while recognizing this alienation is deeper than the capitalist system. The poor need to break free from the dominating class, but they also need to break free from their bondage to sin, which requires trusting in God's promises.

What does practical Christian action look like, then, in a revolutionary situation? Is it legitimate to battle the oppressors with violent action, and to do so from a Christian perspective? Bonino resists any discussion of violence and peace that begins from an abstract starting point. Only the concrete situation should be the starting point. For example, the biblical narrative records several concrete situations where God and his people violently break out of oppressive and dehumanizing situations. If we start with the concrete, it is difficult to deny that there were times in history when violence was appropriate (117–18). But how do we deal with the concrete example of Jesus and his submission to violence for the sake of redemption? Doesn't that provide a different paradigm for revolutionary struggle? It does, but Bonino first unmasks an understanding of love as "tolerance, compromise, or acceptance" and shows how Jesus's demonstration of love involves a willingness to condemn, criticize, resist, and reject. In this way, Jesus took the side of the oppressed and joined their struggle, but he also refused to lead an armed revolt and chose instead to give up his power (123). Because of this, Christians should not be opposed abstractly and categorically to all violence, but nonetheless *nonviolent* action is the most appropriate way to work out Christian obedience in a revolutionary situation (126–7). Whatever the case, Christians should not and cannot remain neutral. Love is never neutral. It moves us to act in concrete situations; it moves us to take sides. What makes Christian faith distinct from a revolutionary mindset, however, is the ultimate hope that motivates present action. For the Marxist, the ultimate goal is socialist revolution, but for the Christian Marxist, revolution may be an immediate goal, but the ultimate hope is the Second Coming of Christ and the consummation of the kingdom of God (130).

In this revolutionary situation, where Christians are joining the revolutionary struggle driven by hope in Christ's return, what is the nature and role of the church? Bonino maintains that the foundation of the church is not any static identity—whether doctrine, structures, or norms—but its concrete, historical task of being a "Church-for-others" (156). Moving away from more static "marks of the church" is fitting in an era of greater ecclesial fluidity, where charismatic, revolutionary, and evangelical identities cut across more traditional lines. In Latin America, this creates an opportunity for churches, regardless of confessional or denominational affiliation, to crystallize their identity around praxis and becoming a church for the poor. For Bonino, this is an urgent task, for "only in the struggle for the liberation of the poor will the Church become the one true Church of Jesus Christ" (162). Amid this struggle, however, the church must not be equated with social and political revolution, for then "either the Church and Jesus Christ are made redundant or the political and social revolution is clothed in a sacred or semi-sacred gown" (163).

Bonino's ecclesiological vision arises from his commitment to the unity of human history and the germinal significance of Jesus's death and resurrection. In his perspective, a more adequate ecclesiology will fuse the creational and soteriological dimensions of human existence. Bonino draws on the language of Reformed theology to relate the "covenant of creation"—which originally placed humanity in relational responsibility to God, each other, and the rest of creation—to the "covenant of redemption," which seeks to restore these relationships and fulfill their purpose in Christ (165). In this view, salvation is a completion of creation, not a departure from it. The redemption accomplished by Christ enables humanity to fulfill their historical and creational vocation to love God, each other, and the rest of creation. Within this Reformed theological framework, Bonino defines the church as "the fellowship of those who embrace a historical task in the freedom of God's forgiveness and sanctification" (169). That historical task is the liberation of humanity to experience the fullness of life and freedom intended by God for his entire creation. This is why the church never exists statically, but dynamically becomes the church wherever Christians confess, celebrate, and enact their commitment to liberation for oppressed humanity. This is the church that witnesses to the already-present-yet-still-coming kingdom of God, the church that performs faithful action in a revolutionary situation.

Bonino, Protestant Theology, and the Mission of Liberation

In *Doing Theology in a Revolutionary Situation*, Bonino laid the groundwork for a distinctly Latin American Protestant theology. Bonino would later build on that foundation in *Toward a Christian Political Ethics* and then attempt a more comprehensive and descriptive account in *Faces of Latin American Protestantism*. In this later work, Bonino doubts whether Western attempts to pinpoint a material principle for Protestantism are adequate, especially for Latin American theology. He argues that doctrines such as justification by faith or the Reformational *solas—sola fide, sola gratia, sola scriptura, soli deo gloria, solus Christus*—usually serve a polemical rather than constructive purpose, and therefore are inadequate for making sense of the struggle for liberation.[13] Bonino admires Paul Tillich for attempting to get to the heart of Protestantism by interpreting justification by faith as an "anti-idolatrous principle" signaling a protest against any absolute claim.[14] But he also agrees with Rubem Alves, who believes Protestantism abandoned that principle in Latin America by absolutizing "the Protestantism of right doctrine" and conservatism.[15] Latin American Protestants have consistently upheld traditional Protestant doctrines, but these doctrines do not actually describe the theological core that unifies and provides a common experience for liberal, evangelical, Pentecostal, and immigrant Protestants in Latin America.

[13] Bonino, *Faces of Latin American Protestantism*, 129.

[14] Paul Tillich, *The Protestant Era* (Chicago: University of Chicago Press, 1957), 163. Quoted in Bonino, *Faces of Latin American Protestantism*, 130.

[15] Rubem Alves, *Protestantism and Repression: A Brazilian Case Study* (Maryknoll: Orbis Books, 1984). Quoted in Bonino, *Faces of Latin American Protestantism*, 130.

Instead of identifying a particular doctrine as this unifying core, Bonino argues that if there is a material principle for Latin American Protestantism, it is mission. To be clear, Bonino is not claiming that any particular *theology* of mission is the material principle, but the practice of mission itself, which is "an ethos that permeates the speech, worship, and life of Protestant communities, a self-understanding manifested in all attitudes, conflicts, and priorities."[16] To relate this back to *Doing Theology in a Revolutionary Situation*, Bonino is asserting that Latin American Protestantism will be true to itself to the extent that it effectively enacts its mission within particular contexts, revolutionary or otherwise. In *Faces of Latin American Protestantism*, Bonino more overtly articulates the trinitarian dimensions of this mission, describing it as "the invitation to participate in faith in the very life of the triune God and hence in the totality of what God has done, is doing, and will do to fulfill God's purpose of being 'all in all.'"[17] In doing so, Christians are "actors or coactors in the divine mission" as we seek to embody justice, mercy, and peace in every area of life and society.[18]

Throughout his entire body of work, Bonino expressed a distinctly Protestant approach to liberation theology in Latin America and beyond.[19] Rebecca Chopp notes how Bonino's perspective on liberation and solidarity with the poor diverges in notable ways from Gustavo Gutiérrez, whom many consider the father of liberation theology. Whereas Gutiérrez embraces solidarity with the poor because the poor manifest God's presence, Bonino embraces solidarity with the poor out of obedience to God's living and incarnate Word to whom the Bible bears witness.[20] This approach reveals Bonino's Protestant, Barthian, and distinctly Latin American way of doing theology, which leads him to interpret and engage with concrete situations in light of the Word.[21] Bonino's distinctive contribution to Protestant liberation theology is his additional commitment to hear and interpret the Word in light of mission and the praxis of liberation.

16 Bonino, *Faces of Latin American Protestantism*, 131.

17 Ibid., 144.

18 Ibid., 142.

19 Leonardo and Clodovis Boff locate Bonino in the foundational stage of liberation theology's development, along with Protestants Emilio Castro and Rubem Alves and Catholics Gustavo Gutiérrez, Juan Segundo, Hugo Assmann, and Lucio Gera, an almost identical list to the primary figures Bonino interacts with in *Doing Theology in a Revolutionary Situation*. Leonardo Boff and Clodovis Boff, *Introducing Liberation Theology*, trans. Paul Burns (Maryknoll: Orbis Books, 1987), 70.

20 Rebecca S. Chopp, *The Praxis of Suffering: An Interpretation of Liberation and Political Theologies* (Eugene: Wipf and Stock, 2007), 167, n. 43.

21 In 1986, Bonino wrote an introduction to the Spanish translation of Karl Barth's *Evangelical Theology*, revealing his indebtedness to Barth, whose theology provided fertile ground for his own development of liberation theology.

Select Bibliography

Primary Sources

Bonino, José Míguez, *Doing Theology in a Revolutionary Situation*. Philadelphia: Fortress Press, 1975.

Bonino, José Míguez, *La Fe en Busca de Eficacia: Una Interpretación de la Reflexion Teológica Latinoamericana de Liberación*. Salamanca, España: Ediciones Sígueme, 1977.

Other Notable Works by the Author

Bonino, José Míguez, *Christians and Marxists: The Mutual Challenge to Revolution*. Grand Rapids: Eerdmans, 1976.

Bonino, José Míguez, *Faces of Latin American Protestantism*. Translated by Eugene L. Stockwell. Grand Rapids: Eerdmans, 1997.

Bonino, José Míguez, *Toward a Christian Political Ethics*. Minneapolis: Fortress Press, 1983.

Secondary Sources

Boff, Leonardo, and Clodovis Boff, *Introducing Liberation Theology*. Translated by Paul Burns. Maryknoll: Orbis Books, 1987.

Bonino, José Míguez, *Faces of Latin American Protestantism*. Translated by Eugene L. Stockwell. Grand Rapids: Eerdmans, 1997.

Chopp, Rebecca S., "José Míguez Bonino: The Conversion to the World." In *The Praxis of Suffering: An Interpretation of Liberation and Political Theologies*, 82–99. Eugene: Wipf and Stock, 2007.

Moltmann, Jürgen, "An Open Letter to José Míguez Bonino." *Christianity and Crisis* 36, no. 5 (March 29, 1976): 57–63.

12

George Lindbeck, *The Nature of Doctrine: Religion and Theology in a Postliberal Age* (1984)

The Making of a Postliberal Theologian

George Lindbeck (1923–2018) never expected *The Nature of Doctrine* to make such a splash. Originally intended as the prolegomenon to a comparative Christian dogmatics, this slim volume demonstrated a new way of doing theology that was neither traditional nor liberal. Building on the work of Hans Frei, Lindbeck proposed a "postliberal" paradigm for understanding religion and Christian doctrine. Although Lindbeck later insisted that postliberalism is primarily a research program rather than a school of theology, his groundbreaking work revealed new possibilities for theologians sharing his dissatisfaction with bifurcated theological methods and a desire for ecumenical collaboration.[1]

As a child, Lindbeck was steeped in both Lutheranism and Chinese culture. Born to Swedish-American missionaries in Loyang, China, illness kept young George from going off to boarding school in Korea until just before his teenage years, which provided more opportunity for him to experience life in Loyang. Immersion within a foreign culture and the confessional fortitude of his parents were two early influences on Lindbeck's personal and theological formation.

Lindbeck's educational journal began at Gustavus Adolphus College in Minnesota, where he graduated with a BA in 1943. Subsequently, he continued his studies for 3 years at Yale (BD, 1946), 1 year at the Pontifical Institute of Medieval Studies in Toronto with Étienne Gilson, and 2 years at the École Pratique des Hautes Études in Paris with Paul Vignaux. During these years, Lindbeck found "unappealing" the work of Descartes, Hegel, Nietzsche, Heidegger, Sartre, and Bultmann, but was increasingly drawn

1 Timothy R. Phillips and Dennis L. Okholm, eds., *The Nature of Confession: Evangelicals and Postliberal in Conversation* (Downers Grove: InterVarsity Press, 1996), 247.

to medieval theologians such as Thomas Aquinas, the Reformers and their neoorthodox progeny, the twentieth-century Jesuit theologians Karl Rahner and Hans Urs von Balthasar, and both Brevard Childs and Hans Frei at Yale with their narrative-canonical approach.[2] In terms of nontheological disciplines, Lindbeck was strongly influenced by the philosophy of Thomas Kuhn and Ludwig Wittgenstein, the sociology of Peter Berger, and the anthropology of Clifford Geertz.[3]

After his stint in France, Lindbeck landed back at Yale, completing a PhD (1955) on late medieval theologian Duns Scotus while teaching courses on medieval philosophy and seminars on Augustine and Calvin. This work launched him into his official teaching career, and although his initial teaching load revolved mostly around philosophy, he enjoyed interaction with theologians Hans Frei, Paul Holmer, and David Kelsey. From 1962 to 1965, Lindbeck received the honor of representing the Lutheran World Federation at the Second Vatican Council, and he later served for two decades on the Joint Commission between the Vatican and the Lutheran World Federation (1968–87).

These experiences nourished the ecumenical roots of *The Nature of Doctrine* (1984), in which Lindbeck delineated a form of Protestant theology that avoided the conservative-liberal conundrum of modern Protestantism. Lindbeck hoped this approach would be better poised to create constructive dialogue with other Christian traditions and non-Christian religions. Later, Lindbeck reflected that the starting point of *The Nature of Doctrine* is "neither biblicist nor experientialist, and certainly not individualistic, but dogmatic: it commences with the historic Christian communal confession of faith in Christ."[4] That said, he also described the book later as "an utter mess" because of how it claims the priority of Christian confession while borrowing copiously from modern terms and concepts.[5]

Whether it's methodologically "messy" or "neat" is a matter of ongoing debate, but *The Nature of Doctrine* no doubt struck a chord with those seeking an ecumenical alternative to conservative and liberal forms of Protestantism,

2 George Lindbeck, *The Church in a Postliberal Age*, ed. James Buckley (Grand Rapids: Eerdmans, 2003), 3.

3 One could argue that Wittgenstein has the strongest influence of all, even when compared to the theologians. James K. A. Smith observes: "Trying to read Lindbeck without understanding Wittgenstein is like trying to read Derrida without understanding Husserl, or trying to read John Calvin without knowing anything of St Augustine." James K. A. Smith, *Who's Afraid of Relativism: Community, Contingency, and Creaturehood* (Grand Rapids: Baker Academic, 2014), 152.

4 Lindbeck, *Church in a Postliberal Age*, 5.

5 John Wright, ed., *Postliberal Theology and the Church Catholic: Conversations with George Lindbeck, David Burrell, and Stanley Hauerwas* (Grand Rapids: Baker Academic, 2012), 71.

one that respects tradition while fully engaging with contemporary thought. Despite the widespread popularity of this book, Lindbeck has not published another monograph, although he has been prolific in writing reviews, essays for edited volumes, and numerous articles, several of which James Buckley edited together as *The Church in a Postliberal Age* (2003). Although many wish Lindbeck had completed the comparative dogmatics to which *The Nature of Doctrine* was intended to serve as an introduction, it remains a paradigmatic work in twentieth-century theology. In the introduction to the twenty-fifth anniversary edition, Bruce Marshall observes: "In the fragmented, even chaotic, world of contemporary Anglo-phone theology, *The Nature of Doctrine* is one of the few books that practically everybody thinks they need to know something about."[6]

Religious Theories and the Promise of Postliberalism

At the outset, Lindbeck identifies three theories for making sense of religion and doctrine. First, cognitive-propositionalism emphasizes the way doctrines make truth claims and how religion is organized according to propositional statements about objective realities. This is the common approach of traditional orthodoxy, and can be classified as a preliberal religious theory, which still holds sway among theologians of a conservative stripe. Second, experiential-expressivism emphasizes the "inner feelings, attitudes, or existential orientations" represented by religious doctrines and symbols (2). Lindbeck traces this approach back to the seminal work of Friedrich Schleiermacher, the father of theological liberalism. A third theory combines the two approaches, as attempted by Roman Catholic theologians Karl Rahner and Bernard Lonergan. Although Lindbeck communicates respect for these theologians, he still considers this a struggling two-dimensional approach in search of a truly three-dimensional alternative.

Of the three theories, Lindbeck recognizes that experiential-expressivism represents a uniquely modern "turn to the subject," engendering habits of thought that "are ingrained in the soul of the modern West, perhaps particularly in the souls of theologians" (7). Given the modern proclivity toward individualism and self-expression, the cognitive-propositional approach was bound to lose ground as the plausibility of objectivity eroded. Despite the prominence of the experiential outlook, Lindbeck laments the way

6 Bruce Marshall, "Introduction," in George Lindbeck, *The Nature of Doctrine: Religion and Theology in a Postliberal Age* (Louisville: Westminster John Knox Press, 2009), vii. All subsequent references will be to this edition, using in-text parenthetical citations.

in which this paradigm begins to blend religions together as symbolizations of the same human experiences. Given his interest in genuine ecumenical dialogue, Lindbeck is not satisfied with any theory that assumes the basic unity of all religions, since this erodes genuine differences in doctrine and practice.

As an alternative, therefore, Lindbeck proposes a cultural-linguistic theory of religion and doctrine. In this theory, doctrines are neither objective propositions nor descriptions of subjective religious experience, but languages that regulate certain forms of life. Rather than an internal idea or feeling, religion is an external phenomenon that shapes internal thoughts and feelings. Just as language enables us to structure our existence, so religion is a comprehensive scheme that brings order and meaning to what we experience. According to Lindbeck, one of the greatest benefits of the cultural-linguistic theory is its symbiosis with nontheological approaches to religion. Since anthropologists, sociologists, historians, and philosophers have, by and large, jettisoned an experiential-expressive theory of religion, the cultural-linguistic theory makes dialogue possible between theology and nontheological disciplines (11).

From a cultural-linguistic perspective, religion is not primarily beliefs or experiences, but the living framework that makes meaningful beliefs and experiences possible. In this way, the cultural-linguistic theory of religion reverses the experiential-expressive theory by showing how an external story or scheme shapes internal experience, not the other way around. As such, it shares some characteristics with the external grounding of the cognitive-propositional theory while avoiding intellectualism. Lindbeck writes: "A comprehensive scheme or story used to structure all dimensions of existence is not primarily a set of propositions to be believed, but is rather the medium in which one moves, a set of skills that one employs in living one's life" (21).

In other words, Lindbeck sees religion as embodied participation in a dramatic narrative that in turn shapes beliefs and experiences. When the situation and context changes, a living religion finds new concepts and symbols to deal with any gaps or anomalies in everyday experience. As an example, Lindbeck claims that Martin Luther's "tower experience" did not lead him to embrace the doctrine of justification by faith alone. Rather, Luther discovered the doctrine of justification in the biblical narrative, and this set the stage for his tower experience. In sum, "First come the objectivities of the religion, its language, doctrines, liturgies, and modes of action, and it is through these that passions are shaped into various kinds of what is called religious experience" (25). If religion produces experiences, not vice versa, then the field is wide open to compare religions as genuinely different cultural-linguistic schemes. In contrast to liberalism, therefore, the goal of studying religions is not to boil them down to common human experiences. Instead, the goal is to encounter diverse forms of life that generate different and sometimes conflicting experiences. This leads to both the challenge and the promise of ecumenical dialogue from a postliberal perspective.

Religious Claims and the Promise of Ecumenism

Lindbeck identifies three primary "interreligious problems—unsurpassability, dialogue, and the salvation of other-believers" (33). When it comes to comparing religions and searching for an unsurpassable one, the cognitive-propositional approach examines the truth or falsity of doctrines as propositional statements. The religion with the greatest number of propositions that correspond to the truth is the one true religion. Within experiential-expressivism, religions are more or less "true" by virtue of how effectively they symbolize human feelings. Since proponents of this approach trace these symbols back to common human experiences, however, Lindbeck evaluates this form of comparing religious claims as relatively weak.

From a cultural-linguistic perspective, religions should be compared on the basis of categorical adequacy rather than propositional truth or symbolic efficacy. In other words, religions should be compared based on the extent to which their structural categories adequately point to ultimate reality and shape life accordingly. Lindbeck writes: "The categorically and unsurpassably true religion is capable of being rightly utilized, guiding thought, passions, and action in a way that corresponds to ultimate reality" (38). Stated otherwise, an unsurpassable religion is the language that best aligns thought and life with ultimate reality. Or to use an additional metaphor Lindbeck introduces at this point, the preeminent religion is the map that best charts reality and leads the map user to the desired destination.

While comparison of religions is a critical part of ecumenical dialogue, Lindbeck underscores another important goal. The purpose of this dialogue is not just conversion to the unsurpassable religion but moving adherents of each religion to be better speakers of their own language and better performers of their own drama. If this is the focus of interreligious exchange, then it is possible for each participant to benefit: Christians can become better Christians, Jews can become better Jews, Buddhists can become better Buddhists, and so on (40). This result is most likely when attention shifts from either propositional truths or a common experiential core to the different forms of life and the languages that describe them. Again, in reaction to the pervading liberal environment of much ecumenical dialogue in the 1980s, Lindbeck insists that the cultural-linguistic approach is stronger than the experiential-expressive one. Dialogue partners who embrace the former method "can regard themselves as simply different and can proceed to explore their agreements and disagreements without necessarily engaging in the invidious comparisons that the assumption of a common experiential core make so tempting" (41). In short, if religious differences don't extend down to the core, then interreligious dialogue remains shallower than it should be.

When it comes to the possibility of salvation outside the Christian religion, Lindbeck treads lightly yet persistently. He expresses dissatisfaction with the "anonymous Christian" proposal of Rahner and Lonergan, but he does so for a different reason than traditional propositionalists. According to Rahner and Lonergan, people can have an inarticulate experience of the divine as a nascent form of Christ's saving grace. For the propositionalist, this is inadequate because faith requires assent to certain essential, propositional truths. For Lindbeck, the anonymous Christian proposal is inadequate because it assumes a common experiential core and minimizes the necessity of encountering an external word (*fides ex audito*). You need to know enough of the Christian language before you can decide whether to embrace it or reject it. This can get blurry, however, because whether a person stutters the Christian language or speaks it fluently, they're still speaking the same language. In fact, Lindbeck insists that when it comes to speaking about God, "all human beings are toddlers" and we never achieve mastery of the language (46–7). The cultural-linguistic perspective on this issue preserves the significance of evangelism, albeit with an emphasis on sharing the Christian story and its distinct language. Lindbeck explains: "The communication of the gospel is not a form of psychotherapy, but rather the offer and the act of sharing one's beloved language—the language that speaks of Jesus Christ—with all those who are interested, in the full awareness that God does not call all to be part of the witnessing people" (47).

Religious Doctrines and the Promise of Pragmatism

After all this talk about religion, what about doctrine itself? Although some traditionalists argue that doctrine plays a diminished role within a cultural-linguistic framework, Lindbeck contends that this theory displays doctrine's usefulness within a culture largely antipathetic to norms of any kind, let alone theological ones (63). Lindbeck is especially concerned to explore how doctrines can stand the test of time while also changing with the times when necessary. He proposes that a cultural-linguistic framework has an easier time accounting for this flexibility because doctrines do not function as first-order propositions, but as second-order rules. In other words, doctrines do not refer directly and unequivocally to the nature of God and reality; instead, they are rules for correctly reading the story of God revealed in the Bible. That story—which culminates in the person and work of Jesus—does not change, but many of the doctrines that help us talk about the story do. Determining which doctrines change and which ones do not is the tricky part, so Lindbeck delineates three different types of doctrine and devotes an entire chapter to test these types with practical examples.

First, doctrines can be "unconditionally necessary" (71). This type of doctrine—like the law of loving God and neighbor—applies in every culture and situation. In other words, there are no conditions that would instigate doctrinal change. Second, some doctrines are "conditionally essential." These doctrines—like pacifism—arose because of particular historical or individual circumstances, and they may or may not be reversible. For example, a conditional doctrine like slavery is reversible because historical developments paved the way. Third, doctrines may be merely accidental but nevertheless permanent because of how habitual or normative they have become. The date of Christmas, for example, is accidental, but it would be virtually impossible to change it.

Which doctrinal type fits the trinitarian doctrines that form the backbone of the ecumenical creeds of Nicaea and Chalcedon? In making his case, Lindbeck distinguishes between the content and form of trinitarian doctrine. While the form or precise terminology of the creeds is conditional, Lindbeck argues for the unconditional necessity of the content because it expresses essential rules for reading the biblical story accurately. Lindbeck identifies at least three "regulative principles" at work in the creeds: monotheism, the historical specificity of Jesus, and Christological maximalism or Christ as the key to understanding God (80). If these rules were abandoned, it would erode the Christian faith. By contrast, Lindbeck comes to a different conclusion regarding Marian dogma such as Mary's sinlessness. Lindbeck classifies this doctrine as "conditionally essential," albeit reversibly so, given its formulation in a cultural milieu with very different perspectives on sin (83). As a more complex example, Lindbeck tackles the doctrine of infallibility, which is the rule that distinguishes who or what has authority over doctrinal formulation and change. While Lindbeck prefers to locate the power of infallibility in the whole church that speaks the Christian language, he realizes that this has more affinity with Orthodoxy and is currently irreconcilable with the biblical infallibility of Protestants and the magisterial infallibility of Roman Catholics (84–90).

Yet if one buys into the cultural-linguistic theory of religion, Lindbeck proposes that the pressure is off to figure out which tradition is ontologically correct when it comes to doctrines like infallibility. The issue is not whether the doctrine corresponds to ontological truth but whether it coheres with the biblical narrative and generates faithful forms of life and worship. As Lindbeck clearly states: "Which theory is theologically best depends on how well it organizes the data of Scripture and tradition with a view to their use in Christian worship and life" (92). In other words, doctrines should be judged based on how well they describe the biblical drama and enable the church to perform their role within it. In fact, it is through performing the biblical drama in worship and everyday life that the church learns the biblical story.[7] All of this has an "intratextual" logic: the biblical world is the lens through which the church understands and lives in the world, yet the church's doctrines and practices are true to the extent that they accurately represent the biblical story.

What Lindbeck calls "intratextuality" others have deemed circular, irrational, relativistic, or fideistic. Lindbeck anticipated these objections and claims that all of them cling too tenaciously to some form of foundationalism. For Lindbeck, there is no foundation independent of the biblical narrative and its presentation of God's revelation in Jesus Christ.[8] To try to find some independent foundation in reason or universal human experience would be to diminish the biblical narrative itself as the source of truth. Therefore, Lindbeck argues for a different kind of reasonableness and intellectual standard that requires a kind of aesthetic skill to discern. "In short, intelligibility comes from skill, not theory, and credibility comes from good performance, not adherence to independently formulated criteria" (117). Showing someone the reasonableness of Christianity, therefore, is more a matter of performing the story beautifully than trying to win an argument. Or to return to Lindbeck's overarching linguistic metaphor, the best way to engage in Christian mission is to speak the Christian language beautifully and learn how to live in ways congruent with the poetry. If the church is faithful in this mission, the hope is that others will want to speak the language. As they do, they too will experience "the ancient practice of absorbing the universe into the biblical world" (121).

[7] This has led C. C. Pecknold to observe the following: "If it can be agreed that 'scripture' might be the first word to come from the lips of a postliberal theologian, a second word might be 'practices,' or arguably better still, 'pragmatism,' the study of practical consequences." C. C. Pecknold, *Transforming Postliberal Theology: George Lindbeck, Pragmatism, and Scripture* (London: Bloomsbury T&T Clark, 1995), 11.

[8] It's at this point that Lindbeck acknowledges his debt to Karl Barth.

Postliberal Theology After Lindbeck

As one might anticipate, Lindbeck's postliberal proposal stirred up mixed reactions among both theological traditionalists and liberals. The first substantial response among conservative evangelicals came from Carl Henry, whose concerns with the ahistorical, anti-propositional nature of narrative theology interacted more with Hans Frei, but nevertheless applied equally to Lindbeck's project.[9] Several additional evangelical and postliberal interlocutors were invited to the Wheaton theology conference in 1995, where it became evident that while some evangelicals resisted postliberalism for a variety of reasons,[10] a growing number of evangelicals were interested in utilizing Lindbeck's insights to move in a "postconservative" direction.[11] These latter evangelical theologians share a concern to appropriately adapt their way of doing theology to a postmodern milieu. For example, Stanley Grenz and John Franke interact appreciatively with Lindbeck as they chart a way to move theology beyond foundationalism.[12] Kevin Vanhoozer counters Lindbeck's proposal by suggesting a "canonical-linguistic" approach to Christian theology, preserving Lindbeck's connection between doctrine and church practice while ensuring that Scripture generates and norms both. With a nod to Lindbeck, Vanhoozer describes his canonical-linguistic approach as postpropositional, postconservative, and postfoundational.[13] Finally, Roger Olson, although interacting less with Lindbeck, shows how postconservative evangelical theology emerged and provides an evangelical alternative to postliberalism.[14]

9 Carl Henry, "Narrative Theology: An Evangelical Appraisal," *Trinity Journal* 9 (Spring 1987): 3–19.

10 For example, see Alister McGrath, *The Genesis of Doctrine: A Study in the Foundation of Doctrinal Criticism* (Grand Rapids: Eerdmans, 1996). McGrath's title is an obvious riff on *The Nature of Doctrine*, but he criticizes Lindbeck for being reductionistic and argues that doctrine does more things than Lindbeck allows.

11 The papers from the 1995 Wheaton Theology were published in Phillips and Okholm, *The Nature of Confession*.

12 Stanley J. Grenz and John R. Franke, *Beyond Foundationalism: Shaping Theology in a Postmodern Context* (Louisville: Westminster John Knox Press, 2000).

13 Kevin Vanhoozer, *The Drama of Doctrine: A Canonical-Linguistic Approach to Christian Theology* (Louisville: Westminster John Knox Press, 2005), 265–305. Vanhoozer also shows how Lindbeck's critique of cognitive-propositionalism and experiential-expressivism fits with Hans Urs von Balthasar's critique of "epic" and "lyric" approaches to theology. Then, taking his cue from Balthasar, Vanhoozer shows how a "dramatic" theory of doctrine can take the performative goal of doctrine identified by Lindbeck and integrate it with "catholic-evangelical orthodoxy."

14 Roger Olson, *Reformed and Always Reforming: The Postconservative Approach to Evangelical Theology* (Grand Rapids: Baker Academic, 2007). Olson also shows how some evangelical theologians were setting the course for postconservatism even before

From a liberal perspective, Lindbeck's postliberal proposal was merely a repackaging of traditional confessionalism. For example, in reflecting on *The Nature of Doctrine*, David Tracy remarks that "the hands may be Wittgenstein and Geertz, but the voice is the voice of Karl Barth."[15] Gordon Kaufman agrees, lamenting that Lindbeck's proposal merely revamps conservative theology and keeps it cloistered within Christian communities.[16] Several other prominent theologians demurred, maintaining that postliberalism is a viable alternative for transcending the traditional-liberal divide. Although this postliberal tribe is often called the "Yale school," a label used to distinguish them from "Chicago school" liberals, George Hunsinger calls this a misnomer.[17] Nevertheless, many who taught and studied at Yale with Frei and Lindbeck identify with the postliberal project. For instance, William Placher followed Lindbeck's lead by modeling an "unapologetic" mode of doing Christian theology, which is "less like a philosophically inclined apologist and more like a sensitive anthropologist."[18] Stanley Hauerwas, although indifferent to the "postliberal" label, shares Lindbeck's conviction that theology and ethics are ecclesial disciplines, since the role of the church is to speak and perform the biblical story.[19] Kathryn Tanner shares the "cultural turn" of postliberal theology, but she takes umbrage with Lindbeck's desire to find certain rules that show the unsurpassability of the Christian religion.[20] Dozens of additional theologians could be mentioned, and although they have varied appreciation of Lindbeck's version of postliberalism, they share his desire "to

Lindbeck, most notably in Bernard Ramm, *After Fundamentalism: The Future of Evangelical Theology* (San Francisco: Harper & Row, 1983).

15 David Tracy, "Lindbeck's New Program for Theology: A Reflection," *The Thomist* 49 (1985): 465.

16 Gordon Kaufman, "Review of 'The Nature of Doctrine: Religion and Theology in a Postliberal Age,' by George Lindbeck," *Theology Today* 42 (1985): 240–1.

17 George Hunsinger, "Postliberal Theology," in *The Cambridge Companion to Postmodern Theology*, ed. Kevin Vanhoozer (Cambridge: Cambridge University Press, 2003), 42–57. Hunsinger also argues that Lindbeck is more revisionist than many postliberals are comfortable with, particularly those who claim close affinity with Barth. He proposes how postliberalism can build on Barth's theology more carefully than Lindbeck does in "Beyond Literalism and Expressivism: Karl Barth's Hermeneutical Realism," in *Disruptive Grace: Studies in the Theology of Karl Barth* (Grand Rapids: Eerdmans, 2000), 210–25.

18 William C. Placher, *Unapologetic Christianity: A Christian Voice in a Pluralistic Conversation* (Louisville: Westminster John Knox Press, 1989), 36. For a more recent work, see William C. Placher, *The Triune God: An Essay in Postliberal Theology* (Louisville: Westminster John Knox Press, 2007).

19 Stanley Hauerwas, *Performing the Faith: Bonhoeffer and the Practice of Nonviolence* (Grand Rapids: Baker Academic, 2004); Stanley Hauerwas, *Working with Words: On Learning to Speak Christian* (Eugene: Cascade Books, 2011).

20 Kathryn Tanner, *Theories of Culture: A New Agenda for Theology* (Minneapolis: Fortress Press, 1997).

recover the significance for Christian theology of Christian specificity."[21] As Jeffrey Stout mused, it may be "too soon to tell" if postliberal theology is a "*cul de sac* or the harbinger of a new theological age," but there is no doubt that Lindbeck was instrumental in stimulating a way of doing theology that moved Protestant theology beyond the tired binaries of modernity.[22]

Select Bibliography

Primary Sources

Lindbeck, George, *The Nature of Doctrine: Religion and Theology in a Postliberal Age*. Louisville: Westminster John Knox Press, 1984.

Lindbeck, George, *The Nature of Doctrine: Religion and Theology in a Postliberal Age*. 25th anniversary ed. Louisville: Westminster John Knox Press, 2009.

Other Notable Works by the Author

Lindbeck, George, *The Church in a Postliberal Age*. Edited by James Buckley. Grand Rapids: Eerdmans, 2003.

Lindbeck, George, *The Future of Roman Catholic Theology*. Philadelphia: Fortress Press, 1970.

Lindbeck, George, *Infallibility*. Milwaukee: Marquette University Press, 1972.

Secondary Sources

Michener, Ronald T., *Postliberal Theology: A Guide for the Perplexed*. London and New York: Bloomsbury T&T Clark, 2013.

Pecknold, C. C., *Transforming Postliberal Theology: George Lindbeck, Pragmatism, and Scripture*. London: Bloomsbury T&T Clark, 1995.

Webster, John, and George P. Schner, *Theology After Liberalism: A Reader*. Oxford: Blackwell, 2000.

Wright, John, ed., *Postliberal Theology and the Church Catholic: Conversations with George Lindbeck, David Burrell, and Stanley Hauerwas*. Grand Rapids: Baker Academic, 2012.

21 John Webster, "Theology After Liberalism?" in *Theology After Liberalism: A Reader*, eds. John Webster and George P. Schner (Oxford: Blackwell, 2000), 57.

22 Jeffrey Stout, *Ethics After Babel: The Languages of Morals and Their Discontents* (Princeton: Princeton University Press, 2001), 301.

13

Sallie McFague, *Models of God: Theology for an Ecological, Nuclear Age* (1987)

Falling in Love with the World

For Sallie McFague (1933–2019), Christian theology and discipleship are concerned with loving God by loving the world. It took several "conversions" and decades of teaching and writing, however, for McFague to settle into her cosmological, ecological approach to theology and Christian living.[1] Nevertheless, this journey established McFague as a leading voice not only in ecological theology but also in metaphorical and feminist theology. Those who encounter her teaching and writing come away with new perspectives on why and how theology matters, not just within our human lives but also to the entire created world.

McFague describes her first conversion as becoming aware of her own existence and the reality of God. She was 7 years old at the time, attending school in her hometown of Quincy, Massachusetts, and from that point on, her experience of God continued to grow and expand. From 1951 to 1955, she studied literature at Smith College, during which she experienced her second conversion. She was reading Karl Barth's *Commentary on Romans* and was suddenly struck by the transcendence or radical otherness of God.[2] She had an overwhelming sense of the "Godness" of God, which she later identified with the "radical monotheism" promoted by H. Richard Niebuhr and the "Protestant principle" espoused by Paul Tillich. McFague does not interpret this experience entirely in positive terms, however, since it kept her from appreciating the immanence and presence of God in the world.

1 All references to McFague's "conversions" are drawn from her autobiographical sketch in *Life Abundant: Rethinking Theology and Economy for a Planet in Peril* (Minneapolis: Augsburg Fortress Press, 2001), 3–14.

2 The second edition of the commentary was translated into English in 1933, the year Sallie McFague was born. Karl Barth, *Epistle to the Romans*, trans. Edwyn C. Hoskyns (London: Oxford University Press, 1933).

After graduating from Smith College, McFague earned several graduate degrees from Yale Divinity School and University, completing her PhD in 1964 on the topic of Christianity and literature.[3] This launched McFague into her long and illustrious teaching career, the bulk of which she spent as a professor of theology at Vanderbilt Divinity School in Nashville (1970–2000). While at Vanderbilt, McFague went through her third conversion, this one inspired by Gordon Kaufman's *Theology for a Nuclear Age*.[4] Impressed by the relevance of Kaufman's approach, McFague decided from that point on to do theology through an ecological lens, shifting from an anthropological to a cosmological paradigm. This was a theological and vocational shift for McFague, requiring just as much ecological literacy as theological acumen.

Shortly after this third conversion, McFague wrote *Models of God: Theology for an Ecological, Nuclear Age*, which won the American Academy of Religion Award for Excellence in 1988. This book combines her earlier work in literature and metaphor with her new concern for ecological attentiveness.[5] Following this work, all of McFague's publications have been permeated by an ecological focus, whether reimagining the contours of traditional theology, as in *The Body of God: An Ecological Theology* (1993), or focusing more specifically on ecological themes, as she did in *Super, Natural Christians: How We Should Love Nature* (1997).

Toward the end of her time at Vanderbilt, McFague experienced her fourth conversion, which she describes in a personal and contemporaneous way: "After years of teaching *about* God . . . I am becoming acquainted *with* God."[6] She describes entering into new rhythms of spiritual direction, meditation, and nature appreciation, all of which began to open up an alternative view on the "abundant life." In 2000, McFague wrote *Life Abundant* and left Vanderbilt to become Distinguished Theologian in Residence at Vancouver School of Theology, where she still resides. Her later work addressed the issue of climate change while reflecting on the dynamic interplay between contemplation and action, divine transcendence and immanence, and love for God and love for the world.[7] McFague's theological and personal journey began with an encounter

3 This was McFague's first published monograph, appearing as *Literature and the Christian Life* (New Haven: Yale University Press, 1966).

4 Gordon Kaufman, *Theology for a Nuclear Age* (Louisville: Westminster John Knox Press, 1985).

5 Her earlier works include *Speaking in Parables: A Study in Metaphor and Theology* (Minneapolis: Fortress Press, 1975) and *Metaphorical Theology: Models of God in Religion and Language* (Minneapolis: Fortress Press, 1982).

6 McFague, *Life Abundant*, 8.

7 Sallie McFague, *A New Climate for Theology: God, the World, and Global Warming* (Minneapolis: Fortress Press, 2008); Sallie McFague, *Blessed Are the Consumers: Climate Change and the Practice of Restraint* (Minneapolis: Fortress Press, 2013).

with God and intensified by falling in love with the world, but the biggest stage in that journey was her realization that these are one and the same.

The Need for New Theological Models

The underlying premise in *Models of God* is that traditional theological models—Father, King, Lord, and so on—are no longer relevant and adequate for life in a late-twentieth-century context. McFague argues that these models actually work against the cultivation and preservation of life in an "ecological, nuclear age." They are patriarchal, hierarchical, and triumphalist models that perpetuate habits of domination and submission rather than encouraging habits of nurture and interdependence. As such, the most important thing for McFague is to find theological models that carry the most contextual relevance, leaving behind a concern for whether or not these models are true in some absolute sense.

To find the most adequate models, therefore, one must accurately understand the cultural context. For McFague, the "new sensibility" that requires new models of God involves the holistic interdependence of all things. We no longer live in an age of the isolated individual or dualistic universe. We live in an "ecological age," which, among other things, means that every singular thing plays a critical role in the interdependent web of life. That web of life is beautiful but fragile, easily disturbed and destroyed by power that ignores or denies this interdependence. The greatest threat to this ecological balance, according to McFague, is nuclear extinction. McFague wrote *Models of God* during the height of the Cold War, when the threat of nuclear attack was causing widespread anxiety. In the midst of that cultural climate, McFague was asking: What kind of theological models represent the opposite of nuclear domination and destruction?

McFague answers that question by pointing to "evolutionary, ecological, mutualistic" models.[8] In other words, the only models adequate for a nuclear age will be cosmological rather than anthropological, organic rather than mechanistic. These models will emphasize the interdependence of all things, including God, rather than perpetuating a sense of hierarchy and dualism. The models of God as King, Ruler, Lord, and Master may have been fitting for a different age and culture, but a new age calls for new models. In fact, McFague suggests, this is the primary task of theology: to deconstruct old

[8] Sallie McFague, *Models of God: Theology for an Ecological, Nuclear Age* (Philadelphia: Fortress Press, 1987), 12. Hereafter, all references to this work shall be noted by employing in-text parenthetical citations.

models and reconstruct new models that are fitting to the perspectives and responsibilities of a particular time and place.

The Nature of Theological Models

According to McFague, all theology is metaphorical theology. In other words, the task of theology involves finding images and metaphors of the God-world relation that fit a particular cultural climate. The criterion for choosing these metaphors is not whether they are true in some ultimate sense, but whether they are imaginatively credible and ethically productive. As a result, metaphorical theology is inherently exploratory, experimental, and provisional. Some metaphors will stick and others will not, which means that searching for adequate metaphors is an ongoing process. If a metaphor proves to have "staying power," it becomes a theological model: "a metaphor that has gained sufficient stability and scope so as to present a pattern for relatively comprehensive and coherent explanation" (34).[9] The goal of metaphorical theology, therefore, is to discover effective theological models. As a whole, McFague defines metaphorical theology as "a kind of heuristic construction that in focusing on the imaginative construal of the God-world relationship, attempts to remythologize Christian faith through metaphors and models appropriate for an ecological, nuclear age" (40).

Within this approach, the process of theological construction involves an ongoing work of interpretation. The theologian needs to interpret both the cultural situation and the Christian tradition in order to generate fodder for imaginative construction. The place of Scripture in this process is not to supply authoritative metaphors and models of God, but rather to provide a paradigm for how metaphorical theology should be done. McFague views Scripture as a "case study, classic, or prototype" of Christian experience and theological expression (43).[10] When theologians experiment with new theological models, McFague argues, they are simply following the trajectory of Scripture itself, which contains a diversity of theological models constructed for a variety of cultural milieus.

The story of Jesus provides the interpretive clues necessary for deconstructing outdated theology and reconstructing relevant metaphorical

[9] McFague unpacks in more detail the relationship between theological metaphors and models in her *Metaphorical Theology*.

[10] McFague acknowledges similarities between her view of Scripture and that of theologian David Tracy. See his *Analogical Imagination: Christian Theology and the Culture of Pluralism* (Spring Valley: Crossroad, 1981).

theology. The way McFague reads the story of Jesus is similar to the interpretive patterns of liberation theology. What the diverse strands of liberation theology have in common, McFague maintains, is the destabilization of conventional divisions and dualisms, the inclusion of outsiders and outcasts, and the deconstruction of traditional hierarchies (47–8). These themes continue to point back to the paradigmatic story of Jesus, since Jesus destabilizes expectations through his parables, includes outsiders in his table fellowship, and makes salvation available to all through his radical identification demonstrated on the cross. In the story of Jesus, therefore, we find "a destabilizing, inclusive, nonhierarchical vision of fulfillment for all of creation" (49).

Inspired by this paradigm, McFague launches into her search for new theological models that will enable us to reimagine God's relationship with the world. In doing so, she again emphasizes the inadequacy of traditional models, paying particular attention to the model of God as king. According to McFague, this model suggests a God who wields distant control of his realm, rules over his human subjects to the exclusion of nonhuman reality, and exercises his rule through militant domination or passive benevolence (66–8). As one replacement for this model, McFague suggests imagining the world as God's body rather than God's realm (69–78). She does not intend for this model to be perfect or permanent, but she does suggest it might have more resonance with the current age than some traditional models. To accentuate this pragmatism and provisionality, she admits to "experimenting with a bit of nonsense to see if it can make a claim to truth" (69). From her perspective, the greatest benefit of imagining the world as God's body is that sin is now inextricably linked to ignoring and breaking ecological harmony. If the earth suffers, God suffers. Protecting and caring for the earth takes on new meaning as a way to love God's body. McFague returns to this model throughout the book, but at this point it functions as a precursor to the primary models McFague explores: God as mother, lover, and friend.

God as Mother, Lover, and Friend

In choosing which models to explore, McFague agrees with Gordon Kaufman that these models should resonate with the new ecological sensibility.[11] She disagrees with Kaufman, however, regarding his willingness to jettison personal models (80). For McFague, it would be a travesty to exclude personal

[11] Kaufman, *Theology for the Nuclear Age*.

models because they are often the most imaginatively potent. Not only do we relate most readily to personal models, but these metaphors also support a view of a God who is "radically relational, immanental, interdependent, and noninterventionist" (83). McFague chooses to imagine God through the lens of three of the most basic personal relationships: mother, lover, and friend. She traces out how each metaphor presents a different portrait of God's love, God's activity, and God's ethic.

As the basis for imagining God as mother, McFague wonders: If God created both men and women in God's own image, then why should we not use both sexes as models to talk about God? God is neither male nor female, so why should we privilege one sex over another in imagining God? In fact, McFague maintains that since God is beyond gender, it is actually idolatrous to restrict theology to male metaphors. In exploring female metaphors, however, McFague is careful to keep outdated notions of femininity from sneaking in and spoiling the creative exercise. When imagining God as mother, she deals with general characteristics of mothering rather than any particular cultural forms or expectations. For instance, she highlights the impartial, giving, nurturing kind of love that mothers express. In classical terms, this is a way of understanding God's *agape* love. God as mother exhibits generative and sacrificial love, connected as intimately to creation as a mother is to her own child. This model accentuates God's creative activity, but from a particular angle. As one who creates by birthing, God is neither totally distinct from nor totally distant from that creation. To return to her earlier metaphor, if creation is God's child, it remains in one sense God's body. This model also impacts how we view God's interaction with the world. How might God's judgment as mother be different from God's judgment as artist-creator? While an artist might be able to maintain critical distance from her work, a mother never has that kind of distance from her child. Indeed, within this model, God's purpose as mother is not to deliver final condemnation or pardon like a judge, but to reorder the cosmic household to ensure that everyone flourishes. In other words, "God as the mother-judge is the one who establishes justice, not the one who hands out sentences" (118). To join in God's mothering work, therefore, is to participate in the cause for justice. We are God's children, but we also share in God's parenthood of the world. McFague calls this "universal parenthood," which involves treating every part of the world, no matter how seemingly insignificant or weak, as a critical member of the cosmic family. Overall, to participate in God's ethic as a mother is to be a preserver: "those who pass life along and who care for all forms of life so they may prosper" (122).

The second personal model McFague explores is God as lover, which highlights God's love as *eros*. As with the model of God as mother, McFague defends this exploration not just because the metaphor of God as lover appears in Scripture, but because this is one of our most fundamental relationships. If God is love, then the world is the beloved, and this creates a unique perspective from which to imagine God's salvific activity. The greatest tragedy for lovers is to be separated, which means that God's greatest desire when it comes to his beloved world is presence and union. The model implies "that the world is valuable, that God needs it, and that salvation is the reunification of the beloved world with its lover, God" (131). In testing the value of this model, McFague emphasizes once again that constructing new models is not a matter of establishing dogmatic truth. Rather, it is an imaginative process of examining how plausible, illuminating, and timely the model can be within an ecological age. One of the strongest elements of the model, in McFague's view, is its emphasis on reciprocity or interdependence. God needs the world just as the world needs God, and both are involved in the reunification process. In fact, sin is the very refusal of relationship in preference for isolation. Sin is a rejection of interdependence and the need for mutual love (139). By implication, salvation is willing participation in a mutual relationship of love and healing. Salvation is not just done for us; we are a part of it. Jesus provides a paradigmatic example of salvation, but he is not the only savior. McFague explains: "if the one thing needed is reunification of the shattered, divided world, there must be many saviors" (150). Within the model of God as lover, the line between salvation and ethics are blurred, because to be involved in the process of healing divisions in the world is to contribute to the process of salvation. Anyone who exhibits radical, inclusive love—especially to people and parts of the world that suffer—is playing the part of lover-liberator.

The last model McFague investigates is God as friend, which focuses on God's *philia* love. In tracing out the possibilities of this model, McFague surfaces three "paradoxes" of friendship that present new ways to imagine God's friendship with the world. First, while friendship is a free relationship between two people, it also involves a voluntary bond of trust and commitment. Likewise, the relationship between God and human beings is free, but it is also a side-by-side commitment with the same goal, namely, "the well being of the world" (163). Second, friendship is a relationship between two particular people, and yet it has an inclusive dynamic, bringing others of similar vision into its fold. In a similar way, God's friendship maintains particularity while remaining open to everyone who shares the desire for reunification and healing (164). Third, while friendship is most natural for children, it requires the adult characteristics of mutuality, reciprocity, and shared responsibility. Consequently, to be God's friend is to be invited into a relationship of childlike trust and mature responsibility (165). God shares with his friends and companions the responsibility to sustain and guide all forms of life. In traditional theology, this sustaining work is linked to God as Spirit, but McFague suggests that the model of God as friend has greater power because it is more personal and less "ethereal, shapeless, [and] vacant" (170). Imagining friendship with God gives us a picture of sitting down to a shared meal as companions (literally: together at bread) while showing hospitality to strangers. The stability of friendship with God gives us a place from which we can be open and receptive to whatever is different, unexpected, and strange. To be God's companions gives us the fortitude to be the world's companions and to fight boldly for justice. McFague concludes: "as friends of the Friend of the world, we do not belong to ourselves nor are we left to ourselves," defying despair while at the same time denying possession (179).

In her conclusion, McFague addresses whether or not these personal models of God—mother, love, and friend—are meant to be a replacement Trinity. While acknowledging some similarities to the tripartite division of God's activity as the creating Father, saving Son, and sustaining Spirit, McFague clearly states that her three models are not meant to establish a "new Trinity." Rather, her purpose is simply to reimagine the relationship between God and the world in a useful, accessible, and illuminating way (182–4). Three models are able to do this better than two, because they avoid any potential dualism and provide ample complementarity. McFague emphasizes that while these may be adequate models of God for an ecological, nuclear age, they are still imaginative fictions that may live for a time only to give way to fresher, more relevant models.

McFague and Postmodern Theology

Models of God is a prime example of constructive postmodern theology. Like other works of postmodern theology, *Models of God* shares a certain "condition" that accentuates the perspectival, provisional, and pragmatic nature of theological knowledge.[12] Given her background in literature and the study of metaphor, McFague's work corresponds with the constructive, imagination-oriented methodology of Gordon Kaufman,[13] which sets

[12] In 1979, Jean François Lyotard was the first to delineate this "postmodern condition" and the shift away from modernity in his book *La Condition postmoderne*. This was first translated into English as Jean François Lyotard, *The Postmodern Condition: A Report on Knowledge*, trans. Geoff Bennington and Brian Massumi (Minneapolis: University of Minnesota, 1984).

[13] Gordon Kaufman, *The Theological Imagination: Constructing the Concept of God* (Louisville: Westminster John Knox Press, 1981). Kaufman is one of McFague's most

them apart from postmodern theology with a more deconstructive bent.[14] While McFague has some interest in dismantling outdated and oppressive theological models, she puts more energy into constructing models that she hopes will resonate with contemporary sensibilities without making claims to absolute truth or transcultural permanence. As such, McFague shares much in common with the cultural-linguistic approach of postliberal theologian George Lindbeck, although Lindbeck ascribes greater authority to the biblical narrative in the process of theological construction.[15]

Given her interest in ecological matters, McFague is widely recognized as one of the mothers of ecotheology and ecofeminism, along with notable Catholic theologians such as Rosemary Radford Ruether.[16] Like other ecofeminists, McFague links patriarchal domination and ecological destruction as different forms of the same drive for oppressive power. In the Preface to *Models of God*, McFague explains how this book is "not a feminist theology in the sense that its guiding principle is the liberation of women," but her perspective as a woman provides "sufficient disorientation from middle-class, mainstream Christianity both to question it and to risk alternative formulations of Christian faith" (xiv). Her subsequent work follows this trajectory, with the ecological focus taking center stage while the feminist agenda mostly remains backstage but informs much of the way she packages and performs her theology.

The themes and concerns Sallie McFague wrestled with in *Models of God* continue to occupy her attention in her present work. In one of her most recent essays, she reflects that in the 70 years since her first conversion to the reality of God and his presence in the world, she has learned many things. But the primary thing she has learned is that loving the world is the same as loving God, because the world is God's body: "The world lives within, for, from, and toward God every minute of every day. Hence, we do not live now

sympathetic critics, but he challenges her, as others do, to explore how her metaphorical theology could be translated into and perhaps even refine conceptual theology. See Kaufman's review of *Models of God* in *Theology Today* 45, no. 1 (April 1988): 95–101.

14 Excellent introductions to the constructive and deconstructive approaches to postmodern theology, in addition to other approaches, can be found in Kevin Vanhoozer, ed., *The Cambridge Companion to Postmodern Theology* (Cambridge: Cambridge University Press, 2003).

15 For two fascinating articles that compare and contrast the theological method of Lindbeck and McFague, see Terrence Reynolds, "Walking Apart, Together: Lindbeck and McFague on Theological Method," *The Journal of Religion* 77, no. 1 (January 1997): 44–67; Terrence Reynolds, "Parting Company at Last: Lindbeck and McFague in Substantive Theological Dialogue," *Concordia Theological Quarterly* 63, no. 2 (April 1999): 97–118.

16 Rosemary Radford Ruether, *Gaia and God: An Ecofeminist Theology of Earth Healing* (New York: HarperCollins, 1992).

on earth away from God, but always, whether in life or death, we all live within God."[17] Sallie McFague is widely recognized for her pioneering work in metaphorical theology and ecotheology, but perhaps her greatest legacy will be the fusion—in both her professional and personal life—of love for God and love for the world.

Select Bibliography

Primary Source

McFague, Sallie, *Models of God: Theology for an Ecological, Nuclear Age.* Philadelphia: Fortress Press, 1987.

Other Notable Works by the Author

McFague, Sallie, *The Body of God: An Ecological Theology*. Minneapolis: Fortress Press, 1993.

McFague, Sallie, *A New Climate for Christology: Kenosis, Climate Change, and Befriending Nature*. Minneapolis: Fortress Press, 2021.

McFague, Sallie, *Super, Natural Christians: How We Should Love Nature.* Minneapolis: Fortress Press, 1997.

Secondary Sources

Armour, Ellen T., "Sallie McFague." In *A New Handbook of Christian Theologians*, edited by Donald W. Musser. Nashville: Abingdon Press, 1996.

Kaufman, Gordon, review of *Models of God* by Sallie McFague, *Theology Today* 45, no. 1 (April 1988): 95–101.

Malone, Nancy H., ed., "A Discussion of Sallie McFague's *Models of God*." *Religion and the Intellectual Life* 5, no. 3 (Spring 1988): 9–44.

McFague, Sallie, "A Brief Credo." In *Life Abundant: Rethinking Theology and Economy for a Planet in Peril*. Minneapolis: Augsburg Fortress Press, 2001.

Reynolds, Terrence, "Two McFagues: Meaning, Truth, and Justification in *Models of God*." *Modern Theology* 11, no. 3 (July 1995): 289–313.

[17] Sallie McFague, "Falling in Love with God and the World: Some Reflections on the Doctrine of God," in *Sallie McFague: Collected Readings*, ed. David Lott (Minneapolis: Fortress Press, 2013), 264.

14

Kwame Bediako, *Theology and Identity: The Impact of Culture Upon Christian Thought in the Second Century and in Modern Africa* (1992)

Becoming an African Theologian

Manasseh Kwame Dakwa Bediako (1945–2008) was the second of nine children within a nominal Presbyterian family in Accra, Ghana. His grandfather was a catechist with the Basel Mission, his father was a police inspector, and the family placed a high value on education. After primary school, Bediako attended the Mfantsipim School in Cape Coast before attending the University of Ghana-Legon (1965–9), where he studied Modern Languages and achieved honors in French. In recognition, the French government awarded him a scholarship for postgraduate study at L'université de Bordeaux III.[1] Bediako was an atheist as he began to study Congolese poet Tchicaya U Tam'si and his expression of négritude,[2] but he experienced a sudden conversion to Christ in 1970, which radically changed his perspective and his academic approach. He began to interpret U Tam'si through a biblical lens and realized how a Christian worldview could lead him to embrace his African identity and heritage rather than relying on European frameworks. In Bediako's words: "In becoming Christian, I was becoming African again."[3]

After his Christian conversation, Bediako began worshiping at an American-led Evangelical Free Church, met and eventually married his English wife Gillian, and enrolled in London Bible College (now London School of

1 Renamed Bordeaux Montaigne University when it became independent in 2014.
2 Négritude describes a cultural, philosophical, and political movement of people seeking to recover their precolonial identity, particularly for French-speaking Africans.
3 Kwame Bediako, "Andrew F. Walls as Mentor," in *Understanding World Christianity: The Vision and Work of Andrew F. Walls*, eds. William R. Burrows, Mark R. Gornik, and Janice A. McLean (Maryknoll: Orbis Books, 2011), 8.

Theology) after finishing his doctorate on U Tam'si in 1973. He was passionate about learning theology and connecting with evangelical Christians worldwide, which led him to attend the Lausanne Congress on World Evangelization in 1974 as a student delegate, where he was involved in launching the International Fellowship for Mission as Transformation (INFEMIT) along with René Padilla, Samuel Escobar, and others. After finishing his bachelor's in theology, Bediako moved back to Ghana and taught for 2 years at Christian Service College (now Christian Service University College) in Kumasi. He was ordained in the Presbyterian Church of Ghana in 1978, which commissioned him to pursue a PhD in theology under the supervision of Andrew Walls at the University of Aberdeen. Over those 5 years in Scotland, he worked on a thesis that he would later revise, deliver as part of the Duff lectures, and publish as his first major book: *Theology and Identity: The Impact of Culture Upon Christian Thought in the Second Century and in Modern Africa.*

Bediako taught for a year at Aberdeen and then returned permanently to Ghana in 1984, serving at Ridge Church in Accra while forming the Akrofi-Christaller Memorial Centre for Mission Research and Applied Theology, which launched in 1987. This educational institution—later renamed the Akrofi-Christaller Institute for Theology, Mission, and Culture (ACI)—was the epicenter of Bediako's life work, and one scholar has appropriately claimed ACI as Bediako's "magnum opus, the bringing together of his methodological, historical, theological, cultural, and pastoral concerns."[4] It was here at ACI that Bediako fleshed out the vision for a distinctly African theology for a post-missionary era, which Bediako explained "is as much a response to missionary underestimation of the value of African pre-Christian religious tradition, as it is an *African* theological response to the specific and more enduring issue of how the Christian Gospel relates to African culture"[5] (xvii).

Corresponding to the founding of ACI, Bediako was invited to be the Alexander Duff visiting lecturer in the Centre for the Study of Christianity in the Non-Western World at the University of Edinburgh. This afforded him the opportunity to reflect theoretically on what was unfolding in Ghana. The Duff lectures formed the bulk of *Theology and Identity* (1992) as well as his next major book, *Christianity in Africa: The Renewal of a Non-Western Religion* (1995).[6] Bediako's third major book, *Jesus in Africa* (2000),

[4] Sara J. Fretheim, *Kwame Bediako and African Christian Scholarship: Emerging Religious Discourse in Twentieth-Century Ghana* (Eugene: Cascade Books, 2018), 151.

[5] Kwame Bediako, *Theology and Identity: The Impact of Culture Upon Christian Thought in the Second Century and in Modern Africa* (Oxford: Regnum Books, 1992), xvii. Hereafter, references to this book will appear in parentheses throughout the text.

[6] Kwame Bediako, *Christianity in Africa: The Renewal of a Non-Western Religion* (Edinburgh: Edinburgh University Press, 1995).

expanded on the themes of his earlier books, offering new perspectives on the history of Christianity in Africa and the relationship between theology and culture.[7] In addition to his teaching and writing, Bediako was passionate about encouraging pastors and advocating for sustainable leadership for the African church, which he did as general secretary of the African Theological Fellowship and the driving force behind the African Theological Institute. In recognition of his academic and institutional achievements, particularly as a champion for African identity, primal religions, and vernacular languages, in 1996 Bediako was elected as a fellow of the Ghana Academy of Arts and Sciences. He continued to work tirelessly for the emergence of a uniquely African and Ghanaian theology until his death in 2008.

What Does Athens Have to Do with Jerusalem? Christianity in Hellenistic Culture

Bediako's central concern in *Theology and Identity* is to determine whether it is theological and historically legitimate to claim continuity between Christianity and pre-Christian religions. The missionary movement in Africa often assumed radical discontinuity between the Christian gospel and primal African religions, and to become a Christian within this worldview required a radical discontinuity of identity. Establishing greater continuity between Christianity and the African religious past, however, would ensure greater unity of self and a posture of abundance toward African cultural traditions. Instead of being a Christian who happens to be African, one could truly be an *African* Christian.

To explore this concern, Bediako turns first to second-century Christianity, which, like modern Africa, was a time of cultural transition characterized by bold theological initiatives, polemicism, and uncertainty. As he investigates this pivotal period in Christian history, Bediako is paying attention to "the Christian's response to the religious past as well as to the cultural tradition generally in which one stands, and the significance of that response for the development of theological answers to the culturally-rooted questions of the context" (7). Christians in the second century lived within a culture of critique, opposition, and ridicule. Within Graeco-Roman or Hellenistic culture, religion and politics were fused together, so to reject Hellenistic religion was to reject political life and authority, and therefore to identify as an outcast. Within the dominant Hellenistic culture, therefore, Christianity

7 Kwame Bediako, *Jesus in Africa* (Akropong-Akuapem, Ghana: Regnum Africa, 2000); republished as *Jesus and the Gospel in Africa: History and Experience* (Maryknoll: Orbis Books, 2004).

was seen as barbaric, superstitious, and separatist, a cult departing from culturally respected religion and tradition.

In response to this critique, second-century Christians faced a choice: they could embrace this barbaric identity and cling counterculturally to the revelation of Christ, or they could try to make a case that Christianity is the fulfillment of all that is true, good, and beautiful in Hellenistic culture. Of the four second-century theologians Bediako explores, Tatian and Tertullian represent the first approach, whereas Justin Martyr and Clement of Alexandria represent the latter approach, albeit with distinct methods and points of emphasis. As such, these second-century examples of how Christianity relates to other religions and cultural traditions provide models for evaluating similar approaches in modern Africa.

Tatian was a Syriac-speaking Christian who insisted on the radical discontinuity between Christianity and all other truths, including Hellenistic tradition. In his *Oration to the Greeks,* Tatian condemned the pagan philosophical tradition and commended radical biblicism as the foundation of the Christian tradition. In doing so, Tatian aligned Christianity with "barbarism," resolutely warning against any attempt to assimilate Christianity to Hellenistic culture. The only option is to convert to Christ and find true knowledge and true humanity in union with the Holy Spirit.

Tertullian, often known as the Latin father of the church, was a northern African theologian who, like Tatian, communicated radical discontinuity between Christianity and Hellenistic religion and culture, which is rooted in idolatry. He rejected the most prominent forms of this culture—theater, public games, and spectacle—as "the Devil's pomp," and encouraged Christians to take an antithetical approach to culture (109). Since all worldly power is alien to the power of God, Christians must remove themselves from it to stay pure and faithful. Bediako identifies Tertullian as a prime example of what Andrew Walls calls "the pilgrim principle,"[8] which "consists in defining Christian authenticity in terms of factors that lie outside of one's natural culture and society" (116). In his *Prescription Against Heretics*, Tertullian asked the question "What does Athens have to do with Jerusalem?" In other words, what does pagan philosophy and culture have to do with Christianity? In a word: nothing. They are diametrically opposed, and Christians must focus on creating their own rule of faith and countercultural way of life.

Justin Martyr, a second-century Greek apologist, took a different approach, desiring to construct a compelling witness to those raised within Hellenistic culture. While not downplaying the necessity of conversion to Christ, Justin

[8] Andrew F. Walls, "The Gospel as the Prisoner and Liberator of Culture," *Faith and Thought* 108, no. 1–2 (1982): 46.

presented Christianity as "the only safe and profitable philosophy," discovered not by developing Greek philosophy but by receiving the prophetic revelation of the Word (141). Although, like Tertullian, Justin discerned the demonic origin of Greco-Roman religion, he acknowledged that some philosophers exhibit partial knowledge of the Word. Whether because of familiarity with biblical literature or the inward illumination of the Word, these Greek philosophers can possess the seeds of truth (151–2). Just as Jewish people can be viewed as believers before Christ, so there are "holy pagans" who witness to the truth of Christ (160). Thus, in Bediako's view, Justin laid the groundwork not for a syncretistic hellenizing of Christian tradition, but the christianizing of Hellenistic tradition (146).

Clement of Alexandria saw even more continuity between Hellenistic tradition and Christianity. In the *Stromatis* and other writings, Clement showed how the Christian gospel related to all the "quests and aspirations—religious, philosophical, intellectual, and ethical—in Hellenistic tradition, as indeed in all human history" (176). His goal was to identify wisdom from all traditions in light of God's revelation, which "absorbs" those traditions rather than opposing them (180). Like Justin, Clement believed that popular religion is misleading and a part of demonic deception, but he places Christianity as the historical fulfillment of the Greek philosophical tradition, much like the Christian gospel is the historical fulfillment of the Jewish Law (201). Christianity is thus a grand synthesis of the Jewish and Hellenistic tradition—Law and Philosophy—which both find their fulfillment in the covenant and wisdom of Christ. Bediako, who based his own approach on Clement, concludes: "He seems to have understood the truth of the Christian gospel not as that of a religious system over against other systems, but rather as the truth of the one beneficent and loving God of all mankind, and capable of apprehension, however minimally, outside of, and prior to, the constituted Christian community" (207).

What Does Accra Have to Do with Jerusalem? Christianity in Modern Africa

Before engaging with several contemporary African approaches to relating Christianity to African culture and religion, Bediako laments the missionary picture of Africa as a place of backwardness and irreligion. This understanding of African culture was an extension of earlier colonial worldviews in which "lower races" needed not only conversion but also elevation into "civilized" culture. In this view, pre-Christian beliefs and religions were valueless at best and harmful at worst, with animism framed as "anti-religious and immoral"

(231). The failure of Christian missionaries to recognize the value of African religious history left the African church without its own distinct theology (237). Most European missionaries failed to recognize how African religions could bear witness to the revelation and activity of God among all people, bearing some similarity to the early Christian Judaizers who did not accept the translatability of the gospel into Gentile cultures (248–9). Consequently, Bediako believes a new generation of African theologians is needed to break away from European hegemony and value-setting and to generate the renewal of Christianity as a non-Western religion.[9]

Nigerian theologian Bolagji Idowu (1913–93) was committed to freeing the African mind from its Western enslavement as promoted by missionary culture. In *Toward an Indigenous Church* (1965), he cast a vision for forming a distinctly Nigerian church under the Lordship of Christ. Bediako contends that the power of Idowu's proposal lies in recognizing how God has already been revealed in the religion of the Yoruba people, which means the revelation of God in the biblical gospel is a crystallization and fulfillment of this previous revelation. In a later work called *African Traditional Religion: A Definition* (1973), Idowu insisted that African theology must begin by understanding its own religious history, which is a form of primitive monotheism (287–8). In doing so, he rejected the common understanding of African religion as polytheistic, arguing that this represents a distortion of true Yoruba religion. For Bediako, Idowu thus proposed a fitting way of synthesizing the wisdom of African religions and Christian revelation.

Kenyan theologian John S. Mbiti (1931–2019) took a similar approach as Idowu, while focusing less on critiquing missionary history and perspective (304). Mbiti distinguished between Christianity, which is culturally embedded, and the gospel, which has transcultural resonance. It is the gospel of Jesus, therefore, rather than Christianity that theologians can indigenize within an African cultural consciousness (308). This process corresponds with the Pentecostal principle that insists on the translatability of the gospel into many languages and cultures. In *African Religions and Philosophy* (1969), Mbiti interpreted African religious traditions as a preparation for the gospel, which represents their fulfillment rather than replacement. In *Concepts of God in Africa* (1970), Mbiti drew on classical theological terms and categories—such as Christology and Soteriology—while interacting with a variety of African source material and cultural values, which Bediako affirms as a fitting method for contextual and ecclesial theology in modern Africa.

9 This links to the subtitle of Bediako's 1995 publication *Christianity in Africa: The Renewal of a Non-Western Religion.*

Congolese and Catholic theologian Mulago gwa Cikala Musharhamina (1924–2012) studied the traditional religion of the Bantu people and concluded "that there exists a deep harmony between the authentic religious aspirations of the Bantu and the Christian message proclaimed by the Catholic Church" (351). In his *Un visage africain du Christianisme* (*An African Face of Christianity*, 1962), Mulago traced corresponding elements between African religious traditions and Christianity, such as the similarity between Mary the mother of Jesus and the queen-mother (*omwamikasi*) within Bantu sacral rule. Bediako stresses how some aspects of Mulago's adaptive method are contrived (366) and others are moot because of the changing political landscape (373), such as creating an analogy between the Pope and the Bantu ruler (Mwami). While the Catholic bishops of Africa eventually repudiated Mulago's method of adaptation in favor of an incarnational method, Bediako still appreciates how Mulago did not assume Western superiority and emphasized African traditional religions as more than a set of beliefs, but a comprehensive identity and life posture.

Nigerian theologian Byang Henry Kato (1936–75), unlike the previous three perspectives, did not have a favorable view of African traditional religions. Similar to Tertullian in the second century, Kato believed that primal religions are man-made and idolatrous whereas only Christianity is truly from God. Any attempt to synthesize these traditions introduces poisonous elements of syncretism and universalism, and the only valid source for theology is the Bible, a method Kato outlines in *Theological Pitfalls in Africa* (1975). Bediako critiques Kato on several levels, whether his weak understanding of general revelation, his limited concern for individual and otherworldly salvation, his ignorance of prophetic teaching and other wide swaths of Scripture, his confusion of unbiblical syncretism with wise synthesis, and ultimately how Kato fails to recognize how African experience can enrich and drive the theological task (407). Bediako references his original encounter and disagreement with Kato at the Lausanne Congress in 1974, and no doubt this encounter influenced the trajectory of Bediako's own attempt to synthesize Christian revelation and African religions in scholarship, teaching, and pastoral leadership.

In the concluding chapter of *Theology and Identity*, Bediako contends that Christian conversion can affirm and stand in cultural continuity with traditional African religions and culture. Standing on the shoulders of second-century theologians like Justin Martyr and Clement of Alexandria and twentieth-century African theologians like Idowu, Mbiti, and Mulago, Bediako places his own contribution within the possibility of synthesis between "Christian religious commitment and cultural continuity" (432). Bolstered by his study of early Christian apologists, Bediako does not claim to be doing anything new. Christian commitment, he argues, has always emerged from the milieu of other religions, and from the moment of Pentecost, Christianity has developed through dynamic practices of translation, indigenization, and engagement with both general and special revelation. Like many of his contemporaries, Bediako communicates a deep love for his culture and the traditions of his people, a love that he believes should not be discarded but rather combined with his love for Christ. This was the motivating force of Bediako's scholarship and his life's work as a teacher and organizational leader: one can be fully Ghanaian and fully Christian.

Diversity in African Christian Theology

Although Andrew Walls may be biased as Kwame Bediako's doctoral supervisor, no doubt he chose his words carefully when he called Bediako "the greatest African theologian of his generation."[10] Many others share this evaluation, praising Bediako for his engagement with vernacular language and concepts, his creative scholarship undertaken in and for the community, and his way of finding a mediating methodology between theologians who dismiss traditional African religion and culture and those who discard historical Christian orthodoxy in exchange for truly African theology. An example of this mediating theological method is Bediako's Christology and his view of Jesus as ancestor, which he developed in later publications such as *Jesus and the Gospel in Africa*. Rather than either completely rejecting the veneration of ancestors or uncritically embracing this practice, Bediako believes Christianity can be at home in African culture by understanding Jesus as the true and mediatory ancestor.[11] In doing so, memory of and reverence for ancestors can be incorporated and fulfilled within ultimate allegiance to Jesus.[12]

Given his mediatory method, it should come as no surprise that Bediako has received critiques from various angles. Evangelical African scholars have critiqued his lack of biblical engagement and his willingness to affirm the

[10] Andrew F. Walls, "Kwame Bediako and Christian Scholarship in Africa," *IBMR* 32, no. 4 (October 2008): 188–93.

[11] Some differing approaches include Nana Oseadeeyo Addo III Dankwa, *Christianity and African Traditional Beliefs* (New York: Power of the Word, 1990); Charles Sarpong Aye-Addo, *Akan Christology: An Analysis of the Christologies of John Samuel Pobee and Kwame Bediako in Conversation with Karl Barth* (Eugene: Pickwick, 2013).

[12] Bediako, *Jesus and the Gospel in Africa*, 20–33.

primal African imagination.[13] Others press him for being overly influenced by Western education and globalized ideologies and not adequately attentive to his local Ghanaian context.[14] Others wonder if he is overly optimistic about the role of Christianity in addressing African social and political issues.[15] But Bediako's theological boldness, wide-ranging scholarship, and institutional investment remain widely respected even by those who might disagree with his theological positions. He preferred not to be identified as a postcolonial theologian, a concept limited by the Western category of colonization, although he stands as an inspiration for African and other Majority World theologians seeking to navigate contextual theology after colonization with faithfulness to the gospel of Jesus. Tim Hartman concludes that Bediako models a way of doing contemporary theology that is "Christological, contextual, cultural, constructive, and collaborative."[16]

An often undervalued aspect of Bediako's legacy is his interdisciplinary engagement and the pivotal role of imagination and the arts in the task of theology. Beginning with his postgraduate study of négritude in the work of Congolese poet Tchicaya U Tam'si and continuing with his admiration for poet and oral theologian Afua Kuma as well as composer Ephraim Amu, Bediako was known for incorporating poems and songs into his lectures and curriculum at the Akrofi-Christaller Institute.[17] In addition, students, friends, and readers of Bediako alike have benefited from his way of seamlessly integrating insights from psychology, sociology, history, theology, politics, literary criticism, and more, taking every thought captive in his attempt to integrate a Christian imaginary with the African primal imagination. Sara Fretheim adeptly summarizes his attempt "to address the probing questions of African poets, intellectuals, and theologians in his efforts to demonstrate the historical and theological roots for an African Christian identity."[18] Despite the dominance of Western theological method during the birth of modern Protestant theology, one may convincingly argue, especially given

[13] Keith Ferdinando, "Christian Identity in the African Context: Reflections on Kwame Bediako's *Theology and* Identity," *Journal of the Evangelical Theological Society* 50, no. 1 (March 2007): 121–43; Kevin Howard, "Kwame Bediako: Considerations on the Motivating Force of His *Theology and Identity*," *Global Missiology* 3, no. 1 (April 2013): 88–90.

[14] James L. Cox, "The Globalization of Localized African Religions: The Case of Kwame Bediako," in *World Christianity in Local Context*, ed. Stephen R. Goodwin (London: Continuum International), 56–65.

[15] Emmanuel M. Katongole, *A Future for Africa: Critical Essay in Christian Social Imagination* (Eugene: Wipf and Stock, 2017), 156.

[16] Tim Hartman, *Theology after Colonization: Kwame Bediako, Karl Barth, and the Future of Theological Reflection* (Notre Dame: University of Notre Dame Press, 2020), xvii.

[17] See Fretheim, *Kwame Bediako and African Christian Scholarship*, 176.

[18] Fretheim, *Kwame Bediako and African Christian Scholarship*, 193.

the shift of gravity within Christianity to the Global South, that the future of Protestant theology lies with scholars and leaders such as Kwame Bediako.

Select Bibliography

Primary Source

Bediako, Kwame, *Theology and Identity: The Impact of Culture Upon Christian Thought in the Second Century and in Modern Africa.* Oxford: Regnum Books, 1992.

Other Notable Works by the Author

Bediako, Kwame, *Christianity in Africa: The Renewal of a Non-Western Religion.* Edinburgh: Edinburgh University Press, 1995.

Bediako, Kwame, *Jesus and the Gospel in Africa: History and Experience.* Reprint, Maryknoll: Orbis Books, 2004.

Bediako, Kwame, *Religion, Culture and Language: An Appreciation of the Intellectual Legacy of Dr. J. B. Danquah.* J. B. Danquah Memorial Lectures. Accra: Ghana Academy of Arts and Sciences, 2006.

Secondary Sources

Aye-Addo, Charles Sarpong, *Akan Christology: An Analysis of the Christologies of John Samuel Pobee and Kwame Bediako in Conversation with Karl Barth.* Eugene: Pickwick, 2013.

Bediako, Gillian Mary, Benhardt Y. Quarshie, and J. Kwabena Asamoah-Gyadu, eds., *Seeing New Facets of the Diamond: Christianity as a University Faith; Essays in Honour of Kwame Bediako.* Regnum Studies in Global Christianity. Minneapolis: Fortress Press, 2014.

Fretheim, Sara J., *Kwame Bediako and African Christian Scholarship: Emerging Religious Discourse in Twentieth-Century Ghana.* Eugene: Cascade Books, 2018.

Hartman, Tim, *Kwame Bediako: African Theology for a World Christianity.* Minneapolis: Fortress Press, 2022.

Hartman, Tim, *Theology after Colonization: Kwame Bediako, Karl Barth, and the Future of Theological Reflection.* Notre Dame: University of Notre Dame Press, 2020.

15

Delores S. Williams, *Sisters in the Wilderness: The Challenge of Womanist God-Talk* (1993)

A Womanist in the Wilderness

Delores S. Williams (1936–2022) was one of the mothers of womanist theology, and her voice continues to guide African American women and many others to survive and find resilience within a wilderness existence. Born in Louisville, Kentucky, Williams grew up in a Seventh-Day Adventist household and went to Central High School, which, until 1956, was the only African American public high school in Louisville. She graduated in 1952 and worked for several years as a reporter at the *Louisville Defender*, an African American newspaper.

After her marriage to Robert C. Williams in 1958, Delores Williams became a member of the Presbyterian Church (USA), devoted herself to raising four kids, and continued her education, graduating with a BA in humanities from the University of Louisville (1965), an MA in the comparative study of religion from Columbia University (1975), and eventually a PhD in theology from Union Theological Seminary (1991), completing this terminal degree 4 years after the sudden death of her husband. During these graduate school years, Williams taught and researched at several institutions, including Harvard University, Drew Theological School, Pacific School of Religion in Berkeley, Muhlenberg College, Fisk University, and Boston University School of Theology. After completing her PhD, she was appointed associate professor of theology and culture at Union Theological Seminary, assuming this faculty position at a time when womanist theology was just emerging as a distinct discipline, led by other African American women with degrees from Union: Katie G. Cannon (who wrote the foreword to the twentieth anniversary edition of *Sisters in the Wilderness*) and Jacquelyn Grant.

Alice Walker coined the term "womanist" in 1983 to describe a Black feminist, memorably stating that "womanist is to feminist as purple is to lavender."[1] Delores Williams began to utilize this term in constructing a theological framework while writing her dissertation, beginning with a 1987 article entitled "Womanist Theology: Black Women's Voices."[2] Over the next 2 years, Katie Cannon, Renita Weems, and Jacquelyn Grant published significant works of womanist scholarship, engaging with the inherent ethical questions of womanist experience, Hagar's story as a biblical paradigm, and Christological questions.[3] Williams developed all of these trajectories and more in *Sisters in the Wilderness*, which created a new standard for biblically engaged, experientially informed, interdisciplinary womanist theology.[4] Other important contributions by Emilie Townes and Kelly Brown Douglas were published soon after *Sisters in the Wilderness*, but Williams's work became the standard for womanist theological method and perspective.[5] In this book, she identifies two African American traditions of reading the Bible and doing theology: the liberation tradition and the womanist tradition, the latter also named by Williams as the survival/quality of life tradition (2–5). Williams critiques the androcentric and patriarchal bias in the Black liberation tradition, centering instead the experience of Black women, including motherhood, surrogacy, ethnicity, and life as a wilderness experience.

Students flocked to Union Theological Seminary to study under Williams, and in 1996, she was appointed the Paul Tillich Professor of Feminist Theology at Union and the first African American woman to be installed into an endowed faculty chair. In addition to teaching and writing, Williams was dedicated to family life, the church, community organizing, and Harlem Initiatives Together. She retired from her teaching post in 2004 and moved to Louisville to care for her mother, later relocating to Nashville to be near her children. She passed away in 2022 at the age of 88, having charted a way through the wilderness for many to follow.

[1] Alice Walker, *In Search of Our Mother's Gardens: Womanist Prose* (San Diego: Harcourt Brace Jovanovich, 1983), xi. Although Walker does not define "womanist" until 1983, Layli Phillips points out that she first used the term in her 1979 publication *Take Back the Night*. Layli Phillips, *The Womanist Reader: The First Quarter Century of Womanist Thought* (New York and London: Routledge, 2006), xix.

[2] Delores S. Williams, "Womanist Theology: Black Women's Voices," *Christianity and Crisis* 47, no. 3 (March 2, 1987). Later published in Phillips, *The Womanist Reader*.

[3] Katie G. Cannon, *Black Womanist Ethics* (Marietta: Scholars Press, 1988); Renita J. Weems, *Just a Sister Away: A Womanist Vision of Women's Relationships in the Bible* (Ann Arbor: University of Michigan Press, 1988); Jacquelyn Grant, *White Women's Christ, Black Women's Jesus* (Marietta: Scholars Press, 1989).

[4] Delores Williams, *Sisters in the Wilderness: The Challenge of Womanist God-Talk*, 20th anniversary ed. (Maryknoll: Orbis Books, 2013). Hereafter, all references to this work shall be noted by employing in-text citations.

[5] Emilie Maureen Townes, *Womanist Justice, Womanist Hope* (Marietta: Scholars Press, 1993); Kelly Brown Douglas, *The Black Christ* (Maryknoll: Orbis Books, 1994).

Womanist Experience and the Biblical Hagar

Williams begins *Sisters in the Wilderness* by rereading Hagar's story in the Bible (Gen. 16:1-16; 21:9-21) as a way of highlighting Black women's experiences and perspectives. Divine liberation is not a feature of Hagar's story as an Egyptian slave of a Hebrew family. Rather, her story is one of survival and striving for life amid slavery, forced surrogacy, and abuse at the hands of Abram and Sarai, God's family of promise. As a result of this harsh treatment, Hagar escaped into the wilderness, thus becoming "the first female in the Bible to liberate herself from oppressive power structures" (18). There in the wilderness, God met her and promised to sustain her, prompting Hagar to also be the first and only person in the biblical narrative to name God, using the words "El Roi," the God who sees me (Gen. 16:13). Unlike some interpreters, however, Williams insists that Hagar did not link this encounter with the God of her oppressors, but with her Egyptian religious tradition (22–4). Williams notes that the biblical text does not present the "angel of the Lord" as a liberating God, instructing Hagar to return to her slave owners where she will raise her son Ishmael (20). Hagar responds in radical obedience to this divine command, embracing this as the most viable path for survival and quality of life.

The second biblical episode featuring Hagar (Gen. 21:9-21) picks up after Isaac, God's child of promise, is born to Abraham and Sarah. To ensure that her son Isaac would receive the full inheritance, Sarah insisted that Abraham cast out Hagar and Ishmael into the wilderness without protection or hope of survival. Again, God met Hagar in the wilderness, reaffirmed his promise, and provided for her and Ishmael. Williams highlights the autonomy and ingenuity of Hagar in overcoming her homelessness and finding an Egyptian wife for her son (30). Thus, Hagar is a model for African American women who have tried to find a way through experiences of slavery, surrogacy, rape, poverty, and other forms of oppression.

Like Hagar, Williams explains how many African American women have experienced "tension in motherhood" (chapter two), beginning with antebellum experiences in which they were forced to fulfill multiple roles of surrogate, nurturer, protector, and laborer. The strength of these women, however, did not equal power, even though they wielded more power than male slaves (36). To endure this situation, enslaved Black women relied on religion, a dynamic that later led to tensions within antebellum society when Black men sought to reestablish their authority. Williams highlights how blues music became a vehicle for reimagining Black women as "mammy-babies" who play a strong, nurturing role yet with dependency on men

(39–42). Reflecting on this transitional time, writers like James Baldwin and Richard Wright critiqued the way Black women relied on and were exploited by religious structures and male preachers (42–5), whereas Black women authors like Margaret Walker and Alice Walker called for women to move beyond these dependencies to embrace "survival intelligence" and "self-realization" respectively (45–51). Williams affirms the portrayal of Black women in Alice Walker's *The Color Purple*, for whom God is "an internal experience rather than a physical manifestation to be worshiped like the man Jesus" (50). Thus, she questions the association of Christianity with a male God and institutionalized religion, preferring the "divine spirit working within" as the locus of religious experience for Black mothers and their search for "self-esteem, autonomy and liberation" (51).

Like Hagar, African American women also experienced coerced surrogacy, which went beyond coercion to bear the children of others to include functioning in roles that ordinarily would be filled by others (what Williams calls "social-role surrogacy" in chapter three). After emancipation, coerced surrogacy morphed into various forms of voluntary yet pressured surrogacy, fueled by social dynamics, poverty, and white cultural standards. For example, Williams recounts the formation of the "Black Mammy Memorial Association," which existed to train Black women in domestic arts for the "nurturing, supporting, and caring for the well-being of white children" (66). While these roles provided employment, they also perpetuated oppressive roles upholding patriarchy and the cultural ideals of white families. Williams worries that new reproductive technologies will support the continuation of classist and racist surrogacy practices, deepening the strain between wealthy and poor women and between white and Black women (73–4).

In chapter four, Williams addresses the persistence of negative connotations with the color Black and by association people with darker skin tones. Whether devil food's cake, blackmail, blackballing, blacklists, or blackening a person's reputation, the color black is commonly associated with darkness and evil in American culture, which plays into what Williams calls "white racial narcissism," a state of mind that "degrades black and elevates white" (78). She explores how this racial aesthetic was deeply embedded within the European colonial mindset, treating both Native Americans and Africans as uncivilized and unreligious based on their darker skin tones. This same mindset informed the eugenics movement in America, "perpetuating the idea of the Negro's inherent intellectual and moral inferiority and white people's inherently superior intelligence and moral character" based on various pseudoscientific proposals such as skull size (93). Williams sees similar dynamics within sociobiology, which "suggests that social problems like racism and pauperism may also be a matter of genes as well as adaptive states in the evolutionary process" (94). The same racist oppression suffered by Hagar continues to plague Black people today, especially women, and Williams calls her readers to declare and demonstrate that "enough is enough" (94). "Thus we can speak of Hagar and many African American women as sisters in the wilderness struggling for life, and by the help of their God coming to terms with situations that have destructive potential" (97).

In chapter five, Williams describes how in white, colonial experience, wilderness was a hostile place needing to be conquered, whereas Black slaves carried the expectation of divine encounter within both physical and symbolic wilderness experiences. After emancipation, however, Williams notes how life became a more hostile wilderness for Black women who had to seek a living for themselves and their families (103). Up to the present day, Hagar continues to symbolize the possibility for both hostility and transformation through divine encounter in the wilderness. In doing so, Hagar synchronizes the sacred and secular dimensions of life as well as the spiritual and political dimensions (106–7). Hagar-in-the-wilderness provides a model of femininity, motherhood, and spirituality that challenges white and historically Victorian ideals, which are patterned after the Virgin Mary and have influenced certain portions of the Black community through "black middle-class channels" (114). Williams insists that Black women need to remember their own history of resistance and find courage, like Hagar, Harriet Tubman, and many others, to "find a way out of no way."

Womanist Theology and Liberation

In part two (chapters six through eight) of *Sisters in the Wilderness*, Williams explains how a womanist theology differs from Black liberation theology, which has been dominated by men. Williams roots her "womanist God-talk" in the conflicted testimony of Scripture, which presents a God who does not eradicate violence or slavery and who liberates some but not others. While Black liberation theology looks to the Exodus as the paradigmatic liberation event for the Hebrew people, womanist theology focuses on Hagar and the wilderness experience as paradigmatic. Williams critiques liberation theology not only for its selective reading of Scripture and its nonliberative elements but also for the way in which it has excluded women and their "re-production" history (140). Black liberation theology may be rooted in Black experience, but it still presupposed and perpetuates Black male experience. Womanist theology begins with the experience of Black women and pursues the question: "What is God's word about survival and quality of life formation for oppressed and quasi-free struggling to build community in the wilderness" (143).

Williams models this epistemological process by interrogating the Christian theological tradition that elevates Christ as surrogate and substitute. Black women cannot accept this vision of redemption, which sacralizes violence and exploitation (142–3). Williams states bluntly: "there is nothing divine in the blood of the cross" (148). Womanists can still look to Jesus for theological insight and salvific themes, but not to his death. Rather, they are guided by "Jesus' life of resistance and by the survival strategies he used to help people survive the death of identity" (145). Womanist theology looks to Jesus's "ministerial vision of righting relations" to craft a similarly peaceful and productive life (146–8). Like Jesus, the power to conquer sin is a dynamic of life rather than death. In articulating this theological vision, Williams utilizes what she calls a "hermeneutic of identification-ascertainment," exploring the biblical events, characters, and themes with which she most identifies and comparing that with the identification of other theologians and the biblical writers (132–3). In her evaluation, Black liberation theologians identify with certain portions of the Bible too uncritically and sometimes in self-serving ways. One is left to wonder, however, the extent to which anyone, womanists included, can avoid selectivity and bias in such a hermeneutical method, since everyone must embrace the continual process of "revaluing value" (150). These different values then inform different ethical principles, which for Williams's womanist perspective revolve around "survival and positive quality of life" rather than the principle of "liberation by whatever means necessary" (155).

Having distinguished her theological approach from liberation theology, Williams turns to show how womanist theology diverges and connects with feminist theology. The differences have to do with definitions of femininity, evaluations of patriarchy, and hermeneutical positions. Whereas feminists tend to appropriate the Virgin Mary as a model of feminine strength and independence from men, womanists are reticent to do so because her character is often linked with a vision of purity and innocence that perpetuates white supremacy (160–2). While feminists rightfully unmask patriarchal power structures, womanists also address ways higher-class women oppress other women and remain silent about oppressive authority structures (164). And regarding hermeneutical commitments, Williams deems that womanists should not merely throw out the Bible like some feminists do, since it "continues to be fundamental in the life, faith and hope of many women" (166). Williams acknowledges that despite being a male story, the Bible still contains life-giving words about liberation and survival. For example, in addition to the story of Hagar and Ishmael, she shows how

Jer. 29:4-7 is a text that informs Black women's drive for survival (172–3). In addition, she advocates for holding the various portraits of God in the Bible in creative tension, like the Seeing God of Hagar and the Liberating God of Moses (174). Despite disagreements with feminists, a womanist perspective shares the critique of violence within traditional atonement theories, the danger of seeing suffering as redemptive, and a passion for resilience amid struggles. Indeed, Williams claims that "to be a Christian is to affirm the life of black Americans and other threatened groups by joining their survival struggle against genocide" (178).

Womanist Leadership and the Black Church

In her final chapter, Williams celebrates the resilience of the "black church" against the deficiencies of what she calls the "black denominational church." While the Black church is invisible, the Black denominational church is visible and exists institutionally. While the Black church is a source of strength and hope, the Black denominational church is riddled with deficiencies. Williams makes a long list of these weaknesses, which include sexism, immoral models of leadership, political collusion, spiritualized proclamation, failure to pool resources and collaborate for social change, homophobia, denial of the AIDS crisis, emotional exploitation of women, overly elaborate church edifices, and the adoption of white American values such as individualism, capitalist economics, classism, and idolization of the nuclear family (183–6). Williams does mention some positive examples within the Black denominational church, but overall, she looks to the noninstitutional Black church as "the heart of hope in the black community's experience of oppression, survival struggle and its historic efforts toward complete liberation" (181). This church may be invisible, but "we know it when we see, hear and feel it" (182), and it "acts as the great judging, healing, fighting, holy Godforce" (185) that drives Black denominations to do righteous and transformative things.

Williams agrees with Patricia Reeberg, who served as the executive director of the Council of Churches of the city of New York, that despite the weaknesses of the Black denominational church, it is sustained by the mothering instinct, volunteerism, and generosity (187). But if the Black institutional church is ever to transcend its cultural confusion and spiritual stagnation, it must stop ignoring Black women's experiences and concerns (189). Williams explores the Universal Hagar's Spiritual Church as an example, which was founded in 1923 by George Willie Hurley as an alternative to Black mainline churches and with room for leadership of Black women. Although this church would be viewed by many as a cult because of its syncretistic elements and the centrality of "Christ Hurley," Williams sees it as one instance—despite the persistence of some androcentric elements—of how the institutional Black church can respect the presence and role of Black women (205).

Despite her frustration with the Black denominational church, Williams ends *Sisters in the Wilderness* on a hopeful note, affirming that Black women "will make a way in the community for the black church to emerge as a God-filled presence, quickening the heart, measuring the soul, and bathing life with spirit" (207). In the Afterword, she outlines four "survival strategies" for Black women: the "art of cunning" or the ability to improvise shrewd wisdom, the "art of encounter" through resistance and endurance, the "art of care" that requires commitment and charity, and the "art of connecting" in which relationships are necessary for survival and quality of life (208–11). "Black men may be the head of the liberation struggle, but black women are the feet that keep the movement going," and it's a movement that turns on trust in God (211).

Womanists in the Wide, Wide World

Throughout *Sisters in the Wilderness*, Williams grounds her theological reflection in the experiences of Black women in the wilderness, which she also calls "the wide, wide world."[6] Like other feminists, the experiential grounding of her theology sets her approach apart from modern theologians who take divine revelation, Scripture, or tradition as their starting point. But it is the *Black* female experience in the "wide, wide world" that sets womanist theology apart from other feminists. As the womanist theological tradition developed in the academy, some shared Williams's interest in the biblical narrative, theological reflection, and the Black church, while others operated more within the spheres of religious studies and African American studies.[7] In the field of biblical studies, womanist biblical interpretation continues to proliferate, from in-depth and intersectional interpretations of particular texts, as in the work of Mitzi J. Smith at Columbia Theological Seminary,[8]

6 See, for example, her use of "wide, wide world" on page 141.

7 Womanists located within religious studies rather than theology are sometimes referred to as "third wave womanists" as a counterpart to "third wave feminists." For example, see Monica A. Coleman, ed., *Ain't I a Womanist, Too? Third Wave Womanist Religious Thought* (Minneapolis: Fortress Press, 2013). For more on these dynamics, see Gary Dorrien, *A Darkly Radiant Vision: The Black Social Gospel in the Shadow of MLK* (New Haven: Yale University Press, 2023), 315.

8 See Mitzi J. Smith, *Womanist Sass and Talk Back: Social (In)Justice, Intersectionality, and Biblical Interpretation* (Eugene: Cascade Books, 2018).

ORPHAN HOLD
DO NOT SHIP

H1 – 000000000405

SBN 9780567718006

Modern Protestant Theology : Introducing he Classics

LIENT	Alternate Sourcing
TATION	TPP Receiving Station 03
ELD	2026 – 10 – 08 14:17

SHELF

If its order arrives, scan this label at a receiving station.

to resources for reading the whole Bible with attentiveness to the stories and perspectives of women, as in the work of Wilda Gafney at Brite Divinity School.[9]

In the fields of theology and ethics, womanist contributions continue to range over a variety of topics and approaches, many focusing on particular themes while drawing from a variety of sources and disciplines.[10] Womanists such as Angela D. Sims and Emilie M. Townes, for example, reflect on Black experience in America more broadly while also drawing on the unique experiences of Black women related to spirituality, trauma, health, and social witness.[11] Joanne Marie Terrell and others have expanded the interdisciplinary nature of womanist theology in dialogue with the arts and other religions.[12] Many womanist theologians have also risen to become prominent leaders in their educational institutions, denominations, or academic organizations and are often the first African American women to hold these positions. For example, Angela Sims is currently the first African American and female president of Colgate Rochester Crozer Divinity School; Emilie M. Townes, who previously served as dean of Vanderbilt Divinity School, was the first African American woman to serve as president of the American Academy of Religion and is currently the first womanist president of the Society of Christian Ethics. Other Black women are writing bold and more popular works of womanist theology and spirituality, though often not using that label, such as Christena Cleveland's *God Is a Black Woman* and Cole Arthur Riley's *Black Liturgies*.[13]

[9] Wilda Gafney has been involved in two large projects, one entitled *Womanist Midrash*, which explores the stories of women in the Hebrew Scriptures (so far in two volumes), and the other a three-volume lectionary entitled *A Women's Lectionary for the Whole Church*. For a helpful introduction to womanist biblical interpretation, see Nyasha Junior, *An Introduction to Womanist Biblical Interpretation* (Louisville: Westminster John Knox Press, 2015). Nyasha Junior, who teaches at the University of Toronto, has also written on interpretations of Hagar in *Reimagining Hagar: Blackness and the Bible* (New York: Oxford University Press, 2019).

[10] For example, see Karen Baker-Fletcher, *Dancing with God: The Trinity from a Womanist Perspective* (Des Peres: Chalice Press, 2007). Baker-Fletcher teaches systematic theology at Perkins School of Theology.

[11] Angela D. Sims, *Lynched: The Power of Memory in a Culture of Terror* (Waco: Baylor University Press, 2016); Emilie M. Townes, *Breaking the Fire Rain of Death: African American Health Issues and a Womanist Ethic of Care* (New York: Continuum International Publishing Group, 1998); Katie Geneva Cannon, Emilie M. Townes, and Angela D. Sims, eds., *Womanist Theological Ethics: A Reader* (Louisville: Westminster John Knox Press, 2011).

[12] See JoAnne M. Terrell, *Power in the Blood: The Cross in the African American Experience* (Eugene: Wipf and Stock, 2005). Terrell teaches at Chicago Theological Seminary.

[13] Christena Cleveland, *God Is a Black Woman* (New York: Amistad, 2023); Cole Arthur Riley, *Black Liturgies: Prayer, Poems, and Meditations for Staying Human* (New York: Convergent Books, 2024).

All of this shows the growing diversity and generativity of womanist theology as pioneered by Delores Williams in *Sisters in the Wilderness*, much of which has developed her trajectory of theological revision in light of the experiences of Black women.[14] Outside the United States, there have been parallel theological developments, such as the "Circle of Concerned African Women Theologians," founded in 1989 under the vision of Mercy Amba Oduyoye, which continues to be "gender-centered, interreligious, interdisciplinary, intersectional and transformative,"[15] as well as less theologically inclined movements such as African womanism and Africana womanism.[16] Although womanist theology is not even 50 years in the making, it has made an indelible mark on modern Protestant theology, unmasking oppressive ways of reading the Bible and modeling alternative methods of theological investigation that draw on the wisdom and strength of Black women.

Select Bibliography

Primary Source

Williams, Delores S., *Sisters in the Wilderness: The Challenge of Womanist God-Talk*. 20th anniversary ed. Maryknoll: Orbis Books, 2013.

Other Notable Works by the Author

Williams, Delores S., "Straight Talk, Plain Talk: Womanist Words about Salvation in a Social Context." In *Embracing the Spirit: Womanist Perspectives on Hope, Salvation, and Transformation*, edited by Emilie Townes, 97–121. Maryknoll: Orbis Books, 1997.

[14] There are some examples that are less revisionist and more attentive to the theological tradition. For examples, see Amy Plantinga Pauw and Serene Jones, eds., *Feminist and Womanist Essays in Reformed Dogmatics* (Louisville: Westminster John Knox Press, 2011).

[15] Circle of Concerned African Women Theologians, "History of the Circle," accessed July 7, 2025, https://circle.org.za/about-us/history-of-the-circle/.

[16] Chikwenye Okonjo Ogunyemi is named as the pioneer of African womanism, which focuses on the identity and struggle of African women within a global community, and Clenora Hudson-Weems was the first to name Africana womanism, which also extends the dialogue to include any women of African descent. Chikwenye Okonjo Ogunyemi, *African Wo/Man Palava: The Nigerian Novel by Women* (Chicago: University of Chicago Press, 1996); Clenora Hudson-Weems, *Africana Womanism: Reclaiming Ourselves* (Troy: Bedford, 1993).

Williams, Delores S., "A Womanist Perspective on Sin." In *A Troubling in My Soul: Womanist Perspectives on Evil and Suffering*, edited by Emilie Townes, 130–49. Maryknoll: Orbis Books, 1993.

Williams, Delores S., "Womanist Theology: Black Women's Voices." In *Black Theology: A Documentary History, Volume II, 1980–1992*, edited by James H. Cone and Gayraud S. Wilmore, 265–72. Maryknoll: Orbis Books, 1993.

Secondary Sources

Cannon, Katie Geneva, Emilie M. Townes, and Angela D. Sims, eds., *Womanist Theological Ethics: A Reader*. Louisville: Westminster John Knox Press, 2011.

Junior, Nyasha, *An Introduction to Womanist Biblical Interpretation*. Louisville: Westminster John Knox Press, 2015.

Kirk-Duggan, Cheryl A., "Womanist Theology as a Corrective to African American Theology." In *The Oxford Handbook of African American Theology*, edited by Anthony B. Pinn and Katie G. Cannon, 267–79. Oxford: Oxford University Press, 2014.

Mitchem, Stephanie Y., *Introducing Womanist Theology*. Maryknoll: Orbis Books, 2002.

Phillips, Layli, *The Womanist Reader: The First Quarter Century of Womanist Thought*. New York and London: Routledge, 2006.

Index